CRISIS AND CAPITALISM
IN CONTEMPORARY
ARGENTINE CINEMA

CRISIS AND CAPITALISM IN CONTEMPORARY ARGENTINE CINEMA

JOANNA PAGE

Duke University Press

Durham and London

2009

© 2009 Duke University Press

All rights reserved

Printed in the United States of America

on acid-free paper ∞

Designed by Amy Ruth Buchanan

Typeset in Scala by Keystone Typesetting, Inc.

Library of Congress Cataloging-in-Publication

Data appear on the last printed page of this book.

To my mother, who taught me to read

Money is the obverse of all the images that the cinema shows and sets in place, so that films about money are already, if implicitly, films within the film or about the film.

GILLES DELEUZE, *Cinema 2: The Time-Image*, 75

CONTENTS

ACKNOWLEDGMENTS

In writing this book I have received advice from many people and financial support from several institutions. Research trips to Argentina were made possible by grants from the University of Cambridge, the Centre of Latin American Studies, and Robinson College. In Buenos Aires a number of people assisted my research. I would particularly like to thank the helpful and generous library staff at the Instituto Nacional de Cine y Artes Audiovisuales; Daniel Sendrós and staff at the Museo del Cine Pablo C. Ducrós Hicken; Sylvia Valdés and Marcelo Albónico from the Universidad de Palermo; the Press Office of the Buenos Aires Festival de Cine Independiente; Julia Choclin at Arte Video who helped me source a number of films; and several directors and producers who kindly gave me copies of their films which were not commercially available at that point, including Daniel Burak, Albertina Carri, César D'Angiolillo, Gustavo Fontán, Aldo Paparella, Raúl Perrone, Ana Poliak, and Lita Stantic.

Laura Podalsky and Michael Chanan made valuable comments on the manuscript, and I appreciate their time and perspicacity. I am very grateful to Geoffrey Kantaris for introducing me to Argentine film a number of years ago and for his support since then. I would also like to thank my postgraduate students at the Centre of Latin American Studies in Cambridge over the past few years—including Philippa Page, Lauren Rea, Ed King, and Jordana Blejmar—who have shared my enthusiasm for Argentine literature and cinema and whose ideas have challenged and shaped my own. I owe a special debt of gratitude to friends and colleagues at Robinson College,

Cambridge, without whom this book would have been written more quickly but much less happily. My final thanks goes to Geoff for his encouragement, patience, and unflagging cheerfulness.

Early versions of some of the material contained in this book have been published in journals and edited volumes, as follows. Parts of chapters 1 and 5 were published in an earlier version in the *Journal of Latin American Cultural Studies* 14, no. 3 (December 2005); the section on *Potestad* in chapter 6 appeared in *Studies in Hispanic Cinemas* 2, no. 1 (2005); a few paragraphs of the analysis of *Los rubios* were published in a much earlier version of this work in *New Cinemas* 3, no. 1 (2005). Spanish versions of chapter 7, and of the analyses of *Hoteles* and *Bar El Chino* in chapter 5, were published in Viviana Rangil, ed., *El cine argentino de hoy: entre el arte y la politica* (Buenos Aires: Biblos, 2007) and in María José Moore and Paula Wolkowicz, eds., *Cines al margen: Nuevos modos de representación en el cine argentino contemporáneo* (Buenos Aires: Libraria, 2007), respectively. I am grateful to the publishers for their permission to reproduce this material.

INTRODUCTION

Since the mid-1990s, Argentine filmmaking has experienced a boom in production that at the time of writing shows no signs of abating. Critics and film festivals worldwide have not been slow to herald a renaissance in Argentine cinema, and accolades, prizes and other sources of funding have secured access for a number of these films to screens around the world. That national production should show such a dramatic increase—from fourteen feature films in 1994 to sixty-six in 2004—is remarkable; that it should do so at a time of severe economic crisis is quite extraordinary.[1]

In December 2001 Argentina's economic recession had reached the point at which the state's policy of convertibility, under which the peso had been pegged to the dollar throughout the 1990s, became impossible to sustain. Financial investors withdrew, and there was a run on banks (*el corralito*), which reacted by freezing deposits, preventing individuals from accessing their savings. A measure of the depth of the Crisis is given by a comparison of GDP levels, which show a drop of almost 20 percent between 1998 and 2002, the sharpest fall experienced by any capitalist country of some significance at least since World War II and "the gravest economic event ever in a country known for the recurrence of crises."[2] The rapid devaluation of the peso and the subsequent "pesification" of savings accounts was accompanied by wide-scale protests and food riots. Argentina had no fewer than five presidents within a period of less than two weeks at the end of December 2001. As a number of commentators have noted, the slogan chanted over and over again during this period—"que se vayan todos" (all the politicians should go)—testifies to the crisis of an entire political system. Marcus Klein echoes the sentiment of many within the country and abroad during the worst weeks of social unrest when he states that "given the depth of the crisis, and the public disparagement of, and hostility towards, the political elite and the political institutions that it caused, it was (and still is) remarkable that Argentine democracy survived at all."[3]

Devaluation also had a significant impact on the financial costs of filmmaking: because film stock and equipment are largely imported, and therefore payable in dollars, many of the costs associated with production virtually tripled overnight. Funds allocated to the Instituto Nacional de Cine y Artes Audiovisuales (INCAA), which had been relatively high between 1995 and 1998, were to suffer cuts of up to 50 percent as the crisis deepened.[4] A number of directors relied on funds given in the form of prizes through international film festivals (the Hubert Bals Fund in particular), while a few were able to secure contracts with private investors or to enter into transnational coproduction agreements. The major success of films made during the Crisis lay, however, in their ability to make aesthetic virtue out of economic necessity. Many of the most celebrated films of this period were made on extremely low budgets, using cheaper film stock and nonstandard equipment: 16-mm, black-and-white, Beta, or (increasingly) digital video cameras. Their styles flaunted the roughness and the informality of their production, made as they were "on the hoof," wherever locations could be found, whenever funds permitted, and with whomever could be persuaded to act or to provide technical assistance for little or no pay. As Quintín suggests, in these films "la pobreza no es un fuera de campo horroroso ni la postal turística de la villa miseria sino la materia misma de las películas" (poverty is not an offscreen horror nor a touristy postcard of the shantytown but the very material from which these films are made).[5] In this respect they demonstrate a clear affinity with cinematic productions of the 1960s in Latin America, which, as Ismail Xavier states, turned poverty "into a signifier" in their representation of underdevelopment and inequality.[6]

This book does not set out to "explain" the boom in filmmaking that, having begun in the mid-1990s, only gathers pace during the Crisis and its aftermath: this task has already been undertaken by others. Critics coincide in referring to the "Ley de Cine" (Cinema Law), which came into force in 1995, as a crucial factor in the growth of Argentine cinema. The new law granted a degree of protection to the national film industry in terms of exhibition and provided significant funds for filmmaking, administered through the INCAA.[7] Diego Batlle also cites as one of the principal motors of growth the explosion of new film schools, from which a number of New Argentine Cinema's most successful directors have emerged.[8] Sergio Wolf points to the importance of the revival of international film festivals held in the country.[9] The Mar del Plata Festival was held in 1996 for the first time in twenty-six years; both this event and the Buenos Aires Festival de Cine Independiente (BAFICI), inaugurated in 1999, have provided a significant space for the exhibition of less commercially viable local films. In addition to these factors, Gonzalo Aguilar draws attention to the rise in film criticism in Argentina during the 1990s, both in film journalism and in academic studies, and particularly the major contribution made by film journals such as *El amante cine* and *Haciendo cine*.[10]

I see no reason not to concur with the majority of critics in their view that Argentina's boom in filmmaking also marks a radical shift from previous filmmaking aesthetics. The role played by film criticism itself in the creation of the phenomenon of "New Argentine Cinema" should not, however, be overlooked. The influential *El amante* enthusiastically proclaimed the advent of a new generation and a wholesale rupture with the old. The predisposition of critics toward the new has resulted in a number of self-fulfilled prophecies: for example, a number of critics went beyond supporting the new directors in written reviews, actively intervening to secure the inclusion of their films in festivals.[11] That the films selected for this study date from the mid-1990s does, however, recognize clear shifts in aesthetics at this time; more importantly for my purposes, from this point onward films began to testify in earnest to the impact of growing unemployment, rising crime, and the expansion of the informal economy. The Crisis of 2001 was the culmination of a longer period of economic troubles and civil unrest, and for this reason I do not create artificial distinctions between pre-Crisis and post-Crisis films, most often reading them together as part of a corpus of texts charting the economic decline of the nation, and its social consequences, over several years.

My central purpose is to explore how cinema has registered, and indeed helped to construct, certain modes of subjectivity relating to Argentina's experience of capitalism, neoliberalism, and economic crisis. Thematic introductions precede the analyses of films presented in this book; to repeat this material here would be redundant, but some words about the range of texts selected, and approaches taken, may be of use. Significant space is dedicated to the films that have become widely associated with the label of New Argentine Cinema. Chapters 2 and 3, in particular, discuss a number of the major productions associated with this corpus of films (too heterogeneous to be called a movement), interrogating the ways in which the themes of the Crisis—unemployment, poverty, debt, and marginalization—are given expression in the forms and styles of these films. Other chapters include discussion of films that do not "fit" the criteria attached by critical consensus to New Argentine Cinema, in an effort to complicate schemas already established: genre films, for example, made against a trend toward "independent" styles, or highly experimental films that do not conform to the minimalism and naturalism most often associated with New Argentine Cinema. Alongside films that have received wide international distribution and recognition, I have consciously sought to include films that have not traveled much outside Argentina but that I consider to have made an important contribution to cultural debates within the country or that are otherwise worthy of more attention than they have received. What unites all of the films examined, including those focused on postdictatorship memory in chapter 6, is their attention to shifts in subjectivity and representation provoked by specific political or economic structures and events. For reasons of space and focus, I have chosen to limit the scope of this book to fiction film, leaving aside the important contribution of documentary film in recent years. I have, however, included a number of films that operate on the border between fiction and documentary, and I return in my conclusion to suggest some important differences between the roles of fiction and documentary film (and video) in representing the Crisis.

Moving beyond the analysis of Argentine film's explicit engagement with economic and political crisis, I explore how—and what—these films can be understood to signify through experimentation with form and genre and with respect to their status as cultural artifacts and commodities with a global industry. What meanings, and conflicts between meanings, are generated by mounting a critique of neoliberalism within a medium produced and distributed in the context of a world market dominated by neoliberal policies and practices? Cinema does not occupy a space external to the events that it registers but is very much part of the economic system, the social relations, and the cultural milieu it might be supposed to depict. This raises important issues for criticism. Fredric Jameson proposes that "far more dramatically than in the sociology of literature, the study of film seems to pose a stark incompatibility between intrinsic and extrinsic analyses, between superstructural and infrastructural codes, between formal readings and just such accounts of the economic and technological determinants of these cultural artifacts." In the theories of film practitioners in the

Third World (particularly those associated with Third Cinema), "technology, or its underdevelopment, is then explicitly drawn back inside the aesthetic message in order to function henceforth as an intrinsic meaning, rather than an extrinsic accident or causal determinant."[12] The analyses presented in this study center on the continuities and the contradictions that emerge in the relationship between "intrinsic" and "extrinsic" meanings in recent Argentine films. Gilles Deleuze considers that "money is the obverse of all the images that the cinema shows and sets in place, so that films about money are already, if implicitly, films within the film or about the film."[13] Films of the Argentine Crisis, often focusing explicitly on the experience of neoliberalism at the periphery of the world economy, provide an ideal corpus for the investigation of the particular kind of reflexivity suggested by Deleuze.

Indeed, money emerges as the universal theme of contemporary Argentine cinema, in which it is commonly owed (*Un oso rojo*), forged (*Una de dos*), swindled (*Nueve reinas*), stolen (*Mala época, Sólo por hoy*), lost (*Rosarigasinos*), extorted through kidnapping (*No quiero volver a casa*), or squandered in desperate and ill-advised enterprises (*Los guantes mágicos*). The analyses I offer here attempt to mediate between these films' discursive engagement with the themes of the Crisis and another—sometimes complementary, sometimes contradictory—set of meanings associated with their status as commodities within the same market that is subject to explicit investigation within the texts.

In line with the reflexive or symptomatic readings I develop in this book, a study of the social issues raised in the films is embedded within an exploration of the metacritical questions they pose for the analysis of film and of cultural texts more generally. Thus the analysis of genre films in chapter 4 leads to questions relating to the politics of genre appropriation from the periphery and to the argument—drawing on Jameson—that these films can be read as allegories of commodification. Similarly, the discussion of post-dictatorship films in chapter 6 engages with theories of subjectivity and spectatorship in order to explore these texts' contribution to memory, a theme that has lost none of its urgency in contemporary Argentine cultural debates. Questions of national and postnational identity addressed in these films are framed within a broader set of metacritical issues concerning the relative importance of national or transnational approaches to film analysis, and the discussion of the collapse of distinctions between public and private spheres in chapter 7 suggests ways in which traditional modes of analysis with respect to political cinema need to be modified to take account of significant shifts in the political sphere, reflected and encoded in the structures of meaning developed in contemporary film.

A critical focus on the nation may seem retrograde in a globalized era in which the frontiers of the state are increasingly eroded and trends in criticism and theory are firmly set toward exploring the transnational and the global and toward deconstructing the center/periphery model along with other "old" binarisms. Many Argentine sociologists concur, however, in pointing to the resurgence of nationalist discourses within popular protests as a result of the Crisis. Crucially, the nation is not associated here with the state but is most often invoked in *criticism* of a state in cahoots with global neoliberalism, which has sold off the country's assets and burdened it with intolerable levels of debt. Alejandro Grimson notes the widespread use of the national flag during antigovernment demonstrations, a phenomenon that, as both he and Maristella Svampa observe, is all the more remarkable given the strong association of nationalist symbols and discourses with the military regime only two decades previously.[14] In the context of the Crisis, a rearticulation of the national became a contestatory exercise, both denouncing the failure of the state and resisting the rhetoric of globalization. Indeed, the Crisis effectively brought about the disarticulation of the "opportunities-for-all" discourses of neoliberalism and globalization, exposing the vulnerability of Argentina as a capitalist country on the periphery of a global economy, where, unlike in Europe, institutions lacked the stability needed to regulate the wholesale restructuring of society under neoliberalism.[15] The Crisis delivered a hefty blow to Argentina's First World aspirations, reinforcing at the same time the specificity of national experience. As Michiel Baud reminds us, "the Argentine crisis did not have very strong repercussions in the rest of the continent, showing simultaneously its exclusive domestic character as well as the decreased and very restricted importance of the Argentine economy on a world or even regional scale."[16]

Svampa argues that a significant effect of the Crisis was its "efecto desnaturalizador" (denaturalizing effect), confronting the country with the consequences of the neoliberal policies aggressively pursued during the 1990s and provoking a revelation that "la brecha social que se había abierto durante los 90 era profundamente ilegítima" (the social rift that had opened up during the 1990s was profoundly illegitimate).[17] The radical critique of neoliberalism that has ensued involves a reassertion of the nation as a strategy of resistance, although exactly how the nation is to be imagined—given the ever-widening gap between rich and poor, brutally exacerbated under neoliberalism—is a dilemma registered in different ways by many of the films discussed in this book.[18] Partly in response to these films' concern with the national, I construct an argument in chapter 1 for the continued importance of national frameworks in the analysis of Argentine film, drawing both on the specificities of context and on theoretical work on the relationship between culture and the public sphere. The second half of the chapter presents two paradigmatic films produced in this period by "veteran" directors, Fernando Solanas and Eliseo Subiela. One consequence of *El amante*'s scathing rejection of the old in favor of the new, with New Argentine filmmakers often presented as an "orphaned" generation, cut loose from past influences, has been a persistent blind spot concerning several important continuities that link contemporary film to previous periods of filmmaking in Argentina. My analysis demonstrates some of the contrasts between filmmaking of the 1980s and early 1990s and the more recent period that is the focus of this book, while suggesting ways in which these rejections and repositionings nevertheless reveal a deep engagement with questions of national culture that represents a significant continuity between the two periods. If, however, the nation is the key theme that unites these films, in contemporary cinema it is—as I argue in chapter 5—not the nation constructed with an appeal to any essentialist categories but most often one that is "extroverted" in the sense explored by Doreen Massey, finding its identity in the particularity of the links it maintains to the outside world.[19]

My conclusion comments specifically on the role of Argentine cinema within the national imaginary, in an era in which culture and politics are becoming increasingly difficult to distinguish. As Jameson contends, in our postmodern era "everything is mediated by culture, to the point where even the political and the ideological 'levels' have initially to be disentangled from their primary mode of representation which is cultural."[20] This is no less the case in post-Menemist Argentina. These films' engagement with their political and economic context is therefore to be found—paradoxically perhaps—in their self-reflexivity: a turning-in on themselves, or on the practices of culture and its industries, that represents an acknowledgment of the already-mediatized realm of politics, as well as a sobering critique of the rapid disappearance of the public sphere. A paradox emerges: whereas much Argentine film has focused on representing the poverty and the suffering associated with Argentina's "Third World" status, such films, and their success on international screens, become fully associated with Argentina's First World aspirations. Although I take issue in some respects with

Jameson's arguments concerning Third World texts as "national allegories," it is clear that, however much these films eschew a national perspective and chart the disintegration of the state, they are always overdetermined as national cultural products made at the periphery of a global culture industry. The contradictions arising from such overdeterminations have been of paramount interest to me in my research into this period of filmmaking. The range of theoretical frameworks appropriated in my analyses of these films—from cultural geography, anthropology, sociology, political philosophy, cultural studies, film studies, and critical theory—reflects an understanding of the cultural, the social, the economic, and the political as fundamentally interdependent spheres whose complex relationships are continually being redefined, both in practice and in our critical approaches to them.

|

NATION, STATE, AND FILMMAKING IN CONTEMPORARY ARGENTINA

THE POLITICS OF NATIONAL FILM STUDIES: THE ARGENTINE CASE

Following the recent leap to prominence within world distribution networks of a few international coproductions from Latin America—and in view of current theories of globalization, which emphasize the flow of ideas, information, and goods across rapidly disappearing national boundaries—it is becoming de rigueur to argue that the nation presents an obsolete framework for the analysis of Latin American film. Although prioritizing the transnational and the global dimensions of filmmaking has undeniable value in combating essentialist notions of the nation, and in challenging the inflexible application of national boundaries in what has always been a global industry, in this chapter I draw attention to some of the limitations of transnational approaches to film criticism. In the case of Argentina it becomes clear that a critical focus on international coproductions often masks the real conditions of film production at a time when this form of funding is not available to (or sought by) the majority of filmmakers and when the state is becoming increasingly involved in the financing and promotion of national cinema. It may also obscure some of the inequalities that still govern transnational exchange in the film industry, in spite of the moderate success of certain international funding schemes such as Ibermedia. I also argue that transnational approaches to film criticism frequently fail to account for the public role of culture within a national context. My objective throughout is to emphasize the inescapably political nature of transnational or globalized approaches within film studies, which can often appear disingenuously to respond merely to an existing set of economic conditions or to the impact of inevitable trends toward greater globalization. That this veiling of ideology beneath a discourse of economic inevitability is also a characteristic of neoliberal discourses should alert us to the very real stakes at play in criticism, especially given the particular importance of the critical (including academic) reception of Latin American films for distribution possibilities abroad.

An emphasis on the extraordinary entry of a handful of recent Latin American films into worldwide distribution networks, and on the cross-border trajectories of their directors and stars, effectively masks the asymmetries of exchange that still limit production and distribution for all but a very few of the continent's films. Among the most celebratory of recent accounts is Stephen Hart's *A Companion to Latin American Film*, in which Hart argues that the international commercial success of *Central Station* (Brazil, 1998), *Amores perros* (Mexico, 2000), *Y tu mamá también* (Mexico, 2001), and *City of God* (Brazil, 2002)—presented as the pinnacle of the continent's achievements in filmmaking—"demonstrated to the world that Latin American cinema had finally come into its own." This occurred, according to Hart, when Latin American cinema began to compete without favors in international distribution networks and in the Oscars; his evident approval of the shift toward private capital in funding, together with the fact that several of the films he presents as evidence of Latin America's "international acceptance," and demonstration of the fact that it has "come of age," are coproductions with Europe and the United States, confirms that the "coming-of-age" he describes really means "opening up to international capital."[1] John King is surely correct to suggest that the extraordinary success of a handful of Latin American directors in recent years tends "to disguise rather than illustrate the very real obstacles that most filmmakers have always encountered in the region."[2] The overwhelming critical attention accorded in recent years to these four films, while they are certainly worthy of extensive analysis, has the unfortunate effect of casting into shadow many other films of merit and drawing a veil over the inequalities of production and distribution that have prevented their greater visibility. Hart cites the Mexican director of *Amores perros*, Alejandro González Iñárritu, who "loathe[s] the government-financed movie-making that seems to operate by the maxim: 'If nobody understands or nobody goes to see a movie, that it must mean it's a masterpiece.'"[3] Underpinning Hart's apoliticized survey is not this particular myth but another: that of the market as a level playing field, as the sole impartial judge of quality, which raises up those films deserving of private finance and international audiences and condemns to obscurity those made only for academic film critics. "Parece innecesario decirlo," writes Beatriz Sarlo: "*el mercado cultural no pone en escena una comunidad de libres consumidores y productores*" (It seems unnecessary to say this: the cultural market does not create a community of free consumers and producers).[4] Perhaps the task of insisting on the inequalities of transnational exchange is not, after all, so unnecessary.

I have already outlined in my introduction some of the production difficulties encountered by contemporary Argentine filmmakers. Equally significant, however, is the fact that the *exhibition* of Argentine films has proven to be a continual struggle in recent years, partly alleviated by changes in state policy. The past two decades have seen the closure of hundreds of independent movie theaters across Argentina. Octavio Getino charts the vertiginous decline of the number of cinema screens in the country from 1,500 in 1975 to just 420 in 1995.[5] Cinemagoing in Buenos Aires and other cities has been dominated since the late 1990s by the presence of new and lavish megaplexes owned by North American and Australian companies, chiefly Hoyts General Cinemas and Warner Village. Their location within ultramodern shopping malls is symbolic of cinema's transformation into a middle-class leisure activity, becoming increasingly associated with the First World aspirations of wealthy Argentines. The entrances to such malls, defended by armed security guards, mark the boundaries between these islands of prosperity and the urban decay and poverty that encircle them, dividing cracked pavements from gleaming marble floors and separating immigrant vendors of fake watches and cheap leatherware from the quiet glamour of designer clothes shops. Often cocooned at the heart of these centers, the new multiplexes are laid with luxuriously plush carpets and boast the latest in audiovisual quality and spectator comfort. Pretrailer advertisements feature exclusive restaurants and plastic surgery clinics, while usherettes with candy-striped uniforms and matching baseball caps sell chewing gum, Coca-Cola, and M&Ms before the film—almost always a Hollywood import—begins.

By contrast, until very recently, the only cinema committed to screening local productions was a run-down city-center theater with ageing technology, where quiet or intimate scenes are still accompanied by the rumble of underground trains below or the clatter of rain on the roof. Aggressive U.S. distribution practices have often all but eclipsed the exhibition of other films in Argentina. Big-budget publicity campaigns prepare the way for each Hollywood blockbuster, and distribution companies flood the country with hundreds of copies of one film at the same time, undercutting the rental prices of the one or two copies typically available of Argentine films. Foreign films are subject to very low import duties, which results, in the words of Jorge Coscia, in "una suerte de dumping frente a nuestra industria cinematográfica" (a kind of dumping vis-à-vis our film industry), which has to compete with films that have already recovered their costs, while Argentine films must often attempt to do so solely within the national market.[6] There is little evidence to suggest, either to Argentine filmmakers or to cinemagoers, that the globalization of the film industry means anything other than its Americanization; nor is there indication of the much-vaunted potential for globalization to erode divisions between center and periphery, producing relationships of mutual dependency rather than domination.

The international coproduction might seem to offer an instance of precisely such transnational dialogue and reciprocity, but coproductions enjoy a position of dominance in the literature that they do not actually occupy in national production across the continent. Ann Marie Stock asserts the "prevalence of coproduction" in Latin American filmmaking, which "has become increasingly transnational";[7] Kathleen Newman likewise observes that "many of the recent feature films considered to be Latin American . . . are co-productions with European companies or institutions."[8] Again, for Marvin D'Lugo, coproductions with European producers and state agencies "have increasingly dominated much Latin American film production."[9] King, in his survey of changing trends in Argentine cinema during the 1990s, claims that coproduction became "the dominant viable route for film-makers" in this period.[10] Michael Chanan refers to "the foreign coproducer, without whom, in Argentina, few films are nowadays made."[11] At least in the case of Argentina, however, current figures simply do not bear out these claims. Although an increase in coproductions is notable during the 1980s, figures in more recent years do not show significant or sustained rises. International coproductions account for only 23 percent of the Argentine films on general release in the country between 1995 and 2006; expressed as a proportion of films *produced* in Argentina, many of which are never screened commercially, this figure would be smaller still.[12]

What is clearly the case, of course, is that those Argentine films that have been widely distributed internationally have been produced with external funding, often Spanish: *El hijo de la novia* (Juan José Campanella, 2001) was coproduced with Spain, and *Nueve reinas* (Fabián Bielinsky, 2000) was financed on the basis of a script-writing competition launched by Patagonik, a multinational production company with significant Spanish interests. To overemphasize the role of international coproductions in Argentine cinema is to overlook the majority of Argentine films that are not financed in this way and that therefore do not receive such wide distribution, thus replicating in criticism the imbalance already existing in the market; it is also often to disregard the very important role of the state in contemporary Argentine production.

Despite the decline of the film industry in the early 1990s and the devastation of the recent Crisis, the state has reemerged in Argentina with significant power to promote the production of local films and to create a space, however limited, for their exhibition. The taxes introduced by the "Ley de Cine" created a new and substantial source of funding for Argentine filmmaking, to be administered by the INCAA. The figures reveal the extent of the resurgence enjoyed by cinema in the wake of this legislation: in 1994 only eleven new Argentine films were released, and between them they mustered less than 2 percent of all ticket sales; in 2000 the number of new films released had risen to forty-four, and their market share had increased by more than tenfold.[13] Although the INCAA's funding was cut at crucial points in the deepening economic crisis, and corruption marred its activities during the 1990s, the institute's support of national filmmaking has been significant. Very few films are currently made in Argentina without loans and grants made available through its funds; even the box-office hit *El hijo de la novia*, nominated for an Oscar, would not otherwise have recovered its costs.[14] More recent resolutions bringing in more stringent screening quotas have redoubled efforts to protect screening time for local films, with greater success.[15] In addition the INCAA has recently embarked on a program to dedicate cinemas to the exclusive screening of Argentine and other Spanish-language productions both at home and abroad, where venues are located as far afield as Paris and Rome.

National cinemas in other Latin American countries also appear to be flourishing in the context of increased state support. Similar legislation has been introduced in Brazil, again with clear results for the national film industry.[16] Even Mexico, which appeared to be pursuing the route of greater privatization for its cinema with the introduction in 1992 of the *Nueva Ley Federal de Cinematografía*, reducing state subsidies for production and phasing out screening quotas,[17] has since passed legislation (the *Nuevo Reglamento de la Ley de Cinematografía*, 2001) to bolster state involvement in the financing of production and to protect screening time for national films, although the implementation of these provisions has been less than straightforward.[18] The impact of public finance is strongly implied by the fact that production in Mexico dropped 40 percent in 2002, when cinema funding was accidentally left out of the state budget, and recovered the following year, when it was reinstated.[19] This pattern, Randal Johnson notes, has repeated itself throughout the history of cinema in Mexico, Argentina, and Brazil, in which periods of success have most often been accompanied by enhanced state support;[20] current figures seem only to confirm the crucial role of the state in financing the production of national films and ensuring their distribution. This role has, of course, produced its own set of distortions and inequalities. Filmmakers in Argentina have often maintained an uneasy relationship with the INCAA, whose decisions over funding have repeatedly been subject to allegations of a lack of transparency, impartiality, or coherent artistic grounds. While far from revealing an unsullied picture of aesthetic discernment and beneficence on the part of state institutions, close examination of the role of state policy and its impact on national production is key to an understanding of Argentine film.[21]

The perceived growth in coproductions across Latin America has led some critics to dismiss national film studies as old-fashioned, nostalgic exercises. Julianne Burton-Carvajal argues that "the prevalence of co-production strategies in the 1980s and 1990s calls the very concept of national cinema into question."[22] Stock claims that "critical discourse remains fixed within national and regional paradigms, while globalization increasingly impacts that body of work known as Latin American Cinema."[23] The argument advanced here—on dubious empirical grounds, as we have seen—represents a call for criticism to abandon old categories in the face of a new, globalized, world order. Pierre Bourdieu suggests that the most insidious operation of the neoliberal program is its ability to project itself "as the scientific description of reality," as an inevitable development rather than the application of a certain set of economic principles. The chief target of neoliberalism's *"methodical destruction of collectives"*—which include unions, cooperatives, and even the family—is the state, "repository of all the universal ideas associated with the idea of the *public.*"[24] Pronouncements made by critics of Latin American film concerning transnational production as the only, or principal, "viable route" reflect something of the hegemony of neoliberal discourses, which have succeeded in presenting themselves as the only possible path for economic development. Doreen Massey observes in this regard the extent to which globalization has "come to have almost the ineluctability of a grand narrative," removing the economic and the technological from political discussion, such that "the only political questions become ones concerning our subsequent adaptation to the inevitability."[25] Careful attention to the language and assumptions of criticism plays an important role in contesting the "inevitability" of the neoliberal model. In a sober passage on globalization David Harvey charges the Left with adopting the discourses of globalization too readily as a description of the state of the world, thereby "circumscrib[ing] its own political possibilities": "That so many of us took the concept on board so uncritically in the 1980s and 1990s, allowing it to displace the far more politically charged concepts of imperialism and neocolonialism, should give us pause. It made us weak opponents of the politics of globalization particularly as these became more and more central to everything that US foreign policy was trying to achieve. The only politics left was a politics of conserving and in some instances downright conservative resistance."[26] The ready replacement in criticism of the national with the transnational not only presents globalization as inevitable and natural but in the context of Latin American cinema even outstrips globalization's own erosion of frontiers in its eagerness to proclaim the death of the nation.

Both Burton-Carvajal and Stock draw on Néstor García Canclini's seminal article, "Will There Be Latin American Cinema in the Year 2000? Visual Culture in a Postnational Era." García Canclini asks, "What remains of national identities in a time of globalization and interculturalism, of multinational coproduction and . . . regional integration? What remains when information, artists, and capital constantly cross borders?"[27] The article has almost exclusively been read as a call for criticism to abandon a restrictive national perspective and embrace a new internationalism. In fact, in the context of the privatization of culture industries, García Canclini argues very strongly for the important role of the state "as a locus of public interest" to prevent the subordination of this to "market forces." He contends that "the question remains as to whether a society's sociocultural sense of itself can be produced like merchandise and accumulated like capital. . . . It is necessary to refute the neoliberals' swift transfer of the responsibility for narrating history and identity to enterprising monopolies and reducing the circulation of those narratives to consumption in homes."[28] As he argues elsewhere, what is at stake here is a properly democratic access to the public realm: a diminished role for the state in relation to information, art, and communication will result in the conversion of these areas of public life into merchandise available to the privileged classes but inaccessible to the majority.[29] As already noted, the situation of the film industries of Argentina and Brazil—the two largest national industries in Latin America—has shifted significantly since the original publication of García Canclini's article in 1993, with a dramatic reversal in the decline of state funding for cinema in these countries. However, his appreciation of the role of cinema within the public sphere in many Latin American countries remains an important corrective to a deterritorialized film criticism that has refashioned his arguments for a very different purpose. It is the public role of culture that is undervalued in a transnational approach to film.

The work of Stock and D'Lugo, among others, has been important in challenging essentialist concepts of the nation. Stock suggests that cinema studies organized around the nation reveal "a critical nostalgia for cultural authenticity." She calls instead for a postnational criticism "which does not privilege origins, which does not insist upon purity, and which is not intent on closure."[30] It is only with a genuine attention to the national context of cinema, however, that the precise dynamics of transnational exchange come properly into focus.[31] As King notes more recently, again in response to García Canclini's article, "there *was* a Latin American cinema in 2000 and . . . the nation remained the principal site for both the production and the reception of movies."[32] In the case of Argentina, calls to write off the nation as a framework for film analysis are premature. This does not preclude, however, analysis that remains sensitive to the nation as a porous entity: specifically, the nation as unfinished project, hybrid, transculturated, marginalized, and positioned as dependent within the asymmetrical structures of globalization. Placing Argentine films within their national context also allows us to locate their complex identity-negotiations, not solely or primarily within the undifferentiated discourse of global flows but within a long and specifically Argentine history of hybridity, one that may be related to but remains distinct from similar histories, such as those of Mexico or of European nations.

Paul Julian Smith concludes his study of *Amores perros* by contrasting trade perspectives and academic perspectives on Latin American film, stating that much of the difference between the two is owing to "their respective biases: business will tend to favour private investment, leftist scholars public protectionism."[33] Masao Miyoshi, in his critique of the reduction of the public and critical role of the university under increasing corporate domination, suggests that the gap may be narrowing between these two perspectives. He notes that, although the postwar introduction of new disciplines and perspectives such as multiculturalism, ethnic studies, and postcolonial studies was a response to existing hegemonies, "there is a large area of agreement between corporate needs (labor control, market expansion, denationalization, privatization, entrepreneurism, and transnationalization) and such cross-border studies."[34] It is vital that there should ultimately be no reconciliation between the two perspectives Smith describes if scholarship is not simply to mimic—and thus legitimize—the maneuvers of the market, which (as Sarlo reminds us) are always self-interested and merely replace one hierarchy (that of the traditional values of art and the academy) with another, no less absolutist for its veiling in an illusory pluralism.[35] However unfashionable the category of "nation" has become, I share Harvey's unease with the swift removal from academic discourse of such "older" terms, including *imperialism* and *neocolonialism*, and their replacement with *transnationalism* and *globalization*. It is, in any case, necessary to insist that these terms are politically marked and not neutral scientific descriptors of the contemporary world.

Further objections to the retention of the nation as an analytical paradigm are voiced by critics addressing postcolonial issues in the study of world cinema and Third Cinema. Gerald M. Macdonald, for whom "the ironic condition that must be drawn from examining national film industries is that the nation is largely irrelevant to the film industry," rejects the tendency toward national film studies that he claims to be particularly associated with the analysis of Third World cinema. He suggests that there is something insidious in the way that "the First World-created world order of independent, territorially discrete, sovereign nation-states is paralleled by our thinking in terms of discrete national cinemas."[36] Likewise, although Paul Willemen does argue for the importance of the nation in Third Cinema, he observes with some unease that "the West invented nationalism" and that its history is bound up with imperialist domination.[37] Given the colonized world's equally long history of resistance in the form of hybridization, recycling, and parody, however, it should not surprise us if, as one of many different strategies of resistance and survival in a world market, its cinema should reflect back to the West an image of the reterritorialized nation. Recent Argentine films, as I will argue in more detail in chapter 5, are often implicated in a dual effort to chart the decline of the state and to question its legitimacy while reasserting national identity and rebuilding a sense of community mobilized around an idea of the nation.

TEXTS OF TRANSITION: INDEPENDENT ART
UNDER NEOLIBERALISM

A concern with questions of national identity and social fragmentation links contemporary Argentine cinema with films of the previous generation, from which they diverge radically in aesthetic terms. Here I trace some of these continuities and ruptures, providing an introduction to New Argentine Cinema by comparing and contrasting its hallmarks with those of filmmaking in the 1980s and early 1990s. Films of this earlier period, whether or not they engage directly with the experience of the 1976–83 dictatorship, frequently explore themes of exile, loss, absence, betrayal, complicity, loneliness, imprisonment, and insanity. They testify to a profound sense of shattered identity, both personal and collective. This experience of fragmentation and dislocation is often expressed in the narrative form of these films, which displace the events of history onto allegorical structures. Thus, for example, practices at a psychiatric hospital in Eliseo Subiela's *Hombre mirando al sudeste* (1986) become symbolic of the torture and repression carried out in clandestine military detention centers during the 1970s. In many films of this period an investigation into the intricate relationships between image, discourse, power, and complicity that allowed the regime to maintain control gives rise to a profound questioning of the language of cinematic representation. The films of Subiela, Fernando Solanas, and Alejandro Agresti, three of the key auteurs of this period, demonstrate a marked skepticism toward the politics of realism, expressing social fragmentation and disorientation through experimentation with surrealist imagery (Subiela), hyperbole and the grotesque (Solanas), or the clash of competing discourses, styles, and genres (Agresti).

These directors, extremely popular in the 1980s with film festival audiences across the world, rapidly began to lose local audiences in the 1990s. Indeed, the first half of the decade saw a general slump in both the production and distribution of national films.[38] Film production was relatively unsupported by the state: typically, loans, rather than grants, were available to filmmakers, and these covered only up to 50 percent of the total cost of the film. To these difficulties were added the problems of distribution in an increasingly competitive market. Cinemagoing had been falling since the 1970s, and hundreds of independent screens were continuing to close across the country.[39] In a reduced market national films lost out to competition from foreign films. In the worst year, 1994, Argentine films failed to attract even 2 percent of spectators.[40] Economic arguments notwithstanding, there is also a sense in which Argentine film becomes estranged from its audience during this period: spectators overwhelmingly opted for Hollywood productions over local films, which were often perceived as too moralizing in tone and too literary in discourse. The success of the films associated with New Argentine Cinema was due in large part to their ability to overcome both financial obstacles and a creative impasse, exploring new forms of aesthetic representation, as well as developing alternative methods of film production. To throw into relief the particular innovations of New Argentine Cinema, in the sections below I read two films by "veteran" directors Subiela and Solanas as texts of transition, which mark the exhaustion of a certain kind of filmmaking that had enjoyed international recognition in the 1980s and early 1990s and point toward the necessity of a regeneration in Argentine filmmaking. The cinematic languages of these two directors succeed in capturing the forms and tones of a crisis in the film industry but prove incapable of the kind of self-renovation that would bring new energy to Argentine cinema in more recent years.

No te mueras sin decirme adónde vas (Subiela, 1995) and La nube (Solanas, 1998) are highly reflexive productions that take as their respective subjects the decline in popularity of national cinema and independent theater in Buenos Aires. Their central concerns—state corruption, globalization, the consequences of rapid and uneven modernization, the increasing division between politics and culture, problems of national identity—are persistent themes in Argentine cinema at the turn of the twenty-first century. However, in their nostalgia for times of greater integration between the spheres of culture and politics, their insistent use of a particular kind of visual trope, and their assertion of a national voice, these films appear to be throwbacks to a previous era of filmmaking.

La nube: A Critique of the Culture Industry

La nube differs little in aesthetic or ideological terms from Solanas's earlier fiction films, such as Sur (1987) and El viaje (1990). Recurrent themes in his oeuvre, stretching back to his renowned documentary collaboration with Octavio Getino, La hora de los hornos (1968), include political corruption in Argentina and the nation's exploitation by foreign powers. While the nation is in many ways the organizing paradigm of his films, it is the nation as an unfinished project, still in search of its own identity, dependent, and ransacked of its natural resources. The rhetoric of La nube is assembled around a nostalgic evocation of the close relationship between art and politics in the 1960s and 1970s, now perceived to be irrevocably shattered. In its portrayal of the increasingly estranged relationship between art and popular resistance, the film draws particular attention to the erosion of public spaces of culture in the 1990s and the withdrawal of state funding, which might have guarded independent art from the ruthless forces of the market. The narrative follows the plight of a modest theater in Buenos Aires, the Espejo, already struggling to pay its electricity bills with the meager takings from dwindling audiences and now under threat of demolition. The Espejo represents just one of the city's many independent theaters that were forced to close in the years leading up to the making of *La nube*. Max and his theater group, full of 1960s idealism about the social function of avant-garde art—but more than a little tinged with contemporary disillusionment—perform to a handful of spectators, the majority of whom have passed retirement age. The film includes scenes from Eduardo Pavlovsky's play *Rojos globos rojos*, first performed in 1994, which also depicts a small theater group under threat of eviction for not paying its bills. *La nube* is perhaps Solanas's darkest fiction film, intended to unveil the truth behind the deceptively affluent 1990s as a decade in which national culture all but disappeared, unemployment rose alarmingly, and the justice system was dogged by corruption and impunity. It gives voice to an acute nostalgia for a bygone era when art "conmovía a mucha gente" (moved many people), playing a significant role in political consciousness and popular resistance.

As if to signal the condition of contemporary art in Argentina, sapped of all vitality by the predatory forces of capitalism and modernization, photography in *La nube* is drained of vivid color to leave gloomy, gray-blue halftones. The film opens with a series of short sequences, edited in reverse motion, in which the citizens of Buenos Aires are seen walking or driving backward through the city's streets. Similar scenes punctuate the narrative of the film at frequent intervals, creating a powerful visual trope for a nation "camina marcha atrás" (moving in reverse gear). Repeated appeals are made in *La nube* to the state to buttress the precarious position of independent art, abandoned in the relentless march toward modernization and commercialization. A local government official justifies the government's plans to demolish the theater and redevelop the area by claiming that they are "recuperando terrenos improductivos" (recuperating unproductive land) in order to build a shopping mall: "algo para toda la gente, ¿no?" (something for everyone, right?). The theater group grudgingly accepts the pointlessness of resistance: what works today, they acknowledge, is "lo que es producto y se paga. Los grandes espectáculos. Lo que se mira en términos de renta y rating" (a product that pays. Big shows. Something that can be gauged by profit and ratings). *La nube* locates itself within an Adorno-esque tradition, lamenting the loss of potential for critique and the danger to high art represented by the culture industry. For Adorno and Horkheimer, "amusement under late capitalism is the prolongation of work. It is sought after as an escape from the mechanized work process, and to recruit strength in order to be able to cope with it again. But at the same time mechanization has such power over a man's leisure and happiness, and so profoundly determines the manufacture of amusement goods, that his experiences are inevitably after-images of the work process itself."[41] Ordinary citizens, we are told in a similar vein in *La nube*, return home exhausted, with no energy to think: for that reason "la cultura hoy es la tele, lo que se puede consumir rápido, como una hamburguesa" (today, culture is television, that which can be consumed quickly, like a hamburger).

The corrupt, neoliberal Argentine state fails in *La nube* to exercise its responsibilities in the protection of high art. In a comic inversion Buenos Aires becomes the circus, the theatrical stage full of pomp and performance, while the Espejo becomes the preserve of rationality. Solanas explains that the three principal spaces of the film—the theater, the psychiatric hospital, and the court—are conceived as different guises of madness: "El teatro como la sublimación, el desdoblamiento, el ensueño, la no realidad. Los tribunales como el escenario donde está depositada la historia de los conflictos y delitos del país. . . . Los tres espacios tenían que ver con una sociedad donde lo irracional viene avanzando" (The theater as sublimation, a psychic splitting, dream, unreality. The courts as the stage on which the history of the nation's conflicts and crimes are played out. . . . The three spaces have to do with a society in which the irrational is on the advance).[42] Dialogue between demonstrators and officials in the court is often sung in the style of recitative, borrowing from the operatic tradition something of its theatrical excess, stereotyping, and artificiality to portray justice in Argentina as a farcical ritual. Solanas introduces the theme of the bankrupt state, which would become an important concern in post-Crisis films. Enrique, in possession of a court judgment that entitles him to the payment of his pension, is told that it has been annulled because "el Estado no puede pagar lo que no tiene" (the State can't pay what it doesn't have). The greatest scandal of recent Argentine economic history, as explored at greater length in Solanas's *Memoria del saqueo* (2004), is the wholesale privatization of national industries during the 1990s and the squandering of the profits. In this context culture—a national resource that could not be sold off quite as easily as the oil industry, the national airline, trains, or the telephone network—has been abandoned, left to occupy derelict spaces and constantly threatened by predatory market forces.

If the state has neglected national culture, the ransacking of its riches has been carried out, *La nube* claims, with the complicity of the Argentine public. In the absence of state support, Solanas suggests that it is up to the public to decide whether the "pasión" of independent theater will die with its last practitioners or become the site of renewed political and cultural opposition. A passage abridged in the film from *Rojos globos rojos* raises the issue of societal complicity in the impoverishment of culture:

> Era un país curioso, la mayoría de la gente inteligente dependía de un grupo de idiotas; era asombroso observar como este grupo de idiotas supervisaba la suerte de los talentosos. Lo increíble es que los inteligentes, para ser aceptados por los idiotas, ¿sabés qué hicieron? Empobrecieron sus ideas. La idiotización de la comarca llegó lenta e inexorablemente. Las ideas cada vez más idiotas de los talentosos producían una enorme aceptación de parte de los idiotas, que premiaban a los talentosos idiotizados con cargos cada vez más prestigiosos.

> [It was a curious country, the majority of the intelligent people depended on a group of idiots; it was astonishing to observe how this group of idiots took charge of the fate of the talented ones. The unbelievable part is that the intelligent ones, so that they could be accepted by the idiots, do you know what they did? They impoverished their ideas. The idiotization of the land took place slowly and inexorably. The ever more idiotic ideas of the talented ones brought about a wholesale acceptance on the part of the idiots, who rewarded the idiotized talented ones with ever more prestigious positions.]

In these lines we might detect an ironic inversion of an oft-cited passage from *Los siete locos* (1929), by Roberto Arlt (who is mentioned in *Rojos globos rojos*). In Arlt's dystopian vision of a future governed by capitalists and technocrats, society has permitted the development of a new hierarchy, in which "la mayoría vivirá mantenida escrupulosamente en la más absoluta ignorancia . . . y la minoría será la depositaria absoluta de la ciencia y del poder" (the majority will live carefully kept in the most absolute ignorance . . . and the minority will be the sole repository of science and power). The minority will ensure that the majority is kept happy by administrating cheap pleasures and the "milagros apócrifos" (apocryphal miracles) with which science will simulate faith and divinity.[43] At the end of the twentieth century Pavlovsky and Solanas imagine a ruling elite that is the depository not of science and knowledge but of ignorance: in a full reversal, a small group of "idiots" now control the fate of the intelligent masses. The compliance of intellectuals in a nonmeritocratic, capitalist regime has led to the erosion of freedom and the depletion of culture.

A measure of success, "ecos de solidaridad" (echoes of solidarity), comes at the end of the film in two forms. The showdown between the demolition workers and the theater's occupants, defiantly threatening to sacrifice their lives to protect the crumbling edifice, attracts a small crowd who throw stones at the workmen until the diggers are forced into a hasty retreat. The special performance organized at the theater attracts a modest but enthusiastic audience, who erupt into applause as Cardenal pronounces his final words, "¡Hay que resistir!" (We must resist!). This very limited expression of support hardly amounts, however, to an optimistic perspective on the future of independent theater in Argentina, and although the narrative closes with a successful performance, the fate of the theater is left unresolved. That *La nube* conceives of resistance as an exercise in obstinacy and conservatism— the jealous guarding of an ever-diminishing space of independence for art— reveals the extent of the cultural impasse to which the film testifies, and which it cannot itself transcend. Solanas's characters appear to resist more by stubborn habit than inspiration, and they stick to their chosen path with little hope of redemption, as suggested by the last intertitle, "Obstinación." For Max, change means capitulation; his pride forbids him to compromise. As he states to the government official, if he were to accept his proposal of a directorship of a new theater with a more "inclusive" program, "habría resistido al pedo toda mi vida" (I would have resisted for nothing all my life). To shield oneself from the possible discovery that one's lifework has been in vain effectively becomes the organizing principle of *La nube*: one that paralyses rather than breathes new life into the arts.

Although Solanas's critique of capitalism and modernity finds echoes in films more typical of the post-1995 period, he employs in *La nube* a certain aesthetic that is rejected by other, often younger, filmmakers as epitomizing an outmoded cinematic language of the 1980s. Characteristic of this cinema is the construction of a highly stylized visual rhetoric, which often fractures space to form heterogeneous, reflexive, and critical texts. Notable, too, is its creation of a narrative voice that assumes the task of speaking to, and for, the nation and the development of a hierarchical relationship between word and image at the service of communicating an unambiguous political message. Closer analysis of these devices will suggest some significant points of divergence in relation to post-1995 cinema in Argentina.

The narrative voice-over of *La nube* is not easily defined as belonging either to a particular character in the story who is also its narrator (intradiegetic) or to a third-person, omniscient narrator strictly outside the story (extradiegetic). This blurring of perspective is crucial to the film's positing of an imagined national community, whose members suffer together at the hands of a corrupt, bureaucratic, and inhumane establishment. The narrator takes no part in the film's events but assumes a position of solidarity with the theater group depicted in the narrative, based on a shared generational and national experience: "esto que voy a contarles nace en la rara pasión que tuvimos por el teatro los de mi generación" (the story I'm going to tell you is born of the peculiar passion those of my generation had for the theater). The narrative voice that emerges is the "national we," as Solanas—whose voice it is—identifies with, and protests on behalf of, the unpaid pensioners, the victims of police violence, the evicted, the ignored, and the exploited. This spilling-over from third-person to first-person narration effectively provides a bridge between the characters and the public. It also adds suggestively to the film's layers of reflexivity, such that when Max declares, in character as Cardenal in the closing sequence of the film, "Lo que más les jode a ellos es que nosotros sigamos defendiendo siempre lo mismo" (What annoys them most is that we carry on, always defending the same), we understand that the play's original lines have been appropriated here not just to refer to the predicament of the Espejo Theater in *La nube* but also to Solanas's filmography as a whole. The use of voice-over, so favored by Solanas in both fiction and documentary films, has been all but abandoned in contemporary Argentine cinema. This reflects a typically postmodern unease with a monologic, didactic perspective that confers a single narrative on disparate events, but it also suggests a growing reticence to imagine the nation in a homogenizing sense or to "speak for" the citizens of an increasingly segregated society.

This deliberate confusion between what is in the story and what is external to it becomes apparent in other ways in the film and forms an essential part of Solanas's cinema of critique. The soulful bandoleon music that often accompanies the transitions between scenes is sometimes simply part of an extradiegetic soundtrack; at other times the singer, Luis, is a character in the story who sings on local radio from his home in a psychiatric institution; at still other times, the same singer performs in front of the camera with his band but remains unconnected to the action. In such instances Luis appears to eschew his role as a character in the film's story in order to accompany its performance and sometimes even to comment directly on it through the tango lyrics. The space marked out by the frame is therefore not unified or homogeneous but includes elements of extradiegetic reflection. Such devices—which often draw on Brechtian aesthetics—encourage the spectator to remain at a critical distance from the issues raised in the film rather than producing an unquestioning emotional response. As Max recollects his

1. Solanas borrows from theatrical staging conventions rather than the cinematic technique of the flashback to fracture time and space within the frame in *La nube*.

last, bitter encounter with his wife some years ago, she appears as a backlit figure in the top right-hand area of the screen, transported to a space a few feet behind him in the cavernous Espejo Theater (Figure 1). Their exchange of recriminations is directly reenacted for us. Solanas plays here with theatrical conventions, in which the stage becomes "split" into different spaces to permit the representation of flashbacks or a dialogue taking place between two characters in different locations. Such devices are uncommon in film, in which the flashback is conventionally used to represent events previous to the film's story, and montage is usually employed to bring together characters talking on the telephone without the need to split the screen. Within *La nube* this overlapping of theatrical and cinematographic languages provides a further instance of the reflexive embedding of performances within other performances in the film, such that many of these textual layers are potentially both the object and source of critical comment: do the citations of Pavlovsky's play comment on Solanas's film, or vice versa? In *La nube*, as in many of Solanas's other films, antinaturalistic devices create a space in which narrative and critique, text and interpretation, are brought together in a search for a genuinely critical, political art. Such transgressions were to become much less common in the more unified and homogenous spaces of neorealist-inspired cinema in the late 1990s.

Essential to Solanas's creation of a cinema of critique is a complex relationship between myth and minutiae. With reference to the specifically localized and historicized nature of much of Solanas's critique in *La nube* (as in *El viaje*), Gustavo J. Castagna claims that Solanas "deja de ser un realizador de cine para transformarse en el columnista de un noticiero" (stops being a filmmaker and becomes a news reporter).[44] From the realistic detail of current political issues—such as the pensions crisis—we are transported to the grander scale of myth, as Solanas draws on magical realist formulae in his hyperbolic representations of an absurdly undeveloped Argentina. Indeed, there is more than a fleeting evocation in *La nube* of the magical realist novels of Gabriel García Márquez: we are told that Buenos Aires has so far suffered 1,651 days of rain, reminiscent of the precision with which the four years, eleven months, and two days of rain are recorded in Macondo in *Cien años de soledad*, and, as in *El coronel no tiene quien le escriba*, the elderly wait in vain for the arrival of their promised pension. These disparate fields of meaning are brought together in quasi-allegorical structures. The incongruity that Castagna finds inappropriate is integral to the film's rooting of the local and specific within a larger, national, or continental perspective; it is a studied incongruity which—in the same way that the prosaic language of complaint is awkwardly rendered in the elevated tones of opera—is intended to distance the spectator and stimulate a critical approach to the film's material. Such underlying faith in allegorical modes of representation is entirely absent in more contemporary films, which express much less confidence about the possibility of generalizing from the everyday.

For all their striking imagery, Solanas's films establish a hierarchical relationship between word and image in which the word enjoys primacy. The humor of *La nube* depends—as it does in *El viaje* and other films by Solanas, stretching back to *La hora de los hornos*—on the repeated use of certain visual tropes based on verbal puns. The touches of surrealism in *La nube*—Max, explaining to a class of drama students how to believe themselves paragons of talent, equal only to God, levitates above them (Figure 2); Cachito, struck senseless by the beauty of Fuló's seminaked body, whispers "me derrito" and dissolves into a puddle of water[45]—are produced by means of a common technique, by which the image is mobilized to illustrate the word, to visualize a metaphor or a turn of phrase. This hierarchical relationship reflects, of course, the clear dominance of the political over the aesthetic in Solanas's filmmaking. By contrast, the majority of contemporary films do not allow the visual and the material to be placed at the service of an explicit political agenda. The films of Lisandro Alonso, for example, shun dialogue almost entirely in favor of the visual. More generally, New Argentine Cinema often resists symbolic or allegorical interpretations: there is no attempt to produce a totalizing vision but, instead, a series of micronarratives, snapshots of everyday lives, which are not subject to the rigorous patterning required by Solanas's Manichean visions. Younger directors were to make no secret of their contempt for such didactic approaches to political

2. *La nube* confirms the primacy of the word over the image, departing from a realist aesthetic as the visual is used to illustrate the verbal (here, becoming like God).

filmmaking. Cristian Bernard's and Flavio Nardini's film *76 89 03* (1999), for example, was marketed as "la primera película argentina que no tiene mensaje" (the first Argentine film not to have a message).

No te mueras sin decirme adónde vas: The Decline of the Dream Machine

Subiela's *No te mueras sin decirme adónde vas* is a less sophisticated film than *La nube*. Indeed, it was voted the worst film of the year in 1995 by readers and critics in a poll organized by the journal *El amante*.[46] The analysis of the film presented here will serve, however, to highlight another series of important contrasts with innovations in post-1995 filmmaking. Like *La nube*, *No te mueras* mourns the erosion of public spaces for mass entertainment, although this time the subject is the decline of cinema itself. The film performs a kind of homage to cinema, looking back to the invention of the first apparatus capable of projecting moving images, exactly one hundred years previously, in 1895. The opening sequence contains a flashback to Thomas Edison's laboratory in New Jersey, where a young assistant reveals his dream of inventing cinema. He is excited by "the possibility of images that provide relief. Images that liberate, images that cure, images that could give back hope. The wonderful possibility of thousands of people dreaming the same dream at the same time. The chance to beat death. . . . A dream-preserver. So that they won't vanish upon awakening, when we return to the horrors of reality."

Later in the film another flashback brings us to the height of cinema's popularity around the middle of the twentieth century. Packed audiences laugh uproariously at the latest film starring Niní Marshall, an immensely popular comic actress who starred in no fewer than eighteen films during the 1940s. This period, often remembered as the golden age of Argentine cinema, is contrasted strongly in the film with the present-day fate of the *cine de barrio*, whose slim takings from a handful of spectators do not even cover its modest costs. Don Mario's cinema in *No te mueras* eventually shares the destiny of many cinemas during the 1990s in Buenos Aires, sold off to evangelical pastors to use for church gatherings.

The film proposes a new invention to take the place of the ailing cinema industry: a "recolector de sueños" (dream collector). Leopoldo (the reincarnation of Edison's assistant, William Dickson) creates a machine that, by means of electrodes, registers the brain's activity during sleep and translates the impulses received into fuzzy images on a monitor. The parallels drawn in the film between William's invention and that of his reincarnated self lead us to recognize the dream machine as the new incarnation of cinema. (Mass fabrication of the machine becomes possible with the money Don Mario earns from the sale of the cinema.) Its precise workings remain a mystery: it is elsewhere referred to as "un traductor de almas" (a soul translator) and appears to have the ability to conjure up past loves or even to predict the future. At the end of the film, Leopoldo tests a prototype for possible entry into the mass market. The laboratory, with its dozens of cubicles, each just long enough to accommodate a single recumbent figure attached to a small monitor, brings to mind both the private spaces of psychotherapy and the ethically disturbing scenario of experiments on humans so often explored in science fiction (Figure 3). For all its power, which is depicted in overwhelmingly positive terms in the film, the dream machine remains a narcissistic invention for a fragmented, individualistic society. It represents an impoverished version of the redemptive power of cinema William envisages, which was always intended to be a social encounter ("thousands of people dreaming the same dream at the same time"). Leopoldo's machine replaces utopia with mere wish-fulfillment, art with a kind of reality show. It is designed to satisfy the demands of contemporary society for continual introspection and an endless flow of raw images.

Subiela's message—disarmingly, or perhaps disingenuously, simple—represents a rather different response to the dehumanizing materialism and commercialism of contemporary society also denounced by Solanas. As Hector Mario Cavallari writes of *Hombre mirando al sudeste*, Subiela's interest in other worlds and hidden dimensions effectively reintroduces the irrational, "para des-centrar la instauración absoluta de ese racionalismo inherente a las formaciones sociales capitalistas" (to de-center the unassailable

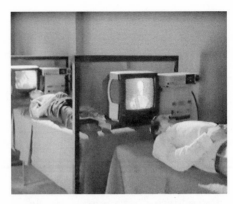

3. The dream machine in *No te mueras sin decirme adónde vas* is an impoverished version of cinema for an introspective, individualistic society; it responds to mass culture's demand for a continuous stream of raw images.

dominion of that rationalism that is inherent to capitalist social forma-tions).[47] Critics of more recent films have been less convinced by the reduc-tiveness, and the political evasiveness, of Subiela's cure for social ills, which appears to propose that "all we need is love."[48] Subiela's abiding interest in universal themes often has the effect of relegating specific political issues to the role of providing local color. The decidedly "touristic" gaze of *No te mueras* contrasts with the more serious, if oblique, treatment given to na-tional tragedy in *Hombre mirando al sudeste*, although in both films a re-liance on certain tropes borrowed from science fiction ensures that their primary frame of reference is not a national one (the trauma of the Argen-tine dictatorship) but a universal one (psychic repression and the cruelty of humanity). The figure of Carlitos in *No te mueras* reveals something of the tension between national and universal discourses in Subiela's work. Car-litos is a robot assembled with imported components—including micro-chips from California—but with "un cerebro argentino" (an Argentine brain) programmed to sing lusty tangos in female company and the ability to make a good *mate*, among other essentials of Argentine cultural know-how. The construction of Carlitos, with hardware from the United States and software from Argentina ("algo así como el ser nacional" [a little like the nation itself], observes Oscar), bears significant resemblance to Subiela's own filmmaking. Within the film's narrative, however, the robot's rhetorical function is to throw into relief the dehumanized existence of Leopoldo and his gradual understanding, through encounters with the spiritual world, that his purpose on earth is to learn to love.

The purveying of this universalist message clashes with the specifically national concerns to which the film alludes, among them the military dictatorship of 1976 to 1983. With apparent tokenism, the film includes a short sequence in which the ghost of Pablo, who was kidnapped and killed during the military regime, is recognized by a newly sensitized Leopoldo as he returns to the favorite neighborhood café of his youth. Catherine Grant, who devotes most of her discussion of *No te mueras* to the analysis of this single scene, notes the seeming incongruity of this "self-contained" episode, which at first sight represents a "pointless diversion from the thoroughly 'apolitical,' 'timeless' or 'New Age' ideology of the rest of Subiela's film." Nevertheless, Grant relates this sequence closely to the utopianism of the film and its desire to provide "resolution," suggesting that what results is "an uncomfortable papering over of rhetorical cracks in this fictional political unit which are being strategically kept open by some of the very people to whom Subiela is attempting to give 'solace.'"[49] Indeed, the film presents with nauseating ease a sentimentalized, spiritualized "closure" to the mourning process. Pablo, magically returned from death, wishes he could tell his mother how proud he is of her, wearing the white handkerchief of the Madres de Plaza de Mayo as she protests against the disappearance of her son; the special favor he asks of Leopoldo, knowing how much it will mean to his mother, is to give her the details of where his body was buried and the names of the five men who were killed with him. Deftly bypassing the urgency of the task of memory after the dictatorship, Subiela suggests instead a breathtakingly apolitical solution: the dead and the disappeared have not gone forever but live on, and if we could only expand our experience to make contact with the spirits who surround us, the work of mourning and that of memory would simply be superfluous.

Subiela's penchant for neatly sewn-up narratives, together with the theme of salvation that pervades his work, invites comparison—*malgré lui*—between the role of the cinema and of the evangelical church that now occupies its building. Don Mario laments the passing of the age of cinema but, thinking of the masses that will flock into the theater under its new management, admits that "la gente últimamente prefiere esos cuentos en lugar de las películas" (nowadays people prefer those stories to films). Beatriz Sarlo, among others, has attributed the phenomenal growth of evangelical Christianity in Argentina to the Church's ability to create community and to generate "sentidos colectivos" (collective meanings) where other institutions, including schools and political parties, have failed.[50] Despite Subiela's derision of the form of religion offered by these mass churches—in a surreal flash-forward, we see row on row of blind men and women, each with dark glasses and a stick, laughing uncontrollably at the jokes of an unseen preacher—church and cinema perform remarkably similar roles in *No te mueras*, providing a focus for collective encounters, a certain set of narratives that make sense of the surrounding chaos and, arguably, more than a touch of the "magic" Subiela wishes to reserve for cinema. For Quintín, that which Subiela condemns as the shallow offerings of evangelicalism are effectively mirrored in the form of *No te mueras* itself: "En un paralelismo increíble, mientras el viejo cine de don Mario se llena seguramente de gente que va a pedir salud, dinero y fertilidad mientras le ofrecen ondas de amor y de paz, Subiela en otra sala nos vende lo mismo por el precio de una entrada" (With astonishing symmetry, while Don Mario's old cinema is filled with people who come to ask for health, money, and fertility in exchange for waves of love and peace, in a theater next door Subiela sells exactly the same for the price of a ticket).[51] As Quintín notes, at the end of the film Leopoldo achieves prosperity and moves to a larger house, his childless wife falls pregnant, and a reunion with the first love of his life gives Oscar the strength to abandon his wheelchair. Subiela, it is argued, exchanges real questions of grave social importance for a kind of New Age optimism, preaching this message with evangelistic fervor. As with the heavily politicized agendas of Solanas's films, this emphasis sits uneasily with artistic exploration, given that—Quintín reminds us—"Predicar es convencer, hacer publicidad, atraparlo todo en una frase, disimular el dolor, la ajenidad y los problemas, las materias de las que se nutre el arte" (To preach is to convince, to advertise, to capture it all in a single phrase, to disguise pain, isolation, and problems, the material with which art is nourished).[52]

In marked contrast to Solanas, Subiela vigorously defends the role of cinema as a form of mass entertainment that should not be sullied by political overdetermination. Reflecting on the unquestioned political function of cinema in his youth, he asserts that "en una época se cargó al cine con demasiada responsabilidad. El cine tenía que hacer la revolución, que el hombre tomara conciencia, y me parece que ahí nos equivocamos. La gente paga una entrada para soñar un ratito, para volar, lo cual no quiere decir que se la estupidece" (at one time cinema was charged with too much responsibility. Cinema had to bring about revolution, to raise consciousness, and there I think we made a mistake. People buy a ticket to dream for a while, to fly, which doesn't make them stupid).[53] Most remarkably, and in contrast to the many contemporary Argentine directors who make their films in conscious opposition to Hollywood conventions, Subiela suggests that "algún día, entre tanta crítica a Hollywood, le vamos a tener que agradecer que haya salvado al cine. Sé que esto que digo puede resultar polémico, pero ellos son magos. Y en cine lo central es la magia. El cine argentino se olvidó de eso" (one day, in the midst of so much criticism directed toward Hollywood, we are going to have to thank them for saving cinema. I know that what I'm saying might be contentious, but they are magicians. And in cinema, magic is central. Argentine cinema has forgotten that).[54] Subiela inscribes *No te mueras* within this line of filmmaking; his reference to the film as "una película fantástica que intenta recuperar una magia que alguna vez tuvo el cine argentino" (a fantasy film that tries to recuperate the magic that Argentine cinema once had) also marks this project, like that of Solanas, as an essentially nostalgic one. By contrast, one of the defining characteristics of contemporary Argentine cinema is its insistence on material reality rather than transcendental matters. This is reflected in a kind of filmmaking that keeps its feet squarely on the ground: as Quintín puts it, succinctly, "la gente no vuela más en las películas argentinas" (people don't fly anymore in Argentine films).[55]

For all its emphasis on images, simulacra, and projections, *No te mueras* belongs—like *La nube*—to a cinematic tradition that privileges the spoken word over the image. Like Solanas, Subiela has often attempted to bring other creative practices (music, theater, literature, sculpture) to bear on the art of filmmaking in an attempt to enrich its aesthetic languages. His films, like those of Solanas, often employ striking visual tropes corresponding to figures of speech. In *Últimas imágenes del naufragio* (1989), for example, the struggles of Estela and her family are given metaphoric weight as they are depicted literally shipwrecked off the shores of Buenos Aires; in *El lado oscuro del corazón* (1992), Oliverio tears his heart from his chest and offers it, still throbbing, on a plate to his lover. While Subiela's debt to literary influences is more evident in other films, *No te mueras* also suffers from a tendency to "explain" its images and an overreliance on dialogue. The film's messages are pronounced in sound-bite form: "sin sueños, no somos más que un montón de vísceras y de miedos" (without dreams, we are nothing but a pile of entrails and fears); "estamos acá para aprender, sin dudas" (Leopoldo) (we are here to learn, there is no doubt); "la gente sin sueños se muere antes" (Don Mario) (people without dreams die younger); "la mente no hace más que crear abismos que sólo el corazón puede cruzar" (the spirit of Leopoldo's father) (the mind just creates chasms that only the heart may cross).

Much post-1995 filmmaking in Argentina was to reject both the explicit political agendas of Solanas's cinema and the magic and universalism of

Subiela's, in favor of a more austere and sober representation of the every-day. Although a pseudodocumentary approach was to prevail over the visual experimentation characteristic of these earlier films, this new cinema never-theless accorded more weight to the visual than the verbal. Although unwill-ing to articulate a clear political message, these films were to establish much more convincing aesthetic relations with the radical cinema of the 1960s in Latin America, itself heavily influenced by Italian neorealism. In production terms, too, the auteur tradition of relatively high-budget films, which had dominated the 1980s and early 1990s in Argentina, gave way to a plethora of independent, collaborative projects on shoestring budgets, again harking back to the ad hoc filmmaking practices of the 1960s. In many ways this new departure in filmmaking represents greater continuity with Solanas's *La hora de los hornos* than his own later films. Instead of lamenting the reduction in state support for culture, New Argentine Cinema simply cut its own budget, using black-and-white images, cheaper 16-mm film, or even digital video. Rather than competing directly with Hollywood styles or asserting a place in mainstream culture, new directors often deliberately chose to inhabit the interstices, making "small" films that signal in their form the interrelations between production, politics, commerce, and aes-thetics that become much more marked outside First World centers of filmmaking.

2

NEW ARGENTINE CINEMA
AND THE PRODUCTION
OF SOCIAL KNOWLEDGE

The relationship between New Argentine Cinema and Italian neorealism has been repeatedly averred by critics but rarely explored in any depth. Parallels are frequently drawn in terms of aesthetic approaches or common themes of unemployment and poverty. David Oubiña finds allegations of thematic similarities more convincing than formal ones: "La conexión entre *Pizza, birra, faso* y *Roma, ciudad abierta* es más bien un referente de precarización. . . . Lo que hay en común entre esas dos películas es esa cualidad del referente y no una idea formal" (The connection between *Pizza, birra, faso* and *Rome, Open City* is really the idea of economic instability. . . . What these two films have in common is a point of reference in reality, rather than any formal similarity).[1] Other critics have drawn attention to the considerable coincidence that does exist in formal criteria, including the use of nonprofessional actors and non-studio locations.[2] Both New Argentine Cinema and Italian neorealism share an impetus to develop low-budget methods of filmmaking; in both cases this impulse arises partly from economic necessity and partly as a deliberate attempt to break away from the technical perfection and industry-based modus operandi often associated with the higher-budget productions of their cinematic precursors. The grainy, unfinished, "ad hoc" nature of these low-budget, independent films expresses with greater eloquence the fissures and imperfections of the present, both in postwar Italy and in contemporary Argentina.

The historical analogy breaks down, of course, when we remember that what was innovative in Italy of the 1940s and 1950s cannot, logically speaking, be innovative in Argentina fifty years later. If the social content of New Argentine Cinema is just as urgent (misery is always new to those on whom it falls), the use of neorealist techniques, although in some ways marshaled to effect a greater austerity, is not new in the same way. It enacts a staged return, a conscious harking-back, to a moment in film history when art and politics, as well as form and content, appeared to enjoy a unique rapprochement. This moment is also played out (arguably already replayed) in the radical social documentaries of the 1960s in Latin America. The principal directors associated with this movement—such as Fernando Solanas, Octavio Getino, and Fernando Birri (who studied at Rome's Centro Sperimentale di Cinematografia before founding his own school in Santa Fe, Argentina)— were profoundly influenced by Italian neorealism. They found the improvised feel and the immediacy of neorealism, together with its anti-industrial modes of production, to be highly suited to the needs of a new, socially committed, and even militant form of documentary filmmaking in Latin America. In contemporary discourses the decade of the 1960s has come to signify a crucial moment of imbrication between the political and aesthetic avant-gardes in Latin America, and this constitutes one of the key points of reference for New Argentine Cinema. The cinematic innovations of both periods—Italian neorealism of the postwar period and then Latin American appropriations of the 1960s and early 1970s under a more explicitly socialist banner—reappear as citations in New Argentine Cinema in the same way that the handheld camera may cite the style of an independent documentary in a film that does not actually engage in documentary practice. Just as the first neorealist films were not transparent windows onto reality but highly wrought works of art, so New Argentine Cinema does not "strip away" representational layers to present us with raw reality but replaces one aesthetic with another; the conscious use of now-iconic neorealist techniques adds a further series of displacements.

In many ways the films associated with New Argentine Cinema reconstruct neorealism under a postmodern, reflexive lens: the use of citation remits nostalgically to a period in which film underwent a crucial revitalization in its form and played a significant role in articulating social change. This nostalgia is accompanied, paradoxically, by an equally postmodern skepticism concerning the social role of art and the possibility of political action in the present. The "new" filmmaking techniques of New Argentine Cinema have, then, as much to do with a crisis in film as they do with a crisis in society, a hypothesis already advanced in my analyses of films by Subiela and Solanas in the previous chapter. If we understand New Argentine Cinema's return to neorealist techniques as a kind of citation system, we must move beyond the simplistic spotting of similarities between themes and techniques to consider what is ultimately being called on or invoked in these incantations: what authority is being drawn on in the use of such quotations and what argument or action they validate. I contend that what is being tentatively re-created or reimagined is a certain kind of anthropological or sociological role for film that is anchored in, and bolstered by, a particular integration of image and thought. New Argentine Cinema borrows from neorealism its rawness and newness in order to present contemporary Argentina as a territory in need of charting, dissecting, and recording and to present film as a tool ideally suited to the construction of social knowledge (or perhaps more accurately, as I will go on to suggest, to the representation of a *crisis* in social knowledge). Taxonomy is a task acquiring some urgency given the economic and political crises of recent years, which have produced a whole host of new social identities, arising from mass unemployment, shifts in migration patterns, and the changing role of the state.

It becomes clear, however, that these films do not "deliver" the social knowledge apparently promised by their semidocumentary or neorealist styles. Indeed, these borrowings are often undertaken with the paradoxical effect of *frustrating* the epistophilic desires usually associated with documentary spectatorship. They draw on structures and discourses of knowledge to explore the limits of epistemology and to deconstruct the relationship between visibility and knowledge. While Emilio Bernini claims that new filmmakers such as Adrián Caetano and Bruno Stagnaro "opusieron una idea del cine como *transparencia* a la opacidad del cine previo, respecto de una realidad contemporánea que debía registrarse" (counterposed an idea of cinema as *transparency* with the opacity of previous filmmaking, with regard to a contemporary reality that needed to be recorded),[3] I suggest that the self-consciousness with which apparently "transparent" modes of representation are used often suggests that the real subject of these films' analysis is not society so much as the gaze itself. My primary interest in this chapter is to explore how cinema's role in relation to social knowledge is reflexively imagined, or constructed, in the form of these films themselves.

Pizza, birra, faso (Caetano and Stagnaro, 1997) has been universally can-
onized as the founding text of New Argentine Cinema. Although the begin-
nings of a radical break with previous styles had already been detected in
Historias breves (1995), a compilation of winning entries for a short film
competition held by the INCAA, it was the screening of *Pizza, birra, faso* that
gave critics the confidence to herald a regeneration in Argentine cinema. In
tracing the film's debt to Italian neorealism, my aim is to bring into focus
the role played by Caetano's film, and New Argentine Cinema more generally, in relation to social knowledge. If I refer more to writing *on* neorealism
than to neorealist films themselves, it is because New Argentine Cinema
establishes a much clearer dialogue with the theory of neorealism than with
its praxis. Attending first to the film's exploration of the interstices in contemporary Argentine society—dealing as it does with marginalized figures,
a group of unemployed youths in Buenos Aires—I will then draw on Deleuze's notion of the "time-image" to interrogate its treatment of another set
of (formal) interstices within the text of the film itself. The exploration here
of the prioritization of discontinuity over continuity, and of observation over
action, both in Italian neorealism (as studied by Deleuze) and New Argentine Cinema will go some way toward laying down a framework for interpreting these films.

The movement of people and traffic in the opening sequence of *Pizza,
birra, faso* is duplicated by a camera in constant motion. This velocity is
stalled at intervals, interrupted by the credits on a black screen before the
next disorientating sequence of city shots begins. In the same way that the
speed of the city is literally paused to give way to the credits, so the film as a
whole attempts to carve a hole in the frenzied time of the city, through which
we may glimpse the lives of those who are not integrated into the space-time
of global capitalism. The city's speed continues unabated, but the film creates a pause, a space for observation: here we may already perceive something of the film's self-construction as a sociological tool, creating a possible
context in which gaps and caesuras can be introduced into the space and
time of the city. The construction of an alternative filmic temporality is also
evidenced by the abrupt transition between the first action sequence, in
which Pablo and El Cordobés board a taxi and rob a passenger at gunpoint,
and the following sequence, in which we see the rest of the group awaiting
their return. Geoffrey Kantaris reads the opening sequence as a meditation
on the space-time compression of globalized capitalism in which, as Fredric

Jameson suggests, time is experienced as "a function of speed."[4] However, crime is the boys' only point of insertion into the space-time matrix of capitalism, and we become aware of the sharp contrast in temporalities between the first sequence and the next, much more indicative of the film as a whole, in which the camera cuts to the group waiting, with nowhere to go and no schedule for getting there. The rapid movements of the handheld camera are replaced with much longer takes; with the movement of cars still visible but reduced to a background blur, and Sandra placed in the foreground, kicking her heels against the wall in boredom, we witness the superimposition of two very different temporalities (Figure 4). Marginalization in *Pizza, birra, faso* is explored primarily as a kind of temporal disjuncture rather than a spatial displacement—more out-of-phase than out-of-place.

Unemployment, as Pierre Bourdieu argues, does not simply cause poverty but "the destructuring of existence, which is *deprived among other things of its temporal structures*, and the ensuing deterioration of the whole relationship to the world, time and space."[5] *Pizza, birra, faso* demonstrates this dynamic of exclusion with great clarity. The film focuses on what Bourdieu would call "subproletarian" members of society who, without the basic security of a job, do not have the "grasp on the present" needed to conceive of a better future.[6] Excluded from society, the youths of *Pizza, birra, faso* are out of control of their own destinies: they have few ambitions or hopes, and those they do hold they seem condemned never to realize, just as El Cordobés cannot fully take hold of his desire to emigrate with Sandra and their unborn child, succeeding only in endangering and eventually destroying his own plans.

If these characters lack a hold on their present, the present is exactly that which *Pizza, birra, faso* is engaged, painstakingly, in producing for its spectators, lest the speed of global capitalism cause us to pass over those who are not integrated into it. As the opening sequences suggest, the present needs to be unveiled in a kind of archaeological exploration, a making-visible of that which has been passed over or covered up, which inhabits the gaps or is left in the wake of modernization. The production of the present is everywhere signaled in the film's style, particularly in those aspects associated with neorealism. The handheld camera seems to collapse the time between action and its recording on camera, producing an unrehearsed effect in which the camera follows the apparently spontaneous movements of its characters rather than following preprogrammed maneuvers. The illusion of a reality existing beyond the frame of the camera is also bolstered by the

4. Two distinct temporalities are superimposed in this shot of long duration from *Pizza, birra, faso*, which contrasts the anomie of the unemployed youths waiting in the foreground with the high-speed flow of traffic in the center of Buenos Aires.

use of nonprofessional actors. The dialogue appears improvised, making use of the natural pauses, interruptions, and overlappings of conversation and couched entirely in the language of the streets. Everything evokes contemporaneity as we are persuaded that what we are witnessing is somehow more real, and less staged, than what we see in more conventional filmmaking. The effect of improvisation is also generated by the film's structure: unlike in conventional crime dramas, we do not experience the climactic robbery of the disco as an event that has already been meticulously planned and rehearsed onscreen for us but find ourselves without preparation already at the scene with no knowledge of what has been planned by the group: we therefore experience the holdup not as an expected repetition but as an improvisation, as if it were being made up on the spot, an effect also created by the amateurism of the criminals, whose robberies are always bungled.

This effect of contemporaneity, a hallmark of New Argentine Cinema, gains significance if we draw some comparisons with constructions of time in other periods of Argentine film history. Sergio Wolf argues that the datedness of much Argentine film stems from its pursuit of realism. If the "golden age" of Argentine cinema from the 1930s to the early 1950s managed to effect the "abolition" of time, this is because this kind of filmmaking "no se proponía como un cine sincrónico" (did not propose itself as a simultaneous cinema): the repetition of types creates a kind of mythic time rather than a historical one. The films made under the dictatorship of 1976 to 1983, Wolf suggests, produced a kind of "frozen time," in which remakes or historical films featured prominently; by contrast, independent filmmaking, including films made toward the end of the 1990s, has often produced "un cine sincrónico," dealing with historical rather than mythical time, and exploring "la idea del *tiempo como puro presente*" (the idea of *time as pure present*). Contemporary cinema often differs from that of the early post-dictatorship period in its incapacity, or unwillingness, to forge links between past, present, and future that, in turn, reveals a crisis in certain kinds of political thought. In films of the 1980s the past (as Wolf observes) becomes "una zona que explica el presente o una coartada que permite establecer una dimensión más completa de las cosas" (a realm that explains the present or a reason that allows us to understand things more completely).[7] But in New Argentine Cinema we rarely see explicit denunciations of the dictatorship or of Menemist policies pursued during the 1990s or, indeed, any appetite for unrooting past causes or laying blame at a particular door. The youths of *Pizza, birra, faso* are not simply victims: the film clearly shows their position within a larger chain of exploitation, as others, hungrier than they, eat the food they discard; we see them dispassionately robbing those with less, as well as those with more. The psychological explanations of behavior advanced in Hollywood cinema are denied to us here: we join the action in medias res, as with so many other contemporary Argentine films, and are afforded no privileged knowledge of the boys' childhood experiences that might explain their current actions. The rigor of New Argentine Cinema lies in its refusal to grant its spectators access to comforting narratives or continuities that are out of reach for the characters themselves. Its gaze deliberately distances us, refusing to create easy identification or satiate our hunger for explanations. Films like *Pizza, birra, faso* seem to suggest that the knowledge base is simply insufficient to support glib theories or schematic representations of history: we need to start again from zero, to make visible that which had been invisible, lost in the gaps, but not in such a way that these new subjects can simply be appropriated for use in old frameworks.

The deliberately antiexplanatory approach of New Argentine Cinema links it both thematically and formally with neorealism as theorized by Deleuze, for whom postwar Italian cinema begins a transition between the "movement-image" and the "time-image." The "movement-image," or more precisely one of its forms, the "action-image," undergoes a crisis in the mid-twentieth century that Deleuze attributes to, among other things, "the war and its consequences, the unsteadiness of the 'American Dream' in all its aspects, . . . the crisis of Hollywood and its old genres."[8] The domination of the "movement-image" reflects a belief in behaviorism and determinism and in the causality of events.[9] But in the collapse of illusions that characterizes the postwar period for Deleuze, "the first things to be compromised everywhere are the linkages of situation-action, action-reaction, excitation-response, in short, the sensory-motor links which produced the action-image."[10] In the "time-image" the interstices, or the cuts, between images do not produce a continuity of action but instead carve time up into a series of discontinuities. D. N. Rodowick provides a helpful gloss of the concept as developed by Deleuze:

> There is no longer a rational interval assuring continuity in space and succession in time. Rather, the force of time produces a serialism organized by irrational intervals that produce a dissociation rather than an association of images. The interval is no longer filled by a sensorimotor situation; it neither marks the trajectory between an action and a reaction nor bridges two sets through continuity links. Instead, the interval collapses and so becomes "irrational": not a link bridging images, but an interstice between them, an unbridgeable gap whose recurrences give movement as displacements in space marked by false continuity.[11]

This kind of dissociative cut is clearly in evidence in *Pizza, birra, faso*: transitions between sequences rarely allow us to construct a temporal framework (do the events take place over a couple of days or several months?), and cuts are not placed at the service of establishing action-reaction schemata. The elliptical structure of the narrative, in which key scenes are left out (such as the ones in which the boys devise their pickpocketing strategy for the job center queue or decide to carry out the disco robbery), leaves room for the insertion of scenes that have no clear narrative or thematic purpose, in which characters merely wait around or observe life around them. Deleuze found cinema of the time-image to be characterized by a privileging of "purely optical situations" over action, in which the character becomes more of a spectator than an actor.[12] We can already see a preference in Caetano's film (which would become much more marked in Trapero's *Mundo grúa*) for a midshot framing all characters together, rather than the close-ups and shot/reverse-shot montage of classical cinema, both of which enhance our understanding of characters' emotional reactions to events: the reduction in such sequences detracts from a behaviorist approach to the analysis of character and action.

In the interstices, the intervals, of film resides the indeterminate: that which confounds action rather than knits it together. In Rodowick's words, "The interval no longer disappears into the seam between movements and actions. Rather, it becomes a ceaseless opening of time—a space of becoming—where unforeseen and unpredictable events may occur."[13] Although New Argentine Cinema, like Italian neorealism, appears to have fashioned itself for an epistemological task, that of documenting new forms of society, its dissociative form and its refusal to indulge our desire for a clear social or political meaning to be imposed on its fragmentary narratives represents a deliberate attempt to stop short of simplistic political manifestos. It constructs, instead, a reality that exceeds the possibility of action, in which the character "shifts, runs and becomes animated in vain, [and] the situation he is in outstrips his motor capacities on all sides" (Deleuze).[14]

In *Pizza, birra, faso* the spectator's own ability to act is also severely circumscribed, reduced to an act of observation. As the film comes to an end with the death of its protagonists, shot by pursuing police officers, the camera moves unexpectedly to occupy a position on the deck of the departing ferryboat Sandra has just boarded. As the ferry draws slowly but inexorably away, the spectator is effectively imprisoned here, in the longest shot of the film, with the camera unwaveringly fixed on its subject. Passive and helpless, we can only watch the aftermath of the shooting from an ever-increasing distance, as police radio exchanges on the soundtrack report the deaths of two young males. This final scene metaphorically confirms the replacement of action with observation: confronted by the bathos and the tragedy of these lives, we become aware of our inability to act and of our condition as spectators. Caetano's film, like many associated with New Argentine Cinema, allows us to glimpse the marginalized, those living in the interstices of the city who are rarely accorded any presence on the big screen, but it also ensures that they remain "other" to us, distant, unexplained, and resisting capture on film, always exceeding the frame of the camera or moving out of sight.

What New Argentine Cinema does to action on the formal level, producing ruptures and discontinuities and subordinating it to observation, it also does in a political sense: as reality exceeds our ability to act coherently in relation to it, the only possible move is to return to observation, to rebuild social knowledge from scratch, while acknowledging the ethical importance of refusing to tame or domesticate these subjects, deliberately allowing them to exceed our knowledge and representations of them. And this is perhaps its greatest debt to neorealism, which, after all, André Bazin describes as "more an ontological position than an aesthetic one": "Whether in the service of the interests of an ideological thesis, of a moral idea, or of a dramatic action, realism subordinates what it borrows from reality to its transcendent needs. Neorealism knows only immanence. It is from appearance only, the simple appearance of beings and of the world, that it knows how to deduce the ideas that it unearths. It is a phenomenology.[15] Phenomenology, with its emphasis on observing the world without presuppositions, provides an apt way to frame the commitment of New Argentine Cinema to portraying an atomized society, as well as the self-reflexive importance it attaches to modes of visuality and perception. It also suggests a way of understanding these films' focus on surfaces, as a deliberate attempt to obscure as well as reveal, to suggest the opacity of film rather than the transparency often, and erroneously, attributed to these texts, given their debt to neorealist and documentary styles.

LA FE DEL VOLCÁN: THE ILLEGIBILITY OF THE IMAGE

Like *Pizza, birra, faso*, Ana Poliak's *La fe del volcán* (2001) experiments with form to raise questions of representation in relation to the experience of social exclusion. Poliak's refusal to reduce the image to a narrative unit, allowing its remainders and excesses to challenge the construction of meaning, draws a line between visibility and legibility in a manner that has a significant bearing on the representation of social marginalization in the film.

The semidocumentary mode of the major part of *La fe del volcán* is employed to explore a friendship across generations between a man in his forties, who earns a living sharpening knives, and a girl of about fourteen, currently working as a hairdresser's apprentice. The part of Anita is played by a natural actress who had previously spent a number of years living on the streets. Ani and Danilo walk through the streets of Buenos Aires, occasionally pausing to look into shop windows, to buy food, or to wait at a crossing. Danilo tells jokes, fantasizes, and does impressions; Ani laughs occasionally, sometimes asks a question, but generally remains taciturn. Most recognizable landmarks of the city are framed out of the telescopic tracking shots that follow the protagonists through the streets. The camera most frequently tracks their progress along the streets from a close angle just behind their heads (Figure 5). Reduced in this way to a series of curbs, traffic lights, and fragments of shop windows, the city becomes unrecognizable and its neighborhoods merge into anonymity. With the velocity of the city reduced to the numbingly slow pace of walking or cycling, the film traces something like an aesthetics of survival: of reduced horizons, of keeping one's head down and trudging through the streets of the city. This "narrative" (nothing of import takes place, and there is no dramatic climax) is framed by another, highly experimental, set of sequences, in which the director herself becomes the subject of the film.

If the scenes involving Ani and Danilo are rarely significant in terms of

5. For the major part of *La fe del volcán* the camera tracks the protagonists closely as they walk through the city, evoking a sense of real time and resisting any attempt to impose narrative shape or meaning on the images recorded.

the information they provide in the form of a plot, certain ideas about their status within the city do become apparent. While the two move through the city, they remain outsiders in it, existing in rigidly marked zones of social exclusion. Ani has never been inside the Abasto shopping center, a flagship modern mall in Buenos Aires: a glittering, climate-controlled oasis of glamour and consumerism in the midst of urban decay. As we become conscious of viewing the city through Ani's eyes, shots of electronic gadgets, video games, and enormous advertisements become esoteric and alienating. Danilo reflects, "No tengo el formato del siglo veintiuno" (I'm not formatted for the twenty-first century). References to a global network society, such as the ad for Aerolíneas Argentinas, underline the extent to which these protagonists (like millions of others) have become, in the words of Manuel Castells, "irrelevant, both as producers and consumers, from the perspective of the system's logic."[16] Maristella Svampa highlights the extent to which citizenship became defined in terms of consumption during the neoliberal 1990s, even becoming crystallized in law in Article 42 of the Constitution, revised in 1994, in which "el individuo es definido como consumidor-usuario de los bienes y servicios que provee el mercado" (the individual is defined as the consumer-user of the goods and services provided by the market).[17] The film seems to be involved in an effort to make visible lives that are often passed over as insignificant, constituting what Beatriz Sarlo has termed "una zona gris de deambulantes" (a gray zone of street-roamers) or, as Castells would put it, "the black holes of informational capitalism,"[18] the language of both theorists suggesting the limits of representation.

The film does not, however, propose itself as a simple exercise in rendering visible the invisible; in fact, it deliberately focuses on the obscured and the uncertain. The feel of an observational documentary is generated by shots of long duration that are entirely unmotivated in terms of the film's action, such as a sequence focusing on a street evangelist who happens to be preaching in a square Ani walks through or a close-up of an apple Danilo is eating. Hollywood's bid for legibility results in the visual signaling of every important detail: nothing significant escapes our attention, as it is placed center-shot or in a close-up; conversely, what is not relevant to the narrative is suppressed. Here, what is marked visually for us often has no narrative significance whatsoever. Paradoxically, perhaps, the pseudodocumentary techniques of *La fe del volcán* are not employed to provide objective knowledge, but to enhance subjectivity, the polysemic, and an uncertainty of interpretation. As Ani and Danilo walk along the streets of the city, they move in and out of different soundscapes, and offscreen sound often remains unaccounted for on the visual track. The interpretation of certain images becomes problematic: for example, are the mannequin shops they pass intended as a symbolic reference to the practice of torture under dictatorship (Danilo suggests to Ani during this scene that his father was a torturer), or are they merely incidental to the space the characters are moving through? Is our interpretation of the scene affected by the knowledge that there does exist a street with several mannequin shops in the shadow of the Abasto shopping center, which Ani and Danilo are circling in this sequence?

In an account of the rise of photography and the cinema, Robert B. Ray observes that "although the longing for strictly objective, and therefore exact, representation had motivated photography's invention, photographs produced precisely the opposite effect—a mute ambiguity that invited subjective reverie." Film, he argues, became involved in an attempt to render the image more legible—to correct its ambiguity—by means of matched cuts and continuity editing. Ray draws on Roland Barthes's concept of a "third" or "obtuse meaning"—that which is present in the image as a remainder, once informational or symbolic meanings are exhausted, and that which cannot fully be expressed in language—to suggest that the insertion of the image into the cinematic narrative is carried out to suppress that excess of meaning: "To the extent that the continuity rules circumscribed the movies' images, regulated their meaning in terms of a single narrative, and vastly reduced their potential complexity, they became . . . *a means of policing photography.*"[19] *La fe del volcán* represents an attempt to restore the illegibility of the image: that which escapes language and narrative, or the properly "filmic" as Barthes understood it.

This attempt is evident from the opening shot of the film, in which a woman (the director) stands, immobile, looking down, against a backdrop of apartment blocks. The shot lasts almost a full minute; only minimal shakes of the handheld camera and a lock of hair moving gently in the breeze make us aware that what we are watching is not a still but a moving image. The length of the shot affords us ample time to examine every detail in the frame and to form hypotheses about the ensuing action or the meaning of the shot, all of which are discarded as the image becomes more and more opaque to us over time. The shot is finally interrupted by an intertitle (bold black type on a white screen), which reads:

Estoy en un piso muy alto
rodeada y llena de vacío.
Tengo que saltar, lo sé.
Pero hacia afuera o hacia adentro?

[I am on a floor high-up
surrounded and filled with space.
I have to jump, I know.
But toward the outside or the inside?]

An abrupt transition takes us to a sequence that is entirely unconnected; although the promise of meaning is tantalizingly held out to us, the legibility of the intertitle only emphasizes the illegibility of the sequence as a whole.

One of the key questions raised for the spectator is the relationship between this prologue and the rest of the film. There is no narrative continuity between them, although a subtle diegetic relationship is established through the use of sound: the squeak of metal against metal we hear (but whose source we cannot determine) is the sound of knives being sharpened by the turning of pedals on Danilo's specially adapted bicycle. The theme of the dictatorship provides a part-association. The director's mother reminds her of her past depression and the suicide attempt she made as a teenager; finally, the director's own voice-over explains: "Cuando tenía catorce años le escribía cartas a mi maestra sin imaginar que la estaban torturando. Hoy tengo siete años más de lo que a ella le dejaron vivir" (when I was fourteen, I wrote letters to my teacher without imagining that she was being tortured. Now I am seven years older than the age to which she was allowed to live). In the main body of the film we are led to understand that Danilo's extravagant theatricality masks a buried trauma connected to the brutality of the military

6. The director rubs her hand across the condensation on a window to reveal the view beyond, in one of a number of images in *La fe del volcán* which play with ideas of interiority and exteriority, transparency, and opacity.

regime and that also manifests itself as survivor guilt. Although this—or any other—link does not exhaust the possible meanings of the framing sequences, which remain elusive to straightforward interpretation, it is also possible to read certain elements of them as a reflexive commentary on the formal composition of the film as a whole.

The first shot and intertitle give way to a sequence in which the director begs, through a closed door and a barred window, to be allowed in to see the apartment she was born in. Once inside the now abandoned and dilapidated shell of an apartment, she bolts and unbolts a door, cautiously and deliberately, as if hesitating over whether to pass through it; she moves uncertainly through rooms. Near the end of the film we return to her image: she stares out of a window misted over with condensation and, as if in a trance, drags her fingers slowly across it to reveal small fragments of the neighboring apartment blocks (Figure 6). Many of these shots suggest ideas of interiority and exteriority, and of transparency and opacity, which are crucial to the film's use of the image. They also play with questions of access and visibility, which, as we have already seen, take on a particularly charged social meaning during the course of the rest of the film.

La fe del volcán ends with an extraordinary single shot of almost ten minutes' duration, which follows Ani trudging silently along a dirt track next to a busy highway, accompanied by a fragmented voice-over, Danilo's, in which he reflects obliquely on a personal and national experience of trauma. The sheer length of this scene produces a heightened perception of the act of spectatorship and explores tensions between interiority and exteriority in relation to the image: the sustained focus on Ani does not result in greater identification but instead emphasizes the inscrutability of this un-knowable other.[20] Indeed, Poliak comments specifically that, despite the closeness of the relationship she developed with her actress, the difference between them in social class and experience did not permit her to "under-stand" the girl.[21] The final sequence causes us, too, to reflect that the entire duration of the film has not sufficed for us to come to know anything of substance about this figure and to become aware of the materiality of her body as something impenetrable and opaque, illegible, resistant to message-making or analysis. As Barthes suggests, "what the obtuse meaning dis-turbs, sterilizes, is metalanguage (criticism)."[22]

If the image here obscures as much as it reveals, it is perhaps because for Poliak, visibility does not necessarily bring knowledge or understanding: her characters deliberately remain "other" to us, and meaning resides in the out-of-field, the offscreen, in past events and inner experience that are in-accessible to us. That the visible can be deceptive is suggested by Danilo's image of the Japanese sword, which cuts so precisely that the head remains unmoving on the neck, and in the repeated references to the image of the volcano, capable of lying dormant for years before erupting. The film hangs back from imposing a narrative because it constructs the relationship be-tween past and present as indeterminable and as a site of trauma. In the light of the dictatorship, film's most ethical role becomes to signal that which lies beyond representation and which is unknowable; as Lyotard says, art in the context of the Holocaust "does not say the unsayable, but says that it cannot say it," as to do otherwise is to allow for its erasure.[23] But in a broader sense, too, the narrative representation of marginalized figures allows them to lose their otherness: in the legibility of Hollywood films their emotions and actions make sense to us, and they become too much like us. For Angelo Restivo, "neorealist aesthetics entails a kind of muteness, where character is not given through dialogue and self-examination but rather through gesture, positioning in space, and architecture."[24] Poliak's charac-ters, like her images, are irreducible to language and narrative, retaining their muteness and opacity, and thereby their polysemy.

MUNDO GRÚA AND THE (AUTO)ETHNOGRAPHIC GAZE
IN NEW ARGENTINE CINEMA

Two sequences from *Tarde de verano* (Raúl Perrone, 2006) and *El árbol* (Gus-tavo Fontán, 2006) may be read as unexpected moments of self-reflexivity in films that for the most part exemplify the naturalism and minimalism that have become the dominant trends in recent Argentine cinema. In *Tarde de verano* a girl repeatedly photographs a beetle, fixing its image with the aid of a digital camera. In *El árbol* an old man peers at a botany book through a magnifying glass, laboriously bringing into focus the unique patterns of ferns and other plant species. These two moments, or modes of visualization, may be read reflexively as representative of a broader relationship between filmmaker and subject. The curious, detached gaze of the characters, studying species and forms by placing them under a lens or fixing them on film, is also the gaze of the filmmaker in New Argentine Cinema, who observes his or her subjects in such a way that their otherness is preserved. This "zoological gaze," as we might call it, is both constructed and subverted in New Argentine Cinema, which (as I have suggested) can be understood as staging a conflict between the visibility of the subject and the illegibility of the image. I contend that many of these films can be read as provisional forms of (auto)ethnography and are at pains to deconstruct the relationship between visibility and knowledge, a hypothesis I will explore here principally with reference to *Mundo grúa* (Pablo Trapero, 1999).

The film accompanies Rulo, a man in his fifties, for a few weeks as he searches for employment and begins a romantic involvement. It was to become paradigmatic of a low-budget approach to making films in contemporary Argentina, shot on grainy black-and-white 16-mm film and using primarily nonprofessional actors, both choices that hark back to the neorealist films of Roberto Rossellini or Vittorio De Sica. Trapero consciously sought to create doubt in the mind of the spectator concerning the boundaries between fiction and reality in the film.[25] Continuity between the on-screen and offscreen lives of the film's characters also unsettles conventional distinctions between authenticity and performance. For example, many details given about Rulo's past in the film, as a guitarist in a rock band, correspond to the biography of the actor who plays him. Much is made in the film of Rulo's membership, when he was younger and rather slimmer, of a 1970s rock group, Séptimo Regimiento, which achieved fame with a single release, "Paco Camorra," before sinking into oblivion. Luis Margani, the actor who plays Rulo, belonged to the real-life band Séptima Brigada, which stepped fleetingly into the limelight with the single of that name.

A number of different techniques combine in the film to produce a kind of documentary effect. These include an observational style, in which a rather untidy, lackadaisical plot replaces the highly organized cause-and-effect relationships of conventional realist fiction. The narrative appears to drift along with the anomie and lethargy of its characters. Loose ends are not always tied up, and the film ends without a sense of climax or closure: Rulo makes his way back to Buenos Aires having left a job in the south but we do not see his arrival, whether he is able to find a new job, or his reencounter with the lady friend who may or may not have waited for him. As so often happens, this kind of narrative ellipsis gives the impression of a reality that exceeds the film frame. In an oft-cited passage Bazin notes the difference between ellipsis in classic montage, which is "an effect of style," and that used in the neorealist films of Rossellini, in which it represents "a lacuna in reality, or rather in the knowledge that we have of it"; this achieves an effect of greater realism, as "it is the same in life: we do not know everything that happens to others."[26] A resistance toward narrative closure is one of the key points of comparison here with Italian neorealist films such as *Paisà* (Rossellini, 1946) or *The Bicycle Thieves* (De Sica, 1948).

Although the events of the film *are* fictional, medium shots and fixed frames give the impression of a hidden camera capturing reality. Trapero has a predilection for fixed-frame two-shots (Figure 7), which means that cuts during scenes of dialogue are kept to a minimum. Critics have referred to the "invisible, almost documentary style" of *Mundo grúa*,[27] almost unanimously emphasizing the transparency of representation in the film, in which the social content, as in many classical documentaries, appears to gain precedence over filming style.[28] This is a significant misreading of the film, however, that glosses over some of the crucial tensions in its aesthetic. Far from being invisible, the camerawork often draws attention to itself, suggesting the importance of the mode of observation, not just of the subject portrayed. The sheer length of many of the shots produces a sense of unease in the spectator accustomed to more conventional editing techniques. The presence of the filmmaker and a voyeuristic relationship with the subject is suggested by shots such as the one in which the camera is self-consciously positioned behind a curtain blowing in the breeze. The filming style is not at all uniform throughout; in the opening scene of the film, for example, the camera is the hypermobile, handheld camera that has become a cliché of documentary work, typically following the movements of actors a couple of seconds behind and not always registering sound at audible levels.

The diversity of shots used throughout the film, many of them associated with nonfiction film, suggests that they are being used precisely to connote documentalism rather than simply to represent their subject. Simultaneously, however, the film refuses to indulge our desire for knowledge. One of the most striking departures from filmic convention in *Mundo grúa* is the virtual absence—save for a couple of very brief instances—of point-of-view

7. Trapero avoids unnecessary cuts in *Mundo grúa* with the use of fixed-frame two-shots.

shots. When characters look at photos, watch television, or interact with each other, the camera remains fixed on them as the object of the gaze but very rarely the possessor of it. As spectators we are denied knowledge of what Rulo is able to see; this technique works to undermine conventional processes of identification. Rulo, like many other protagonists in New Argentine Cinema, is a character to be looked at, with scientific curiosity and perhaps affection, as one might look at an animal in a zoo, study a bug specimen, or conduct an animal-behavior experiment. Characters often remain irreducibly Other in this way, objects of scrutiny but rarely of knowledge gained. Close-ups, where they do occur, suggest only inscrutability, serving only to remind us that the truth remains inaccessible to us; faces become more of a barrier to representation than signifiers of subjectivity.

Catherine Russell reminds us of the extent to which the zoo is historically and discursively linked with colonial ethnographic practices. The rather telling motto of the World's Columbian Exposition held in Chicago in 1893, "To See Is to Know," indicates, as she suggests, "the coextensive discourses of science, visuality, imprisonment, and imperialism that governed the display of native peoples."[29] Many recent Argentine films adopt some of the forms and techniques of ethnographic practice but ultimately suggest that "to see is *not* to know." Emphasis is often placed on observation, with every-day life placed under the magnifying glass in an attempt to dissect its nature. Examples abound, although the most obvious would be Lisandro Alonso's almost dialogue-free study of a day in the life of a woodcutter in *La libertad* (2001) or Caetano's *Bolivia* (2001), which captures the racial and sexual tensions rife in a small neighborhood bar. These films are ultimately antiallegorical, however, in a specific sense. James Clifford understands ethnography to be inescapably allegorical, as "realistic portraits . . . are extended metaphors, patterns of association that point to coherent (theoretical, esthetic, moral) additional meanings."[30] Thus individuals and their stories always mean more as subjects of ethnographic study than they do as individuals, and these meanings are not additional to the ethnographic text but intrinsic to its form. But the films of New Argentine Cinema invariably hesitate at the point of locating their individual studies within a larger, overarching, ethnographic narrative. Individuals or particular images are not easily interpreted as "representative" of anything broader than themselves, refusing the allegorical impetus of ethnographic narrative. On the one hand, these films testify to an urgent need to reconstruct a social and cultural imaginary in the context of national crisis, but on the other, they recognize the impossibility of doing this without recourse to delegitimized discourses or theories. This emphasis on the everyday is consonant with the postutopian vision of Latin American modernity portrayed by Martín Hopenhayn in *Ni apocalípticos ni integrados*, where he expounds on the value accorded to nuance and detail in the context of the collapse of grand social projects:

> La cotidianidad se convierte en el receptáculo natural de expectativas que han debido abandonar los pastizales de la liberación total. . . . El mini-malismo se ha convertido en un valor bien visto para la acción de todos los días. Todo gran proyecto es tildado de pretencioso o irrealista, y resurge la valoración del matiz, el detalle, la coyuntura.

> [Everydayness becomes the natural receptacle for hopes that have had to abandon the pastures of total liberation. . . . Minimalism has become a well-respected value for everyday action. Every grand project is branded as pretentious or unrealistic, and greater value is accorded to the nuance, the detail, the particular.][31]

This crisis of social knowledge and representation is articulated in a variety of ways in *Mundo grúa*. First, the protagonist does not become a social actor. We do witness something in the film of the exploitative nature of contemporary, "flexible" working practices, and the film also records the activities of a local trade union, but no specific argument is advanced in relation to this theme. Treated in a documentary, this might have been "unions can protect against capitalist exploitation"; in a fictional narrative it might have been "the human spirit rises above (or succumbs to) the indignity of modern labor practices." But the crisis-resolution structure of conventional realist film, whether fiction or documentary, is entirely absent from *Mundo grúa*. Unemployment in the film is hardly a social theme at all, merely the particular condition of an individual life. Second, the everydayness of the images presented does not dramatize social relations through the use of polarizations, such as rich/poor, modern/traditional, urban/rural, exploiter/exploited. In the opening sequence of the film, for instance, the neighborhood depicted as a backdrop to the crane is neither luxurious nor a slum; the presence of the crane connotes progress, but this is tempered by the use of black and white, which is suggestive of the past or perhaps of timelessness. There is an indeterminacy in many of the images that impedes our ability to read them allegorically in Clifford's sense.

Clifford argues that "ethnographic writing is allegorical at the level both of its content (what it says about cultures and their histories) and of its form (what is implied by its mode of textualization)."[32] In the case of New Argentine Cinema the meaning implicit in its form, I would suggest, is contradictory: the need to catalogue new social marginalities, but to do so consciously from a position of no-knowledge, as if recording the biochemical makeup and behavior of a new species.

In one sense, however, New Argentine Cinema does retain the allegorical structure of traditional ethnographies, which, as Clifford contends, is one of loss and salvage, enacting "a redemptive Western allegory."[33] The Other is lost in the world but saved in the text.[34] Russell notes the nostalgia implicit in the zoological gaze, arguing that the zoo "constitutes another instance of the salvage paradigm: it emerges at the moment when animals begin to disappear from daily life, and species become extinct."[35] Many recent films in Argentina are governed by a similar impulse to catalogue and preserve an ever-shifting conglomeration of marginalized, migrant figures, particular trades that are becoming obsolete in the context of rapid technological advance, or traditional neighborhoods and ways of life under the threat of extinction. One of the clearest examples here is provided by the work of Poliak, whose films center on forms of labor now being eclipsed by modernization, such as the neighborhood knife sharpener in *La fe del volcán* or, in

Parapalos (2004), the job of retrieving balls and replacing skittles in a pre-automated bowling alley.

Although it appears to be concerned only with the present, and to eschew historical themes, New Argentine Cinema consistently bears witness to loss and a rupture with the past. For this reason the generation gap is a key theme in recent Argentine cinema, and it is not uncommon for filmmakers to film their own parents and grandparents in work that touches on the autobiographical. Starting from zero means employing a minimalist aesthetic but also starting with the self or one's family. This becomes one of the most prominent motifs of New Argentine Cinema, which often uses family members or friends as actors or as part of the production team, at least partly as a cost-saving tactic. Poliak films herself in *La fe del volcán* and records her mother's voice recalling her daughter's childhood depression; *El árbol* is a minimalist portrait of the director's own parents, set in the house in which he was born and brought up; Trapero films his own grandmother in *Mundo grúa* and again in *Familia rodante* (2004); the apartment Rulo lives in in *Mundo grúa* is actually that of the director's deceased grandmother. Russell notes that

> a prominent theme in contemporary personal cinema is the staging of an encounter with the filmmaker's parent(s) or grandparent(s) who embody a particular cultural history of displacement or tradition. . . . The difference between generations is written across the filmmaker's own inscription in technology, and thus it is precisely an ethnographic distance between the modern and the premodern that is dramatized in the encounter—through interview or archival memory or both. One often gets the sense that the filmmaker has no memory and is salvaging his or her own past through the recording of family memory.[36]

This encounter between the modern and the premodern is dramatized to particular effect in *El árbol*, in which older forms of visuality, including old slides of the family, stand in implicit contrast to the filmmaker's own use of technology. Indeed, in a particularly self-reflexive mode the film's aesthetic is constructed around the use of magnifying lenses and the projection of shadows onto a screen, as in the many sequences that focus on the patterns created on the patio floor or its walls by sunlight filtering through the leaves of a tree (Figure 8). A further displacement in technology is encoded here, given that *El árbol* was actually shot on digital video and therefore does not actually make use of the apparatus traditionally associated with filmmaking

8. Many shots in *El árbol* focus on the projection of shadows onto a background screen, composing a self-reflexive aesthetic that engages with older forms of visual technology such as slide projection or analog cinema.

and cinematic projection. The film's themes of memory, nostalgia, the proximity of death, and an ethnographic encounter between generations are here consciously articulated through technological difference.

It is in these films' relationship with *auto*ethnography that many of the tensions inherent in their aesthetic are brought most clearly into focus. Whether centered on family narratives (*Mundo grúa, El árbol, Familia rodante*)—all of which articulate generational ruptures—or on the filmmaker's Other in class terms (*La libertad; Mundo grúa; Pizza, birra, faso; Bolivia*), these films in part "own" their subjects as belonging to their own world and, simultaneously, distance them as belonging to a different time, culture, or class. To what extent can we interpret the ethnographic gaze of *Mundo grúa*, of *Pizza, birra, faso,* or of *Bolivia* as a postmodern reluctance to construct the Other as knowable? Or are these films' lower-class subjects treated as Other because they cannot plausibly be integrated into a coherent national imaginary, given the increasing polarization of rich and poor under neoliberalism and the growing social segregation it has produced?[37]

The complexity of New Argentine Cinema's treatment of its subjects takes on a further dimension if we recall the extent to which these films are consciously produced as much for an international market as a domestic one. Given that European film festivals have supplied significant funding for Argentine films, and provided crucial points of entry into distribution networks, autoethnography becomes not merely an exercise of charting one's own cultural practices but, crucially, of doing so for an imagined European or North American audience, as well as for a local one. Here the salvage paradigm becomes associated not with an imperial gaze but with a postcolonial one. Mary Louise Pratt defines autoethnography in a way that makes clear its coextension with postcolonial textual resistance:

> If ethnographic texts are those in which European metropolitan subjects represent to themselves their others (usually their conquered others), autoethnographic texts are representations that the so-defined others construct *in response to* or in dialogue with those texts. . . . They involve a selective collaboration with and appropriation of idioms of the metropolis or the conqueror. These are merged or infiltrated to varying degrees with indigenous idioms to create self-representations intended to intervene in metropolitan modes of understanding. Autoethnographic works are often addressed to both metropolitan audiences and the speaker's own community. Their reception is thus highly indeterminate.[38]

Pratt's definition speaks to the strabismic gaze of these films, made with one eye on Europe and the other on Argentina. New Argentine Cinema certainly seems to supply a First World demand for images of poverty and social unrest in the Third World. The deliberate failure of these films to produce social knowledge, however, can be understood as a form of resistance to First World epistephilia. In contrast to the great Latin American social dramas to have reached North American and European screens in recent years—such as *City of God* and *Amores perros*—the gaze of New Argentine Cinema is self-doubting, contingent, and provisional. These filmmakers' refusal to present themselves as authentic, "insider," interpreters of their own culture becomes both a poignant expression of crisis of social knowledge, on a local level, and, on a global one, an act of resistance toward First World inscriptions of other cultures, embedded in the imperial collusion of visibility, knowledge, and power.

3

LABOR, BODIES, AND CIRCULATION

Some of the most poignant moments of *Pizza, birra, faso* are afforded by the youths' adoption of the language of political activism, a language that echoes anachronistically from a bygone era of collectivized struggle. "Nos tenemos que independizar" (We have to become independent), Pablo proposes; either that or go on strike: not to resist exploitation by an employer but by their taxi-driving partner-in-crime. Córdoba, for his part, objects to working the trains again after privatization. The language of political ideology and activism, voiced by boys who are fully alienated from the contexts of business and trade unions, comprises media clichés and gestures that shape their aspirations in the same way as the crime movies they watch. Such language highlights the painful gap between these aspirations to coherent action and the miserable ineffectiveness of the boys' attempts to take control over their lives.

Unemployment in Argentina more than tripled in the decade leading up to the Crisis, reaching 21.5 percent in May 2002.[1] This raw statistic, however bleak, does not even begin to account for widespread *under*employment in these years or for the significant rise in unregistered employment, in which workers are not protected under contracts from dismissal and have no access to social benefits.[2] The increasing difficulty of survival during the 1990s for many sectors of society is registered everywhere in contemporary Argentine cinema. If protagonists of 1980s films were often writers and intellectuals, more recent films chart the fall of the middle classes and their forced resort to unskilled or semiskilled jobs as dog walkers (*Silvia Prieto*), pizza-delivery boys (*Buena Vida Delivery*), hairdressers' apprentices (*La fe del volcán*), girls turning unhappily to prostitution as a last resort (*Hoy y mañana*), or youths contracted on a daily basis to hand out promotional flyers and free samples (*Un día de suerte*). Caetano's *Bolivia* and the films of Martín Rejtman discussed in this chapter provide particularly interesting perspectives on the "precarización" (growing uncertainty) of work during this period. It is a paradox that work, despite the value it acquires in the context of scarcity, nevertheless becomes increasingly less central to constructions of identity in a manner similar to that experienced in affluent "postwork" societies. As these films suggest, greater instability in Argentina has perhaps only exacerbated trends in evidence across the postindustrial world that are continuing to produce radical changes in subjectivity.

Bourdieu argues that "casualization profoundly affects the person who suffers it: by making the whole future uncertain, it prevents all rational anticipation and, in particular, the basic belief and hope in the future that one needs in order to rebel, especially collectively, against present conditions, even the most intolerable."[3] Alejandro Grimson posits the experience of repeated economic crises in Argentina as a crucial shaping factor in what might, very provisionally, be considered a form of national identity, paradoxically based on the shared experience of "experiencias disgregadoras" (experiences of disintegration). He argues, for example, that the experience of hyperinflation in the late 1980s, in which prices rose by the hour, "transforma todas las nociones de tiempo, especialmente el presente, el futuro y la planificación" (transforms all notions of time, especially the present, the future, and planning), producing a "cortoplacismo" (short-termism) that, in turn, "implica que el horizonte de la vida social y política se achica hasta desaparecer" (means that the horizon of social and political life shrinks to the point of disappearance).[4] In this chapter I explore shifts in subjectivity that have resulted from dramatic transformations in modes of labor and consumption in Argentina since the mid-1990s. It is striking that while much documentary production in recent years has centered on the successful mobilization of workers' collectives in the aftermath of the Crisis, fiction film has focused almost exclusively on the increasing instability of work and the failure of traditional modes of collective activism. Perhaps because of its greater reliance on narrative form, fiction film—as we have already seen in the case of *Pizza, birra, faso* and *Mundo grúa*—has most often explored the negative impact of casualized labor and unemployment on the narratives of individual lives and on the possibility of collective action.

FILMING LABOR AND THE LABOR OF FILM:
BOLIVIA AND LISANDRO ALONSO'S TRILOGY

Bolivia (Caetano, 2001) exemplifies the meticulous detail with which the everyday practice of work is visualized in contemporary Argentine film. As employment becomes scarce, the tools of trade and the prescribed movements and rhythms of labor become worthy, it would seem, of sustained observation and even stylization. The clock on the wall of the bar marks out the beginning and end of the long workday, measuring its quieter periods and its busier ones. The length of the shots will decrease as work picks up and increase again at times of rest. Despite the long hours worked by bar owner and employees alike, they work productively and without complaint: the alternative is, as Enrique warns Rosa when she turns up late to work one morning, no job at all. The grueling nature of their working lives is more than counterbalanced in the film, however, by the poetic manner with which they are often represented. The precredits prologue is composed of a series of still images, focusing on the typical tools and contexts of labor in a Buenos Aires neighborhood café-bar: a standard espresso coffee machine; a stainless-steel jug for steaming milk; the counter adorned with paper serviette holders, sugar dispensers, and a glass shelved unit for the display of fresh food; a modest-sized charcoal grill with heaped ashes left over from the previous day; a chopping board, knife, tongs, and basters for the preparation and cooking of meat; behind the scenes, a basic storeroom with an old gas hob bearing well-used pots and pans (Figure 9). The accompanying voice-over is that of Enrique explaining to Freddy the nature of the job for which he has just been hired.

Where Christian Gundermann finds "the disjointed sound and image, the hard, bleak quality of the dry cuts" in this sequence to express "the desolation of use objects in disuse" and therefore a kind of alienation within an era of commodity fetishism,[5] I would suggest an alternative reading that places these shots—and the film as a whole—squarely within the context of the sharp rise in unemployment and economic austerity that marked the turn of the century in Argentina. These first scenes create a sense of expectation—the tools are poised, ready for action, their fulfillment of their function promised—and accord a kind of poetic grandeur, through the use of still close-ups, to these humble tools patiently awaiting human use in productive labor. The defamiliarizing effect of this technique noted by Gundermann is less at the service of contesting commodity fetishism and more in the interests of according dignity to human labor, approaching its

9. Worn tools await human laborers at the beginning of the day in the small café-bar of *Bolivia*.

practices step by step (still by still) with a sense of rediscovered awe. Far from representing " 'loose' objects, that is, elements that are not connected with the diegesis or the plot in a traditional manner,"[6] my reading would therefore place this opening sequence at the heart of the film's meditation on, and homage to, labor, its tools, and practices, and therefore draw attention to its engagement with a precise socioeconomic context, that of Buenos Aires at the start of the twenty-first century. The context in which these objects are defamiliarized is perhaps less signally one of commodity fetishism (as Gundermann would have it) than one of the revalorization of any form of labor in the context of severe and increasing unemployment.

Where we might have expected a critique of the harsh working conditions under which Freddy is employed, with low pay and no contract, *Bolivia* curiously opts for a more positive portrayal of labor, which is not seen here as dehumanizing but rather as a source of satisfaction. Richard Sennett contrasts the positive vision of routine depicted in Diderot's *Encyclopaedia* (1751–72), which accorded a dignity to labor and allowed workers to take control over their actions, with the much more negative portrayal of routine as dehumanizing and destructive in Adam Smith's *The Wealth of Nations* (1776).[7] Negotiating a line between these two extremes, Sennett suggests that, in the contemporary world of flexible capitalism, routine does offer the possibility of creating a coherent narrative for one's life: "We are hardly disposed now to think of routinized time as a personal *achievement*, but given the stresses, booms, and depressions of industrial capitalism, it often became so. . . . Routine can demean, but it can also protect; routine can decompose labor, but it can also compose a life."[8] It is this rather more optimistic portrayal of work, which by regulating a life may also give it meaning, that emerges in *Bolivia*, in a context in which "the stresses, booms, and depressions of industrial capitalism" have such an unequivocal bearing on the everyday. We might recall, for instance, the repeated shots of the clock on the wall, marking time throughout the film: a time to work, a time to eat, a time to rest.

Furthermore, the film's most stylized sequences evoke the simple pleasure of losing oneself in the physical demands of work, of allowing the rhythms of labor to erase other cares. At the height of the working day, a slow-motion sequence, accompanied by a traditional Andean song on the soundtrack, interrupts the predominantly realist aesthetic. We are shown shots of Enrique making coffee for a customer, Rosa washing a plate at the sink, Freddy cleaning his hands with a rag and wiping down the counter before seizing a few spare seconds to drink water and to look out across the bar. As well as taking these shots out of rigid time and therefore suggesting their iterability, the slow-motion treatment lends an epic, lyrical quality to the everyday tasks depicted. The intense activity of the bar and the small, insignificant movements of the characters are captured and slowed up for us so that we can appreciate the poetry of labor in motion. Discussing this sequence and focusing particularly on the lingering shot of Freddy taking a drink, Gustavo Noriega comments that the effect is to give Freddy the cinematic treatment not normally accorded to the "other": this sequence acts as "un pequeño desafío, el de sacar a 'ellos,' los que nosotros no somos, los desposeídos, de su imaginaria cárcel cinematográfica que es el registro documental, inmediato, sin modificaciones y regalarles por una vez los beneficios de la posproducción" (a small act of defiance, removing "them," those who aren't "us"—the dispossessed—from the imaginary cinematic prison constructed by the immediacy and the unmediatedness of the documentary register, and granting them the privilege of postproduction work).[9] It is manifestly honest labor that lends Freddy this dignity, his demeanor contrasting with that of the rather self-pitying band of locals who frequent the bar, out of work or too depressed to work, and drinking away their few remaining pesos.

In a similar manner to *Pizza, birra, faso* and many of the other films analyzed in the previous chapter, *Bolivia* is involved in a kind of staging of the contemporary and the social that has as much to do with a renovation in cinematic language as it does with the object of its gaze. This renovation is achieved, in the case of *Bolivia*, by a redemption of the material and the everyday for the purposes of lyricism. Rather than depicting "the desolation of use objects in disuse" (Gundermann), I propose that *Bolivia*'s attention to the tools and receptacles of labor should be read in relation to the materialist aesthetic of the film as a whole. Caetano's discovery of the lyrical potential of the everyday and the material, which suggests a certain positioning of art in relation to social and political crisis, resonates strongly with the ideas expressed in the work of Pablo Neruda. I quote at length here from Neruda's celebrated manifesto, "Sobre una poesía sin pureza" (On an Impure Poetry), as the reader familiar with *Bolivia* will be able to grasp the peculiar aptness of these words and the materialist conception that informs them:

> Es muy conveniente, en ciertas horas del día o de la noche, observar profundamente los objetos en descanso: Las ruedas que han recorrido largas, polvorientas distancias, soportando grandes cargas vegetales o minerales, los sacos de las carbonerías, los barriles, las cestas, los mangos y asas de los instrumentos del carpintero. De ellos se desprende el contacto del hombre y de la tierra como una lección para el torturado poeta lírico. Las superficies usadas, el gasto que las manos han infligido a las cosas, la atmósfera a menudo trágica y siempre patética de estos objetos, infunde una especie de atracción no despreciable hacia la realidad del mundo.
>
> La confusa impureza de los seres humanos se percibe en ellos, la agrupación, uso y desuso de los materiales, las huellas del pie y de los dedos, la constancia de una atmósfera humana inundando las cosas desde lo interno y lo externo.
>
> Así sea la poesía que buscamos, gastada como por un ácido por los deberes de la mano, penetrada por el sudor y el humo, oliente a orina y a azucena salpicada por las diversas profesiones que se ejercen dentro y fuera de la ley.

[It is appropriate, at certain times of the day or night, to study objects at rest: wheels that have traveled long, dusty distances, carrying heavy loads of vegetables or minerals, coal-yard sacks, barrels, baskets, the handles and knobs of a carpenter's tools. The eloquence with which they speak of their contact with man and the earth provides an important object lesson for the tortured lyrical poet. The scratched surfaces of hand-worn things, the often tragic and always pathetic air of these objects, arouses a powerful kind of attraction toward the realities of the world.

In them we see the confused impurity of human beings, the gathering, use, and disuse of materials, footprints and fingerprints, proof of a human presence that saturates things from within and without.

The poetry we seek should be like this, worn by the work of hands, as if by the skin's acid, permeated with sweat and smoke, smelling of urine and lilies, infused with the various trades we practice within the law or outside of it.][10]

Caetano's *Bolivia* adopts just such a poetics of observation, and of impurity, in its search for an aesthetic that can approach the tragedy and pathos of human experience and account for the messiness, the worn-out ("gastada") quality, of existence in the shadow of the law or on the brink of ruin. The low resolution of the images and the black-and-white film stock perfectly capture the rough-hewn, timeworn nature of the objects and lives that enter the frames.

If New Argentine Cinema, as I have been suggesting, is as much about the renewal of a cinematic language as it is about a response to shifting social realities, the trilogy directed by Lisandro Alonso provides perhaps the clearest example of a kind of reflexivity (a turning-in) that is not antithetical to social engagement (looking outward). Instead, conventional distinctions between these two approaches are collapsed in Alonso's work, which insists on cinema's synecdochic relationship with society and the economy, subject to the same forces it depicts on its screens and not external to them. The film's exploration of the relationship between labor and subjectivity extends from the protagonists to the filmmaker himself.

Alonso's daringly minimalist *La libertad* (2001) has aroused more academic than popular interest. An observational-style depiction of twenty-four hours in the life of a woodcutter, the film studies its subject with a thoroughness of detail and a lentitude of pace that create the effect of events occurring in real time. *Los muertos* (2004), although bearing more traces of a linear plot, continues in a similar, mesmeric vein, as we follow the ex-prisoner protagonist on a journey along a series of rivers and streams in his canoe. While some critics have been lured into assuming that Alonso's project was essentially a documentary one, exploring the potential of minimalism and real-time filming to achieve a greater sense of realism, his reflexive agenda is made fully explicit in *Fantasma* (2006). This film brings together Misael and Vargas, the protagonists of *La libertad* and *Los muertos* respectively, for a screening of *Los muertos* in the Centro Cultural General San Martín in Buenos Aires. As Deborah Young of *Variety* comments rather caustically, the film's "willful lack of content" makes it "unlikely to travel outside fests presenting crit pics for the cognoscenti."[11] My reading of reflexivity across all three films of the trilogy will focus on the filmmaker's exploration of precisely such a position of extreme marginality in relation to the market, both for his characters and for the films themselves as cultural artifacts.

The analogy between the toil of the solitary woodcutter and the labor of the independent filmmaker has already been established in the insightful studies of *La libertad* published by both Gonzalo Aguilar and Christian Gundermann. For the latter, "la mayoría de los planos de la película, que se dedican a la actividad artesanal del protagonista hachero, se convierten en una especie de metáfora del oficio cinematográfico en condiciones pos-industriales" (the majority of the film's sequences, dedicated to the traditional skills of the woodcutter protagonist, become a kind of metaphor for cinematic art in a post-industrial world).[12] Aguilar also reads *Los muertos* as a metaphor for Alonso's own filmmaking, arguing that "así como el protagonista se aleja del pueblo ahogado por un medio en el que el único contacto con los demás hombres o mujeres es el de la transacción económica, el realizador sale intencionalmente en su búsqueda para hacer un cine diferente, lejos del cine-institución" (just as the protagonist flees the town, stifled by an environment in which economic transactions provide the only form of contact with other men and women, so the director steps out in a conscious quest for a different kind of filmmaking, far from the cinema-as-institution).[13] For both writers the films' focus on modes of survival in the wilds—the expert excision of honeycomb from a hive, the opportunistic seizure and slaughter of a goat, the roasting of an armadillo—sketches out the possibility of autarky. In a similar manner Alonso's own films, largely produced and distributed through noncommercial channels, deliberately renounce the market in their search for a genuinely independent form of art. Interestingly, the films avoid a dramatization of this choice: as mainstream culture is never denigrated within *La libertad* or *Los muertos* as a seductive but less worthy alternative, Alonso's depiction of rural isolation has little of the nostalgia that we might expect; neither does he present either his characters or his films as consciously rebelling against the System (this would re-introduce, of course, a hackneyed Hollywood theme). The films celebrate the peripheral and the artisanal without overtly denigrating the mainstream and the mass-produced; unlike Solanas's *La nube* (see chapter 1), they do not stage a lament over the death of high art, displaced by the culture industry, but instead display a quiet confidence in the viability of the lesser-trodden paths they have chosen, relishing their niche at the margins of the market.

Fantasma both reinforces and complicates the analogy of the solitary laborer-filmmaker suggested by the first two films and their critics. It certainly makes explicit the reflexive impulse behind Alonso's work, shattering

10. The protagonist of *Los muertos* watches himself on screen in Alonso's highly reflexive *Fantasma*, sitting in the same auditorium as many of the spectators who are also watching him.

any illusions of transparency created by his pseudodocumentary approaches. Such illusions might not have had such enduring power had Alonso not been obliged by Cannes to cut the final sequence of *La libertad*, in which Misael looks straight into the camera and laughs, clearly interacting with the filmmaker and displaying a gaiety and abandon that conflicts with the development of his character throughout the film as taciturn and reserved (a character that, as a natural actor, we have assumed to be his own). *Fantasma* eschews the rural locations of Alonso's first two films to document a screening of *Los muertos* to which both Misael and Vargas are invited. Watching Vargas in *Fantasma* watching himself as he appears in *Los muertos* (Figure 10), we become aware of a series of mises-en-abyme. It is not simply that the protagonist of one film becomes a spectator of the next; *Fantasma* also reflects on *Los muertos* as a cultural artifact, meditating on the conditions of its exhibition and its reception. The screening of *Los muertos* filmed in *Fantasma* takes place in the Sala Leopoldo Lugones, a well-known venue for art film frequented by *porteño* cinephiles, and—indeed—the venue in which *Los muertos* was screened on its release a few years previously.[14] Thus the play with mirrors extends even further: viewers of the newly released *Fantasma* would be watching the film in the very same theater in which Vargas is watching *Los muertos*, and in which they may well remember having seen *Los muertos* themselves. Moments of self-parody punctuate *Fantasma*, as the tiny audience of three (Vargas, plus two employees of the theater) shift rather uncomfortably in their seats during the film, which is evidently seeming rather long to them; the caretaker-usher leaves halfway through, and the woman can express only a vague and rather dutiful enthusiasm in her congratulations to Vargas. Again, the film comments on its position at the very margins of the entertainment industry, reflecting perhaps on the walkouts commonly occasioned by Alonso's films, even at Cannes.

Further refractions are suggested by the extensive filming of interiors of the cultural center that houses the Sala Lugones: the labyrinthine building becomes an architectural allegory for the culture industry and Alonso's position within it. The gleaming marble foyers are frequently abandoned for the neglected back stairs, the gloomy corridors with flickering strip-lights, the projection room, shabby washrooms, and untidy dressing rooms. Of the several different elevators that feature prominently in the film, the one with brass doors and automated announcements is clearly intended for the visiting public, while the others, more basic, are for staff and maintenance use. Like Misael and Vargas, wandering through the less presentable parts of the building, Alonso chooses to inhabit the dingy and forsaken spaces of the culture industry, to travel in the service elevator rather than the official one, and to take us backstage with him.

However, *Fantasma*'s multiple mirrorings also have the effect of breaking down the analogy between the reclusive protagonists and their director and, by extension, of undermining the autarkic paradigm. "¿Por qué nos inquieta que Don Quijote sea lector del *Quijote* y Hamlet espectador de *Hamlet*?" asks Borges. "Creo haber dado con la causa: tales inversiones sugieren que si los carácteres de una ficción pueden ser lectores o espectadores, nosotros, sus lectores o espectadores, podemos ser ficticios" (Why does it trouble us that Don Quixote should be the reader of the *Quixote* and Hamlet the spectator of *Hamlet*? I believe I have found the reason: such inversions suggest that if the characters of a fictional story can be readers or spectators, we, their readers or spectators, can be fictitious).[15] In the mise-en-abyme of *Fantasma*, however, what disturbs us is not the possibility that we, as spectators, may be as fictitious as Vargas but the knowledge that he, as a natural actor, is as real as we are. With that knowledge comes the recognition that Vargas, although physically inhabiting the same space that we inhabit, belongs in social, cultural, and economic terms to a very different world. The analogy between the solitary laborer and the independent filmmaker breaks down, of course, even in the earlier films, because only one of these is free to exercise choice. Aguilar misses this distinction when he claims that "Misael es el nómade que huye de la ciudades para encontrar su hogar en la naturaleza y su sustento en los árboles" (Misael is the nomad who flees from the cities to find his home in nature and his sustenance in the trees):[16] while Alonso is deliberately crafting his films in opposition to a dominant mainstream aesthetic, Misael and Vargas are less consciously resisting consumer culture or urban lifestyles than using their skills in the necessary task of making ends meet.

Indeed, there is much evidence in all three films to suggest that Alonso is deliberately drawing attention to the differences between the world of the filmmaker and spectators and that of the characters in a way that seeks to provoke reflection on questions of social and cultural exclusion rather than to celebrate marginality and asceticism. In *Fantasma*, for example, Vargas and Misael are not given the red-carpet treatment of film stars but are left to find their own way to the cinema screen. Vargas stumbles on the aftermath of a wine reception; as he stubs out a cigarette in a half-empty wine glass and drinks the dregs of another, we are afforded a telling image of his exclusion from the lofty circles of high culture. Misael, too, has to find his own champagne, which he cracks open alone in a workshop somewhere in the depths of the building, with only a television for company. All the characters in the film pass their time looking: at others, at the building, at the film. In the undisguised curiosity of the caretaker-usher, who stares obtrusively at Vargas until the object of his attention moves uncomfortably away, we are forced to recognize something of our own unblinking gaze. The style of all three films reveals a similar attention to the gaze, with the camera's movements markedly given independence from the action recorded. This independence can be seen when the camera lingers in empty spaces after the character has left in *Fantasma*, or when it pans across the landscape in *La libertad*, registering images of Misael as if by chance before abandoning him in order to finish its own arc, or, as in *Los muertos*, when it remains fixed on the child, staring at his grandfather, without following the direction of his gaze.[17] As Aguilar notes, the contemporary, urban sound of electronic music used in the closing credits of *Los muertos* (also used at the beginning of *La libertad* and at both beginning and end of *Fantasma*) immediately highlights the difference between the observer (to whose urban world such music belongs) and the observed.[18]

By means of reflexivity Alonso raises ethnographic questions concerning the relationship of these protagonists with their director and their audiences. What are the ethics of transplanting Misael and Vargas from their rural environment to place them under observation in a temple to high urban art? How can we maintain a vision of their hermitlike existence, close to nature and untouched by consumer society, when we know that these protagonists have been contracted to act on film, offered wages as an incentive to leave their usual jobs aside for the duration of the shooting? By turning his documentary subjects into actors, Alonso acknowledges as impossibilities two paradigms that seemed to underpin his filmmaking: first, that the camera simply observes without constructing (the documentary illusion) and, second, that film can fully step out of the market (the autarkic reading). It may be made with less money, but it is money nonetheless. As spectators who have paid our dues—a lower price, admittedly, than for entrance to a multiplex—we cannot but wonder whether we might ourselves be the ultimate object of Alonso's parody and of Misael's laughter, staying in our seats to the very end and congratulating ourselves on choosing to inhabit the lonely, neglected, and uncomfortable salons of high art.

MARTÍN REJTMAN: MODES OF LABOR AND SUBJECTIVITY IN (PRE)CAPITALIST ARGENTINA

Martín Rejtman's oeuvre, although universally identified with New Argentine Cinema, is at several points aesthetically at odds with the more clearly neorealist-inspired projects that dominate the canon. Although his films share some of the asceticism of these productions—low budgets and long takes with minimal editing—the dialogue is deliberately antinaturalistic, and the economy of the plot, together with rapid transitions between scenes, draws us far away from the sense of "real time" constructed by many productions associated with New Argentine Cinema. The relationship between Rejtman's films and these others is clearly established, however, in the influence of his first feature film, *Rapado* (1991), which for many years was the "missing referent" of New Argentine Cinema. Readily acknowledged as the most important precursor to this new wave of filmmaking by the directors and critics who managed to see it—at one of very few screenings before its release in Buenos Aires in 1996—*Rapado* has attained something of a cult status, due at least in part to its semiclandestine circulation. No commercial copy of the film existed in video or digital format until April 2006.

Rapado represents a significant point of rupture in the recent trajectory of Argentine cinema. Rejtman proposed to "empezar de cero" (begin from zero), leaving behind "lo discursivo, lo artificial, lo pretencioso, lo falsamente político o lo ideológico" (the discursive, the artificial, the pretentious, the falsely political or the ideological) in a quest to allow a story to tell itself, free from the overdetermined, didactic narratives he considered characteristic of Argentine cinema of the time.[19] *Rapado*'s most obvious legacy is its minimalism, and this was to become a powerful model for subsequent filmmakers of how a coherent aesthetic approach could be developed to cope with, and indeed deliberately to reflect, a shoestring budget. There are certainly echoes of neorealism in Rejtman's first film. Exteriors, often of the street, dominate the mise-en-scène; the plot contains several loose ends; the camera moves only when necessary to keep its subject within the frame; and dialogues are shot with a medium fixed frame, eliminating the more conventional shot/reverse-shot syntax.

But the most significant legacy of *Rapado* for New Argentine Cinema is perhaps its refusal to indulge our desire for knowledge: we are accorded no privileged insight into his characters' lives, and their emotional responses—if they have any—remain a matter for guesswork on the part of the spectator. Although *Silvia Prieto* (1998) and *Los guantes mágicos* (2003) replace, to some extent, the experimentalism of *Rapado* with a more conventional aesthetic, the gaze in all three films—like those of Trapero and Alonso already explored—is the gaze of the outsider, the anthropologist. Like both of these directors, Rejtman's decision to "empezar de cero" relates not just to a minimalist aesthetic but to a measured, studious approach to his subjects suited to the task of producing social knowledge. As I will argue, Rejtman's particular concern is the circulation of commodities within the economy and how bodies, through labor and consumption, become involved in complex processes of exchange and reciprocity.

Of Rejtman's critics, however, David Oubiña is not alone in considering that his films deliberately hold back from saying anything of substance about the society of their time. With reference to *Rapado*, Oubiña comments that

> el realizador no utiliza al personaje de Lucio para hacer un discurso sobre su generación, ni pretende denunciar la decadencia moral mediante el robo de la moto, ni hace del film un vehículo para reflexionar sobre la clase media. . . . Las imágenes no están ahí en lugar de otra cosa y el film no es un medio para comunicar algún contenido que debería buscarse en su profundidad.
>
> [the director does not use the character of Lucio to deliver a speech about his generation; nor does he intend to denounce moral decadence through the theft of a motorcycle; nor does he turn the film into a vehicle to reflect on the middle class. . . . The images are not there in place of anything else and the film is not a medium for the communication of some content that must be unearthed.][20]

Such conclusions seem to be substantiated by Rejtman's discourse on his own work, in which he declares his intention to leave behind the obviously political or ideological in search of a more honest kind of filmmaking,[21] one that also recognizes that "el cine es superficie, porque más allá de la pantalla no hay nada" (cinema is surface, because beyond the screen there is nothing).[22]

The initial difficulty of reading Rejtman's films within their socioeconomic context is that they do not deal with the extremes that—both pre- and post-Crisis—have filled screens in Argentine cinema. No one is poor, and there are no spectacular plunges from riches to destitution. As he says, "Todo era medio" (Everything was average).[23] The world of his films is not fully recognizable as that of contemporary Argentina living through the Crisis, yet it does bear remarkable similarities to it: it has been made strange through processes of abstraction and an externalizing anthropological gaze. His films represent, I will argue, a study in miniature of the relationships between the economic and the social under capitalism and the particular variants of these to be observed in Argentina at the turn of the twenty-first century; as befits a study, or a theoretical model, its validity is based on an investigation of the norm and the median rather than extremes of experience. In other words, there are processes of abstraction and displacement at work that render the films' relationship with their context complex; nevertheless, their treatment of the nature of work, the relationship between work and identity, and the dynamics of production, labor, and circulation, resonate strongly with recent shifts in the capitalist world, particularly with social transformations in Argentine society from the 1990s onward. If we look for the drama of the Crisis in Rejtman's films, we look in vain: here is no powerful indictment of the exploitation of the downtrodden under capitalism. His films are populated neither by the rich nor by the poor but by people somewhere in the middle. But it is precisely Rejtman's attention to the middle, the average, in which pendulum swings are minimal, which makes his films so revealing of the ways in which particular economic systems profoundly affect subjectivity and social relations.

Many critics have noted the attention given in Rejtman's films to the circulation of objects, which are caught up in complex networks of exchange. These relationships, however, have not yet been sufficiently theorized: by drawing on Marx's understanding of capitalist circulation and the work of anthropologists on alternative economic systems, I aim to explore in greater depth the relationship between Rejtman's films and their socioeconomic context. What will emerge in this reading is a vision of Argentina as caught between market and nonmarket systems, between the developed First World and the developing Third World.

Many of the transactions in which Rejtman's characters become involved reveal much about the circulation of commodities, money, and labor in capitalism. In *Los guantes mágicos* Piraña becomes aware of an opportunity to invest in high-tech shares and persuades Alejandro to provide some of the capital. Alejandro, who has no money, sells his taxi to Luis, who gives him $4,500 for it so that he can invest this in shares with Piraña; meanwhile, Alejandro carries on driving the taxi but splits the profits with Luis. Alejandro's car is to be converted into cash and back again once more, as Piraña persuades him and Luis to partner with him in another not-to-be-missed investment opportunity: a vast consignment of one-size-fits-all "magic gloves," shipped from Hong Kong in time for an unusually cold winter in Buenos Aires. We need to become capitalists, Piraña tells them, and reinvest. These transactions provide a textbook example of how capital, according to Marx, is produced from the introduction of money into the circulation of commodities. Simple commodity exchange (C-M-C in Marx's formula, or "selling in order to buy," which is based on use value and consumption) does not produce profit, even when conducted via the medium of money; capital is produced when the transaction begins with money as its starting point (M-C-M′, or "buying in order to sell dearer," a transaction based on exchange value and circulation).[24] As Marx observes, "The ceaseless augmentation of value, which the miser seeks to attain by saving his money from circulation, is achieved by the more acute capitalist by means of throwing his money again and again into circulation."[25] After the success of this first consignment, Piraña insists that they reinvest the profits in more gloves. Things start to go wrong, however: when Alejandro cannot sell his car the second time, he borrows money from a loan shark; when the car is eventually sold, he has to give the money he earns back in the form of interest payments. As the second consignment of magic gloves arrives too late to sell that year—the cold snap has well and truly passed—Alejandro (who has lost his livelihood) has to find another job as a coach driver. The film ends on a hopeful note, however, as his fellow driver comments on the changing weather: the cooling air surely means that winter, and therefore profit, is on its way.

Both *Silvia Prieto* and *Los guantes mágicos* explore the circulation of labor and consumption within capitalism in ways strongly reminiscent of Marx's theorizations:

> The capitalist class is constantly giving to the working class drafts, in the form of money, on a portion of the product produced by the latter and appropriated by the former. The workers give these drafts back just as constantly to the capitalists, and thereby withdraw from the latter their

allotted share of their own product. . . . From the standpoint of society, then, the working class, even when it stands outside the direct labour process, is just as much an appendage of capital as the lifeless instruments of labour are. Even its individual consumption is, within certain limits, a mere aspect of the process of capital's reproduction.[26]

This role of the worker in "the production and reproduction of capital" is clearly to be witnessed in the life of the protagonist of *Silvia Prieto*. Silvia works as a waitress in a café-bar, but when she reflects on her work, or recounts her experiences in the café—always reduced to a simple statement of the total number of lattes and espressos she has served—we most often see her not serving but *consuming* coffees in another café-bar. In fact, a considerable amount of screen time is dedicated to the characters' consumption of food and drink, in homes, cafeterias, fast-food stalls, and Chinese all-you-can-eat buffets. Silvia's labor, as an "appendage of capital," is rewarded with wages that are then spent on products produced by other workers and make their way back into the hands of the café-owning class. With her first paycheck from the bar she goes to Mar del Plata for a weekend, but the only activity we see her taking part in is drinking in a café.

The emphasis on food in *Silvia Prieto* is perhaps not entirely accidental, as it is in food that we can appreciate the clearest links between production, consumption, circulation, and the reproduction of labor that assures the continued supply of workers for capitalism. Marx makes the connection explicit:

The capital given in return for labour-power is converted into means of subsistence which have to be consumed to reproduce the muscles, nerves, bones and brains of existing workers, and to bring new workers into existence. . . . The individual consumption of the working class is the reconversion of the means of subsistence given by capital in return for labour-power into fresh labour power which capital is then again able to exploit. It is the production and reproduction of the capitalist's most indispensable means of production: the worker.[27]

The burgeoning of the service industries and the middle classes in Argentina under Menem is clearly evident in *Silvia Prieto*, with the middle class also caught up in this cycle of consumption, labor, and production that keeps the economy going and provides profit for those at the top of the pyramid. When Silvia meets—in a café—another woman she has discovered who shares the name, the second Silvia Prieto is pleased to hear what Silvia does for a living, replying, "Ah, igual que yo. Servicios para la clase media. Yo soy profesora de canto" ("Ah, the same as me. Services for the middle class. I'm a singing teacher"). Such "services for the middle class" abound in Rejtman's films, from massages in *Silvia Prieto* to health spas, yoga classes, and professional dog-walking in *Los guantes mágicos*. Characters both provide these services and avail themselves of them in ways that insistently draw attention to the circulation of money, goods, and services within the economy.

In his *Spaces of Hope*, David Harvey reappropriates (and to some extent revises) classical Marxist models of the circulation of labor in order to explore subjectivity and the role of the body in contemporary theoretical debates. Harvey focuses on Marx's distinction between "the laborer (*qua* person, body, will) and labor power (that which is extracted from the body of the laborer as a commodity)," arguing that this leads to the question, "What effect does the circulation of variable capital (the extraction of labor power and surplus value) have on the bodies (persons and subjectivities) of those through whom it circulates?"[28] This, I would argue, is precisely the question that informs Rejtman's films, which explore how subjectivity and social relations are profoundly affected by economic phenomena.

That bodies, and not just the labor extracted from them, are very much caught up in circulation is clearly demonstrated in *Silvia Prieto* and *Los guantes mágicos* by the emphasis on another kind of consumption: drugs. Among the many quick fixes that the characters persuade each other to try in order to counteract stress or depression are a range of relaxants (marijuana, whisky, tobacco) and a catalogue of pharmaceuticals that they self-prescribe and pass on to others. As well as remedies, characters share afflictions and addictions: Susana in *Los guantes mágicos* tries to help Cecilia overcome depression but ends up depressed herself, at least partly because she is no longer needed once Cecilia's depression has lifted. Characters buy and sell to each other, with no need of media publicity, often adopting the language of advertising. Brite, in *Silvia Prieto*, reels off the benefits of Garbuglia's apartment as if she were a real estate agent, including its "pleno centro" (right in the center) location, "contra frente, luz, poco ruido, . . . completamente amoblado" (facing the front, light, quiet . . . fully furnished), before mentioning the price, "más las expensas, claro" (plus bills, of course). But the characters also exchange their neuroses, and even their partners, in a way that imitates the circulation of commodities. As Oubiña observes, Lucio's stealing in *Rapado* of another motorcycle after his own is stolen is not an act that produces reflection of a moral nature in him but a simple one of exchange. He observes someone else breaking a chain to steal a bike and imitates his action.[29] This dynamic governs all of Rejtman's films, in which, as Oubiña states, "todo parece regirse por una mecánica del contagio. . . . Los personajes no sólo intercambian objetos o parejas sino que también se transmiten depresiones y enfermedades" (everything seems to be governed by a dynamic of contagion. . . . The characters do not only exchange objects and partners but also depression and illnesses).[30]

Within this economy people become as exchangeable and recyclable as objects, as suggested by the ease with which Cecilia and Brite swap husbands in *Los guantes mágicos* or the nonchalance with which Silvia takes on the job (and even the uniform) of a girl who had died at her post only a few days before. This exchangeability of people is often marked aesthetically in Rejtman's films by the use of matched shots. In *Los guantes mágicos* the similarity between repeated shots of Alejandro's taxi on several trips to the airport draws attention to the different combinations of characters being transported: Valeria's promotion to the front seat reflects her position as Alejandro's current partner, with Cecilia relegated to the back (Figure 11). At the end of the film the splicing together of two other very similar shots, the first of Alejandro driving a coach and his fellow driver asleep and the second of the two men with their roles reversed, reinforces this idea of exchangeability (Figure 12). That human subjects have been reduced to the status of objects is also suggested by the fact that it is sometimes the movement of an object, and not its owner, that becomes the plot motor in *Silvia Prieto*. The china doll discarded by Silvia is picked up by a teenage boy who has no relation to the plot of the film, but the camera follows him home and then to a nightclub; it then switches to one of the band members whom, on her return home, we discover to be the daughter of the second Silvia Prieto, and thus the main plot resumes.

Sociologists have paid much attention in recent years to the effects of shifting economic patterns, and particularly the nature of work, on subjectivity and on the social identities that may arise from, or condense, particular forms of subjectivity. As the ties linking capital and labor are loosened under a shift described by Zygmunt Bauman as that of "heavy capitalism" to "light capitalism"—the former characterized by the prospect of lifelong employment in the same company (Ford, as always, provides the classic example) and the latter by uncertain and insecure job prospects—so social identities are cast adrift from the work in which they had been anchored in the industrial era.[31] While, as Martín Hopenhayn explains, work became central to personal and social life during industrialization, giving meaning to both

11–12. The juxtaposition of matched shots in *Los guantes mágicos* emphasizes the exchangeability of people, who are swapped as freely as goods and services in the film.

of these, more recent developments in the nature of work in a postindustrial world have caused a breach in this relationship, with work no longer able to perform its erstwhile functions of providing a framework for personal realization and sustaining a sense of social identity: "Hoy día la nueva oleada descentra todo eje de integración y reconocimiento, y en esa dinámica crece la tensión entre esta centralidad simbólica del trabajo y un mundo en que el trabajo se va haciendo más escaso y discontinuo" (In our time the new wave decenters every axle of integration and recognition, and within that dynamic we see a tension growing between the symbolic centrality of work and a world in which work is becoming scarce and intermittent).[32]

Beatriz Sarlo is not the only critic to have noticed the similarity between the plot of *Rapado* and that of Vittorio De Sica's Italian neorealist classic *The Bicycle Thieves* (1948), whose protagonist also has his bicycle stolen. As Sarlo notes, however, this point of comparison also reveals an important cultural shift: "en la película de Rejtman, lo que se roba no es un medio de trabajo sino de identificación" (in Rejtman's film, what is stolen is not a means of work, but of identification).[33] The absence of the world of work in *Rapado* tells us much, she argues, about the place of work, a "scarce commodity," in Argentina of the 1990s:

Aunque conserva un lugar clave desde el punto de vista de la inserción social, ocupa una posición completamente subordinada desde el punto de vista cultural, y no es un espacio de identificación. Hoy es difícil que un núcleo de construcción de la identidad sea alguna ocupación profesional o laboral.

[Although it retains a key role in terms of social insertion, it occupies a completely subordinate position in cultural terms, and is not a space of identification. Today it is difficult for work or a professional occupation to provide a nucleus for the construction of identity.][34]

In *Silvia Prieto* the transience of employment in a precarious labor system is matched by low expectations and commitment in workers, who move on from one short-term job to another on a whim. As Bauman suggests, "The place of employment feels like a camping site which one visits for just a few days, and may leave at any moment if the comforts on offer are not delivered or found unsatisfactory when delivered—rather than like a shared domicile where one is inclined to take trouble and patiently work out the acceptable rules of cohabitation."[35] Silvia is identified with the companies she works for—first as a waitress, then handing out promotional sachets of soap powder—by means of a uniform; both Brite and Armani take their names from the brands with which they are associated. But these associations are empty signifiers standing in for a more genuine kind of loyalty and identification with the workplace and pointing to a more general crisis in identity. The use of names and uniforms acquires a certain pathos within the film, particularly as we see Silvia, who initially disliked the unattractive yellow overalls she had to wear in the bar, decide to don them on her weekend away to Mar del Plata. Her horror at discovering that other women share her name suggests that her own identity is anchored to little else.

In *Los guantes mágicos* work fails to provide a vehicle for fulfilling personal ambition and identity, as all the characters find it impossible to climb higher than the first couple of rungs on the employment ladder: Alejandro drives a taxi, but it is an old Renault 12; Valeria loves her job as an air stewardess but doesn't manage to progress from charter and domestic flights to international ones; Luis is a film star but in pornographic movies; Piraña wants to be a musician but has to content himself with making a homegrown CD. If there is—rarely—a long-term strategy for building a career, it is frustrated. Bauman explains that, in the postindustrial era, "work has changed its character. More often than not, it is a one-off act: a ploy of a *bricoleur*, a trickster, aimed at what is at hand and inspired and constrained by what is at hand, more shaped than shaping, more the outcome of chasing a chance than the product of planning and design."[36] The reference to the trickster here is illuminating, as contemporary Argentine cinema is full of examples of *la viveza criolla*, that particularly Argentine kind of entrepreneurialism that doesn't play strictly by the rules and may also involve fraud or deception. This theme links *Los guantes mágicos* with other films, such as Leonardo Di Cesare's *Buena Vida Delivery* (2003), that take the Crisis as an explicit referent, showing the opportunism—at once admirable and despicable—that was to ensure the survival of some at the expense of others.

According to Bauman, the precariousness of relationships in the labor world leads to "the fading and wilting, falling apart and decomposing of human bonds, of communities and of partnerships."[37] Rejtman's films likewise demonstrate a continuity between the short-term alliances made at work and those of a personal nature. Instead of "patiently work[ing] out the acceptable rules of cohabitation," characters continually separate from each other, move out, and form alliances with the nearest available new partner, while remaining in the same social circle in a way that, although treated comically in the films, consistently reveals superficiality. Coincidence is often mistaken for destiny and leads to fleeting forms of association, like the group in *Los guantes mágicos* who spend the weekend at a spa in Brazil and discover that they are all Sagittarians, which provides them with enough reason to form an exercise group, which they attend for a while. Valeria repeats several times that she likes being with Alejandro because they are both in the public transport sector, as if this were something more than a simple coincidence and therefore a sufficient reason for moving in together. Alejandro is offered accommodation in Luis's flat because Piraña insists that he is an old classmate of his brother's, and he continues to live there even when Luis returns to Buenos Aires and it is clear that they had never met. In *Silvia Prieto*, Marta, who meets Garbuglia on a TV dating show, decides to continue the rather awkward, media-driven courtship so that she can fulfill her dream of having a wedding party. Cohabitation arrangements —whether moving in or out—are made either on a whim or on the basis of economic convenience rather than romantic attachment: Rejtman's characters are never seen displaying affection for each other. This superficiality governing personal identity and social relationships is matched by the films' objectifying gaze: characters are two-dimensional, lacking in depth, appearing emotionless.

Yet Rejtman's reflection on the impact of "light" capitalism on social relations should be held in tension with another key theme in his work, which contrasts First World capitalist economic relations with those of Argentina, which—I will argue—is positioned as primitive in comparison. The Argentine economy is depicted in these films as a hybrid system in which a capitalist market economy exists alongside (and is often bypassed by) alternative systems, specifically the gift economy and the barter economy, which are frequently associated in economic anthropology with early or tribal societies. The Buenos Aires we see is caught between two forms of society that we might variously express as First World and Third World, market and nonmarket, developed and developing, modern and traditional, cosmopolitan capital and tribal village: handicapped by the operation of these more informal systems and unable to move into a full market economy but stripped of the nonmaterial benefits the more traditional systems represent in terms of a sense of genuine community or loyalty.

The many complicated networks of exchange set up between the films' characters would provide rich material for an anthropological study of economic and social relations in contemporary Buenos Aires. Significantly, in many of these, goods and services are exchanged directly without recourse to money as a medium. In *Los guantes mágicos* Cecilia is given a dog by Daniel, the professional dog-walker, which had been left with him when its owner died; Susana takes it off her hands to give to Alejandro as a birthday gift. Daniel's present to Alejandro is free dog-walking services for a month, but as he lives too far away, Alejandro's taxi services are contracted to transport him, for which Cecilia offers to pay as her own present. Only one of these transactions (the last) actually involves money. Barter systems are most often used in countries that do not have a formal currency or whose currency is experiencing instability; during the Argentine Crisis, barter clubs were used extensively as a mode of survival. The widespread use of barter in Rejtman's films points to the cracks in Argentine capitalism. In capitalist terms, of course, these transactions are not profit-making, being based entirely on use values rather than exchange values; they are deliberately intended to bypass money as an unreliable medium.

It is, however, the gift economy that often provides the best model to explain the circulation of objects in Rejtman's films. In a gift economy goods and services are given without an explicit condition of reimbursement or exchange. Implicitly, something is expected in return, whether goods, favors, or a nonmaterial benefit, such as loyalty. Thus tribal leaders might present gifts of food and jewelry to their own tribes in order to ensure their support. We see much evidence in both *Silvia Prieto* and *Los guantes mágicos* of the operation of a gift economy, but its principles are continually perverted. Not one of the gifts really costs the givers, who are interested more in the appearance of generosity than in the formation of genuine relationships. For example, Silvia opts for the biggest bottle of shampoo as a present for the second Silvia Prieto, entirely unbothered about the quality of the product, explaining to the shop assistant that "me interesa quedarme bien" (I'm interested in looking good). Sometimes the gifts given do not even belong to their givers: Piraña offers Alejandro the use of his brother Luis's flat while he is away, at no cost to himself, and profits from it himself by taking pay in the form of free taxi rides. Nor are the gifts wanted or appreciated by their recipients. Brite is insulted by the china figurine she receives from Gabriel and passes it on to Silvia as a present, who discards it. Most significant, characters often try to gain profit on the gifts they receive, in a move that, as Lewis Hyde observes, is not permitted in societies based around gift economies: the gift is meant to be consumed, not invested for growth or profit.[38] Silvia, who steals a jacket from Armani, gives it to Gabriel as a gift, as a man's jacket is of no use to her; Gabriel sells it to Marcelo for $75, pretending that he had bought it in Los Angeles; Armani sees Marcelo with the jacket and challenges him, eventually agreeing to buy it back from him for $100.

Hyde notes that "capital earns profit and the sale of a commodity turns a profit, but gifts that remain gifts do not *earn* profit, they *give* increase. The distinction lies in what we might call the vector of the increase: in gift exchange it, the increase, stays in motion and follows the object, while in commodity exchange it stays behind as a profit."[39] The characters' attempts to gain profit in the absence of capital, by turning gifts into commodities, testify both to the weakness of the Argentine economy and to the fragility of the societal relations that might have constrained dishonest profiteering. As Hyde argues, "Where someone manages to commercialize a tribe's gift relationships the social fabric of the group is invariably destroyed."[40] Rejtman's vision is far from nostalgic; he is not holding Argentina up as a model of the close ties of premarket social communities; instead, he is showing how the rules of community are consistently violated. This is a society that is impoverished principally because it has forgotten how to give, receive, and reciprocate.

It is also one that is poised between these more informal economic systems and First World–style capitalism. If the image of cohabitation served earlier to suggest a lack of commitment in relationships, it may also be employed here to evoke the lack of distance in *porteño* society, in which the characters are shown living on top of each other in a way more reminiscent of an extended family home than a city. Indeed, Buenos Aires is represented in the films as a village where ex-partners continually rub shoulders with each other and each other's new partners, old classmates continually bump into each other, and all relationships are conducted in a public arena. When the porn actor Luis realizes he needs to return to Canada to find work, he makes a significant statement about Argentina:

> No es un país serio. . . . Acá no hay industria. ¿Y sabés por qué? Porque en este país somos todos como hermanos. Yo hago una película acá, al día siguiente salgo a la calle, todo el mundo se da vuelta y me señala con el dedo. En Canadá, es otra cosa. Allá sos más anónimo. En un país desarrollado, es otra cosa.

> [This isn't a serious country. . . . There is no industry here. And do you know why? Because in this country it's as if we're all brothers. If I make a film here, and the next day go out, everyone turns and points at me. In Canada it's another story. There you're more anonymous. In a developed country it's another story.]

There is little in the Buenos Aires depicted in the film of the distance and anonymity that most theorists consider essential to the development of a market economy, given that we prefer to socialize with family and friends but do business with strangers.

Rejtman's superimposition of different economic models results in a depiction of Buenos Aires as backward and parochial but lacking the benefits of trust and loyalty that often characterize the close-knit communities of nonmarket economies. Marcel Mauss's stated intention in writing his pioneering study of the gift economy was also to argue for a "return to the old and elemental" in his own society, to recover the social benefits enjoyed by "primitive" communities, and to prevent a descent into "frigid utilitarian calculation."[41] Rejtman's vision is not nostalgic in this manner: what emerges under his more neutral gaze is not a full-scale critique of capitalism, nor a defense of it, but a dissection, intelligent and often witty, of the relationships between the economic and the social in contemporary Argentina. What he does share with Mauss is an appreciation of the interconnectedness of these spheres. Like Mauss, who states that in "primitive" or "archaic" societies, "social phenomena are not discrete; each phenomenon contains all the threads of which the social fabric is composed,"[42] Rejtman treats aspects of the economy as "*total* social phenomena" in the sense that they are, at the same time, economic, social, and moral, suggesting that an approach exploring the integration of these phenomena is as valid now as it was then and as appropriate to "developed" societies as to "early" ones.

4

CRIME AND CAPITALISM
IN GENRE CINEMA

In *El cuerpo del delito: Un manual*, Josefina Ludmer explores the importance of crime as "uno de los instrumentos más utilizados para definir y fundar una cultura" (one of the tools most commonly used to define and found a culture). Crime acts as *"una frontera cultural* que separa la cultura de la no cultura, que funda culturas, y que también separa líneas en el interior de una cultura. Sirve para trazar límites, diferenciar y excluir" (*a cultural boundary* that separates culture from nonculture, which founds cultures, and also draws lines within a culture. It serves to trace limits, to differentiate and to exclude). It becomes, she suggests, a critical tool par excellence, being a phenomenon that is at once historical, cultural, political, economic, legal, social, and literary: it allows us to read in fiction the complex and paradoxical relationships between the subject, beliefs, culture, and the state.[1] One of the most sustained of Ludmer's analyses centers on the figure of Juan Moreira, a gaucho immortalized in a series of legends and cultural representations, from his death in 1874 to the present day. Ludmer contrasts the "peaceful" gaucho of José Hernández's *La vuelta de Martín Fierro* (1879), who returns from exile to recommend "la pacificación y la integración a la ley por el trabajo" (pacification and integration into the law through work) with the violent popular hero of Eduardo Gutiérrez's serialized novel *Juan Moreira*, published in the same year. Read together, in the context of Argentina's rapid modernization and the internationalization of its economy at the end of the nineteenth century, they demonstrate two possible paths for the popular within the liberal state, "para hablar nada más que del uso de la fuerza o del cuerpo, para la economía y para la violencia" (to talk precisely about the use of force or of the body, for the purposes of the economy or for violence).[2] I propose to extend Ludmer's symptomatic reading of crime narratives to the analysis of a selection of Argentine films from the more recent neo-liberal era. The readings that emerge will demonstrate the extent to which crime remains a powerful tool in articulating the conflict between national and international economic interests and in imagining the relationship between the individual and the capitalist state in a globalized world. The films under discussion draw on internationally recognized genres—the crime thriller, the western, and film noir—but also maintain a dialogue with two specifically national stories, both of which date back at least as far as these versions of the legend of Juan Moreira: the criminal state and economic injustice.

The "just criminal" arises where legality and morality diverge. As Ludmer shows, the violent gaucho of Gutiérrez's *Juan Moreira* started off on the right side of the law, but two incidents involve him in committing "just" crimes and drive him to serial acts of lawlessness. The first murder is of a man who refuses to honor a debt; the second is of a representative of the state who wrongly imprisons him. Ludmer observes that the novel

> no hace sino repetir la leyenda del criminal heroico llevado a una vida de delito por una injusticia o por cometer un acto que el estado, pero no la comunidad, considera criminal. Quiero decir que hasta aquí Moreira podría ser un Billy the Kid o un Jesse James, que aparecen en Estados Unidos en la década de 1870 con la modernización tecnológica . . . en momentos de descontento rural con la nueva política económica y junto con organizaciones políticas agrarias que se definían como populistas.

> [merely echoes the legend of the heroic criminal led to a life of crime by some injustice or by committing an act that the state—but not the community—considers to be criminal. I mean that thus far, Moreira could be a Billy the Kid or a Jesse James, who appear in the United States in the 1870s at the same time as technological modernization . . . at moments of rural discontent with the new economic policy and together with agrarian political organizations that defined themselves as populist.][3]

At the turn of the twenty-first century in Argentina, both economic injustice and the abuse of state power produce similar figures of criminal heroes whose actions endear them to the community while provoking the retribution of the state or—more often—of shadowy forces defending the interests of corporate business, which are able to marshal all the powers of pursuit and punishment once associated only with the state.

Marcelo Piñeyro's *Caballos salvajes* (1995) presents a paradigmatic narrative of the "just crime" in contemporary Argentina. In the opening sequence José, holding a gun, threatens a bank manager and demands a large sum of cash. Nothing is quite as it appears, however: José is in fact only demanding the return of a deposit of $15,344, made eighteen years ago, which the bank has refused to honor; the only person he is threatening to kill is himself; even his taking of Pedro as a hostage is simulated. This "asalto al revés" (upside-down holdup) confounds the bank and the media, who swoop in to cover the "crime." Even more indigestible to the system is the decision made by José and Pedro to distribute the money they inadvertently took in excess of the amount owed (about $465,000) to the workers of a multinational company who have been made redundant. They become people's heroes overnight as they scatter hundreds of dollar bills over the stunned crowd "en nombre de los muchos estafados de nuestro país" (in the name of the many cheated people in our country). The introduction of a second protagonist, Pedro, allows the much older and wiser José to educate him (and us) in the interconnectedness of the "System," which brings together political and economic forces and embraces all kinds of corruption— drug trafficking, money laundering, the exploitation of workers—in the name of power and profit. It is never clear in the film whether the hit men pursuing Pedro and José are associated with the police, the secret services, or the bank; this indeterminacy reinforces the all-pervasive power of the System, which admits of no clear distinctions between criminality and the state.

When Pedro accuses him of being a Marxist, José responds: "Soy mucho más antiguo que eso. . . . Soy anarquista" (I'm much older than that. . . . I'm an anarchist). In the light of Pedro's late-twentieth-century skepticism concerning the validity of social theories that appear to have lost both power and relevance, anarchism is presented in the film as a much more viable principle, one that has stood the test of time and now seems even more relevant than ever. Brought to Argentina by Italian members of the burgeoning immigrant population, anarchism played a prominent role in workers' organization from the 1880s until becoming virtually eclipsed by Bolshevik success. In the cultural sphere anarchist ideas underpin the imaginary world of Roberto Arlt's novels, the most well-known of which is *Los siete locos*, published in 1929, the year of the Wall Street crash. During the 1920s and 1930s, when Arlt published his major works, events repeatedly emphasized

Argentina's vulnerability within the structures of an ever more globalized economy, and opposition mounted against the liberal internationalist policies that had largely prevailed since the mid-nineteenth century, increasingly framed in these decades as antinational. It is perhaps unsurprising that the ideas explored in Arlt's work should have inspired another generation of Argentine artists, both writers and filmmakers, in the context of the widely perceived failure of the neoliberal project of the 1990s.

As Idelber Avelar observes, crime becomes a narrative tool in Arlt's work, in which the crime of the individual always throws into relief the much greater corruption of the capitalist state: "His plots are always triggered by some illicit or ill-intentioned borrowing, ransacking, or sheer robbery, as if the very possibility of storytelling depended upon an alteration, however minimal and illusory, in the peaceful equilibrium between the wealthy and the destitute. Such alteration always comes from lawbreaking: petty robberies that stand as a pale miniature of the institutionalized robbery upon which the entire polis functions."[4] In recent Argentine films the "just crime"—always in the form of robbery—has often accentuated the injustice and corruption of the state in precisely this way. In José Glusman's black comedy *Cien años de perdón* (2000), characters already in financial ruin launch a kidnapping operation to keep a creditor at bay; the title of the film, taken from the proverb "Quien roba a un ladrón, tiene cien años de perdón" (He who robs a thief deserves a hundred years of forgiveness), clearly suggests the comparative insignificance of a smaller misdeed in the context of a greater wrong and the moral defensibility of individual retribution against an exploiting class or an unethical state. The film's unusual narrative twist is that the known corruption and brutality of the police has the unexpected effect of uniting criminal and victim in their common desire to keep the law at bay. Mauricio's mother repeats his father's adage, "Siempre es mejor un mal arreglo que un juicio bueno" (A bad private arrangement is always better than a good court judgment); the aggrieved parties agree to resolve their own conflict because calling the police will only result in the ransom ending up in *their* hands. An honorable robbery also features in *Nueve reinas* (Fabián Bielinsky, 2000), in which characters work together to con another who had previously swindled his brother and sister out of their inheritance. The deeply flawed hero of *Un oso rojo* (Adrián Caetano, 2001) also challenges simple ethical positions with regard to crime when he reluctantly takes part in a bank robbery in order to safeguard the precarious finances of his family, which has been threatened with eviction and left unprotected by the state.

That the nature and motive of these "just" crimes—and often the initial wrong they redress—are overwhelmingly economic suggests the extent to which the more treacherous, far-reaching, and unpardonable crime of the state is also perceived fundamentally as an economic one. The state appears in these films as deeply corrupt or is made conspicuous by its total absence from the narrative. Although most of the films discussed in this chapter contain a form of dénouement, this rarely comes in the form of the agents of the state solving or punishing crimes. For the most part, the state in recent Argentine cinema has lost its sovereignty to such an extent that the dramas we see are played out entirely in the absence of the disciplining—much less the nurturing—functions of the state. Punishment is more likely to be meted out by other individuals or by all-powerful supranational corporations that have taken over the role of the nation-state in regulating social behavior, in the interests of maintaining an environment suitably stable for the production of capital. The state is depicted as criminally negligent of the needs of its citizens, whether for security or welfare. Where the police do play more than a very incidental role in the narrative—as, for example, in *El bonaerense* (Pablo Trapero, 2002)—they are portrayed as trigger-happy bunglers or as sinister, self-serving figures of terror and corruption. More often, punishment in the form of vengeance is provided by unidentified armed men who, as in *La cruz del sur* (Pablo Reyero, 2002) and *Caballos salvajes*, are probably members of drug rings or the henchmen of corporate tycoons rather than law-enforcing agents of the state.

As well as confronting the question of the state's domestic failings, then, crime narratives also demonstrate the interpenetration of the local and the global in contemporary Argentina and the state's subservience to financial interests, particularly foreign ones. Nationalist readings are suggested by many of these films, in which homegrown criminals are pitted against evil institutions with global reach. Many of them can be read as examples of the kind of "conspiracy narratives" Fredric Jameson reads as attempts "to grasp our new being-in-the-world,"[5] unconscious allegories of the world system, like David Cronenberg's *Videodrome* (1983): beyond the explicit content of this film, which narrates the "classical struggle between a small businessman and entrepreneur and a great faceless corporation," Jameson maintains that it can be read to refer allegorically to a broader encounter between the individual and the global web of hidden social, economic, and technological orders that remain hidden from him.[6]

Nationalist readings are also suggested by these films' appropriation of, and deviation from, established international (or, more accurately, Hollywood) genres such as the crime thriller, film noir, gangster movies, and the western. These reworkings provide the principal focus of the analyses in this chapter, which explores the interplay in the texts between internationally recognized codes and local meanings rooted in the socioeconomic climate of pre- and post-Crisis Argentina. In many cases these films present conscious citations that, displaced and distorted, reflect rather different images of crime and society back to the metropolis. Reappropriations of genres arising originally at different points in time and space provide particularly rich pickings for a kind of cultural archaeology that seeks to mine the complex relationships between text and context. The mediations between the local and the global at the aesthetic level in these films (as well as in their narrative content) produces multiple readings: intersecting, superimposed, and contradictory.

NUEVE REINAS AND EL AURA:
SIMULATION AND REALITY IN THE CRIME THRILLER

Nueve reinas (2000), Fabián Bielinsky's highly successful crime thriller, has been praised by critics and audiences alike for achieving a genuine synthesis between artistic merit and commercial viability. The ease with which the film was taken up in international distribution networks has—perversely, perhaps—led many of its academic critics to concentrate their efforts on resituating the film within its Argentine context. Gabriela Copertari's complex reading of *Nueve reinas* examines the film's rather problematic resolution as a "demand for justice," which "synecdochically represents the broader social demand for justice existing in Argentine society as a response to the deception of disillusionment produced by 'the promise of globalization.' "[7] Searching not only for allegories of present economic failures but also for antecedents in Argentine culture, Deborah Shaw suggests that we might understand the film's layers of artifice, together with its appropriation of a foreign-born genre for national ends, as Borgesian devices.[8] Geoffrey Kantaris points to connections between the film's explorations of simulation, forgery, fantasy, and criminality and those of Arlt's fiction.[9]

By contrasting the textual politics of *Nueve reinas* with those of Bielinsky's second feature-length film, *El aura* (2005), I aim to explore further the rather contradictory relationship these films hold with the social and cultural contexts of their production. Arlt's critique of capitalism, and the association of cinema, fantasy, simulation, and crime in his fiction, will serve as tools to dissect and oppose these two films, which, I will argue, produce fundamentally different images of crime in contemporary Argentina. The rhetoric of *Nueve reinas* establishes a number of parallels between con men, capitalism, and cinema, all of which draw on the power of illusion. While the film draws attention to the precariousness of financial systems under late capitalism and their vulnerability to corruption, a rather different reading of the film's politics reveals at the heart of its representation of crime a nostalgia that works to reinforce the logic of capitalism. *El aura*, an unlikely sequel to Bielinsky's first film, systematically destroys the illusions set up in *Nueve reinas* to produce a much darker vision of crime with significantly greater social and psychological realism, one that forces us to reconsider the relationships between crime, capitalism, and cinema that have informed most readings of *Nueve reinas* to date.

The relationship established in *Nueve reinas* between criminal deception and cinematic illusion constitutes a self-reflexive twist on a popular genre. Performance in *Nueve reinas* is indistinguishable from the real thing, both for the film's characters and its spectators. Marcos, Juan, and their various accomplices are, first and foremost, confidence tricksters who rely on a convincing performance to pull off their scams. While Marcos appears to be the more experienced and devious, Juan possesses an even more enviable attribute in this line of work, his "cara de buen tipo" (nice-guy face). The closing scene of the film reveals the extent to which we as spectators have been successfully duped: Juan, not Marcos, emerges as the master swindler, who has managed to cheat his girlfriend's brother into giving up part of a stolen inheritance that was rightfully hers to share. This last twist in the tale invites reflection on the status of film as illusion and performance. The camera, we realize, has shown us only part of the truth, deliberately leading us to draw false conclusions. The con man's most valued skills—telling a convincing story, giving a good performance, selling an illusion—are also those of the filmmaker. Both are involved in the purveying of fictions, relying on their ability to persuade us of their veracity.[10]

Perhaps the most significant contribution to the genre made by *Nueve reinas*, however, lies in Bielinsky's addition of a third term to this exercise in illusion and credibility: the money system itself. *Nueve reinas* abounds with symbols of value: notes, stamps, and checks "stand in" for money, which is itself a symbol of value. The film depicts a system in which money has become thoroughly dematerialized. The severing of links between money and precious metals, or other tangible commodities, provides the opportunity for ever more daring and undetectable acts of fraud: reduced to digits on a screen, money can easily disappear and reappear. As David Harvey argues, in recent decades the severing of links between the financial system and both production and a material monetary base has produced a crisis of value; it "calls into question the reliability of the basic mechanism whereby value is supposed to be represented."[11] Money becomes a fiction, just so many bits of printed paper that refer only to themselves: the simulacra of value.

The fragility of a dematerialized financial system is suddenly revealed in the film's climax. The swindles of small-fry crooks such as Juan and Marcos are finally eclipsed by corruption at the heart of the financial system itself. As the two protagonists arrive at the bank to cash their check for $450,000, they discover locked doors and a crowd clamoring outside. It is explained to them that the bank's board of directors sold the assets and took off with $11 million the night before. Everything until this vital turning point has been bound by a simple dichotomy: is it real or counterfeit? Success up to this moment in the film has been entirely determined by a character's ability to pass fakes off as real and to recognize false or genuine items correctly in order to evade the tricks of others. But when Marcos, failing to grasp the import of what has happened, thrusts Vidal Gandolfo's check in front of a bank employee and asks, desperately, whether it is genuine, he receives the reply, "¿Eso qué carajo importa?" (What the hell does that matter?). The precious check, which—as Valeria reassures Marcos—is "un cheque de caja certificado por el banco. Es lo mismo que efectivo" (a cashier's check, certified by the bank. As good as cash) is worthless. Only Juan, wise to the ephemerality of money and tipped off about the imminent bank crash, is able to continue playing the system in an unstable world; Marcos makes the fatal mistake of believing that money has a tangible value. When Juan, trying to avert possible suspicion by voicing skepticism about the proposed (fictitious) deal, says "Esto no es real" (This isn't real), Marcos replies, "Esto es lo más real que te pasó en la vida, pelotudo. Son 450 lucas. Esto es más real que vos y yo" (This is the realest thing that has ever happened to you, you jerk. It's 450 big ones. This is realer than you or me). His unwavering confidence in the value of money and the possibility of making it big—"Es una oportunidad, una sola, una en un millón, en toda tu vida" (This is an opportunity, *the* opportunity, one in a million, the one of your life)—becomes his downfall.

The argument that capitalism produces its own criminals is Marx's. As he writes in *Capital*, "The criminal breaks the monotony and everyday security of bourgeois life. In his way he keeps it from stagnation, and gives rise to that uneasy tension and agility without which even the spur of competition would get blunted. Thus he gives a stimulus to the productive forces."[12] This idea is given much greater force in Arlt's fiction, in which the swindler and the forger become emblematic figures of capitalism. As Ricardo Piglia observes, in Arlt

> el dinero otorga un poder infinito y es la única ley y la única verdad en una sociedad que es una jungla. Entre los ricos y los pobres están los estafadores, los inventores, los falsificadores, los soñadores, los alquimistas que tratan de hacer dinero de la nada: son los hombres de la magia capitalista, trabajan para sacar dinero de la imaginación.

> [money bestows an infinite power and is the only law and the only truth in a society that is a jungle. Between the rich and the poor there are the swindlers, the inventors, the forgers, the dreamers, the alchemists who try to make money from nothing: they are men of the capitalist magic, who work to extract money from the imagination.][13]

Making money from nothing becomes even more possible in a system in which money is becoming increasingly estranged from the production of goods and services, a trend Harvey calls "paper entrepreneurialism," exemplified by the currency speculation, corporate mergers, and takeovers that have presented hitherto unimaginable opportunities for moneymaking as the financial system rapidly folds in on itself.[14]

Both crime and capitalism are allowed to flourish in *Nueve reinas* in a deregulated environment in which the authority of the state is subsumed into the higher authority of capital. The state is entirely absent in the film. The only agents of the law that appear in the film's frames are impostors hired by either Juan or Marcos to lend credit to their operations. The absence of the state suggests a collusion with middle-class corruption that is particularly notable in the film's exploration of the interior space of the hotel, which is the setting for much of the action. The camera pans and tilts to take in the scope of the atrium lobby of the quietly lavish Hilton in Puerto Madero, passing slowly over clean, gleaming surfaces of glass and marble. This sterilized, ordered space contrasts with the chaos of the streets outside; intrusions that might threaten its air of respectability are not welcome. It does not surprise the viewer that the coughing, vomiting old forger, Sandler, should be banished to a locker room and quickly bundled into an ambulance. Conversely, however, it would seem that the hotel is only too happy to number among its honored guests a wealthy Spanish businessman about to be deported to Venezuela, almost certainly for the shady nature of his dealings.

The rapid and apparently straightforward translation of *Nueve reinas* into a Hollywood remake (*Criminal*, Gregory Jacobs, 2004) suggests the reiterability of the film's story and themes in an international context. Indeed, the postmodern profusion of simulacra and the dematerialization of money under late capitalism, together with the challenges to the state's sovereignty posed by supranational corporations, are themes that echo across the developed world. Bielinsky did not intend *Nueve reinas* to provide any kind of commentary on "el ser nacional" (the national character), but he acknowledges that the film has been taken up within Argentina as a specifically national tale. He finds this reception fascinating, as "esta modalidad de robo se da en todas las grandes ciudades del mundo, pero no en todas las ciudades el público lo tomaría como una especie de ilustración de algo genérico" (this kind of theft takes place in every large city in the world, but not in every city does the audience take it as an example of a native trait). Bielinsky attributes this to an identification on the part of the audience with the characters: "Es como si dijeran 'Esos no son marginales, son decididamente parte de nosotros'" (It's as if they were saying, "Those aren't marginal figures, they definitely belong to us").[15] In the post-Crisis context, however, it is less the action of two individual crooks and more a *systemic* corruption that strikes a particular note of resonance in Argentina. With chilling prescience *Nueve reinas* exposes the fragility of the financial system; the crowd that gathers outside the bank, shouting for access to their accounts, prefigures scenes that were to become all too familiar during the economic collapse of 2001–2.

This postdated provision of a very real historical referent in the form of the Crisis creates something of a problem for criticism. The obvious parallel has decisively shaped readings of the film, both in Argentina and beyond. Sergio Wolf and others draw attention to the misreading that this historical accident has encouraged: "Ahora, la película es leída como real pero *Nueve reinas* es una historia de enorme artificialidad, de artificios que se suman a otros artificios" (Now, the film is read as real, but *Nueve reinas* is a hugely artificial story, about one artifice after another).[16] In the context of the reading developed here, however, the anchoring of the film to a referent in reality need not be understood as antithetical to its exploration of artifice. Its crucial revelation of the artificiality and simulation at the heart of the money system suggests the inherent instability of banking practices and currency values that was to be most catastrophically proven in the Crisis. Piglia considers that el funcionamiento de la bolsa de valores y la fluctuación de los "intereses" y los flujos de dinero y las alzas y la inflación, todo el circuito de circulación monetaria, tiene mucho que ver con la circulación de informaciones y con qué cosas se dan a conocer y con el tipo de lenguaje que se usa, la jerga, y esa circulación de palabras produce inmediatamente movimientos financieros. Las cosas son al revés de lo que parecen, el lenguaje hace funcionar las finanzas. . . . Todo tiene mucho que ver con la confianza, con el crédito, en definitiva con la creencia.

[the functioning of market values, the fluctuation of "interests," the flows of money, rises in prices, inflation, the whole system of monetary circulation, has a lot to do with the circulation of information and with what gets known and the kind of language used, jargon, and that circulation of words immediately produces movements of money. Things are the other way around than they seem: language puts finance in motion. . . . Everything has a lot to do with confidence, with credit, particularly with belief.][17]

For Piglia the model of fictions circulating in society becomes a powerful representation of the way the capitalist economy functions. Given the system's dependence on fiction and belief for its stability, economic crashes such as the one experienced in Argentina in 2001 are as much the result of a sudden crisis in trust and belief as in "real" events. For many it came as a shock to realize that money deposited in banks did not exist in material form; relying as they do on the premise that not all customers will want to withdraw their savings at the same time, banks participate in the virtual flows and exchanges that underpin global finance systems. Both the *corralito* of December 2001 and the subsequent pesification of savings revealed the apparent materiality of money and the value of a currency to be fictions— fictions that could no longer be sustained in a country on the brink of economic collapse.

The placing of the film within the context of the events of the Crisis is therefore entirely in keeping with its critique of the simulations inherent in finance capitalism. The amorality of *Nueve reinas* is the amorality of capitalism, in which profit justifies the overlooking of exploitation and inequality. The film charts the dissolution of personal morality at the prospect of financial gain; as Marcos explains, everyone has a price: "Lo que hay son tarifas diferentes" (What there is, are different prices). Characters frequently use the language of ethics to distinguish between grades of criminality: Washington sells all manner of fake checks, watches, software, and perfume from his black briefcase but is insulted when asked for a gun, pronouncing "Yo no soy un delincuente" (I'm not a criminal); Juan, having deprived an old lady of $100, reacts indignantly to Marcos's surprise at his honesty in placing her gift of a ring into the joint coffers, saying, "No soy chorro" (I'm not a thief). That such posturing is merely part of the con man's performance becomes clear when Marcos convinces the stamp specialist that he will telephone him about handing over his share of the deal because "entre nosotros los delincuentes las cosas funcionan así, de confianza" (between ourselves, criminals, things work like that, on trust). These phrases act as empty markers of erstwhile social and moral codes that lose all authority when pitted against the prospect of rapid accumulation of money.

Yet against this anticapitalist analysis of *Nueve reinas*, a rather more conservative reading of the film's politics may be developed, which constructs the text as one that ultimately shores up the tenets of capitalism. The film intends to shock the viewer into the unsettling recognition that the apparent normality of city life conceals depths of unseen criminal activity. The underhand dealings of *Nueve reinas* do not take place in some criminal underworld but in the common public spaces of the city: gas stations, downtown bars, hotel lobbies, the street. Educating us as viewers to "read" the signs of the city, Marcos provides a verbal commentary in the form of a voice-over— by which means we understand that we, the viewers, are really the intended addressees—to brief shots edited in rapid succession showing pickpockets, speculators, and contrabandists at work on the streets of Buenos Aires:

> Están ahí, pero no los ves. Bueno, de eso se trata. Están, pero no están. Así que cuidá el maletín, la valija, la puerta, la ventana, el auto. Cuidá los ahorros. Cuidá el culo. Porque están ahí y van a estar siempre. . . . Son descuidistas, culateros, abanicadores, gallos ciegos, biromistas, mecheras, garfios, pungas, boqueteros, escruchantes, arrebatadores, mostaceros, lanzas, bagalleros, pequeros, filos.

> [They are there, but you don't see them. That's what it's about. They're there, but they're not there. So watch your briefcase, your suitcase, the door, the window, your car. Watch your savings. Watch your backside. Because they're there and always will be. . . . They're opportunists, petty thieves, lock-pickers, go-betweens, illegal bookies, shoplifters, bag-snatchers, wallet-lifters, tunnel-diggers, window-forcers, muggers, mustard-squirters, pickpockets, smugglers, gamblers, grabbers.]

As Bielinsky explains, the criminal activities listed by Marcos in this sequence are specialties that figure in pre-1950s police manuals, now largely dropped from the lexicon.[18] The film as a whole betrays a nostalgia for a time when criminals were gentlemen and swindlers were specialists who took pride in the artistry and intelligence of their work, when thieves were consummate professionals and not the desperate and unemployed. In this rather anaesthetized—or aestheticized—vision of white-collar crime, the only threat posed by Bielinsky's criminals is the danger of being charmed and hoodwinked out of one's savings. Juan and Marcos do not inspire fear but admiration. In the context of rapidly growing violence in turn-of-the-century Buenos Aires, *Nueve reinas* becomes an anachronistic exercise in displacement. Like the glossy, polished surfaces of the hotel, the film effectively aestheticizes crime, reflecting back a reassuring order to tame the increasing chaos outside its frames. Rather than making us uncomfortable in our seats, the film ultimately soothes us with a version of crime that responds to a strict meritocracy: the most intelligent wins. The dénouement impresses us with its neatness and thoroughness; nothing of the senselessness, the desperation, or the random nature of crime in contemporary Argentina is allowed to permeate the text of the film, which consistently ignores the role of economic misery in the growth of thefts and violent attacks. Ultimately, *Nueve reinas* leaves the logic of capitalism untouched. Its organization obeys the structure of the capitalist dream, in which the worker of today is the millionaire of tomorrow.

In the light of this aestheticization, invoking Arlt becomes incongruous. In contrast to those of *Nueve reinas*, Arlt's inventors, forgers, and criminals are desperate individuals who struggle against the meaninglessness of modern bourgeois life. Theirs is an existential anguish born of economic destitution. The respective protagonists of *El juguete rabioso* (1926) and *Los siete locos* (1929), Silvio and Erdosain, are trapped in a system that does not allow them to advance in spite of their abilities. Arlt's vision of capitalism is one in which intelligence is certainly not rewarded: Silvio, for example, is unable to gain employment in the Escuela Militar precisely because of his intelligence. Crime in Arlt is shot through with the misery of marginalization and unacknowledged talent: it is not devised by tidy professionals but by madmen gripped by illusion and despair.

Crime, capitalism, and cinema are certainly brought into a series of mirroring relationships in *Nueve reinas*. But although the final narrative twist reveals to us the illusion that the film has forged for us, two more important illusions are left unshattered, relating to crime and to capitalism. Ultimately, Bielinsky's film encourages us to believe the most insidious lies of capitalism: that the most intelligent, resourceful, and talented *deserve* to win and that these are the only assets needed to rise from poverty to riches. In the end crime becomes subject to the same dematerialization as capitalism in *Nueve reinas*, and we are encouraged to engage not just in the usual form of cinematic disavowal but also in another kind of disavowal, of the film's socioeconomic context. In Bielinsky's aestheticized version no one suffers, no one is hungry, no one is driven to desperate acts in order to survive, and no one dies.

Five years later, *El aura* was to offer a vision of crime that could not be more different. The opening credits of the film lead us to expect a criminal act orchestrated with the same skill and neatness as those of *Nueve reinas*. Shots of the taxidermist at work, using sharp instruments with care and dexterity, pan across to newspaper crime headlines; a Vivaldi concerto on the sound track enhances the air of calm professionalism and precision exuded by the whole sequence. A little later, the protagonist, standing in a queue to collect a meager wage, explains to a colleague his hypothetical plan to rob the museum. The events he describes are simulated for us onscreen by other actors while both men stand and watch: his imagination conjures up a heist that is played out around him in flagrant disrespect for the conventions of classical cinematography, in which the camera does not "lie" to us, and real and imagined events are not brought together on the same set. When the robbery is over, the scene returns to normality, with one of the gang members standing meekly in the queue behind them. The whole event has been enacted with clockwork accuracy, efficiency, and minimal fuss, with the robbers' careful plans and teamwork ensuring a clean and easy getaway.

The unusual shooting of this scene, which does not use camerawork or editing to erect boundaries between the real and the imagined, immediately suggests the collusion of cinematography in simulation and in producing the perfect crime. It is an equation that the rest of the film will explore by contrasting this set of simulations with reality. The heist in which the taxidermist becomes personally involved, hundreds of miles away in a Patagonian backland, initially appears to call on all the skills—logical deduction, confidence trickery, and a phenomenally detailed memory—for which we admired the characters of *Nueve reinas*. As plans are put into action, however, a crucial slip in the details turns a professional operation into a bloodbath; we see the protagonist visibly shaken and undone by the events that unfold at a pace he cannot control and in the hands of ruthless men who do not hesitate to kill even their fellow gang members. The reality of crime is distinctly different from its imagined version.

This contrast suggests a reading of *El aura* as a deliberate deconstruction of the aestheticization of crime at work in *Nueve reinas*. In *Nueve reinas* illusion replaces reality with consummate ease: so many of the performances we initially take to be "real" are eventually revealed as illusions. The unbreachable gap that emerges between illusion and reality in *El aura* arguably owes more to Arlt than the perfect simulations of *Nueve reinas* do, particularly to his vision of the rather insidious role of cinema in creating and sustaining capitalist fantasies. Erdosain, in *Los siete locos*, is obsessed by the gap between his mundane existence and the plots of the North American films he watches, "donde el pordiosero de ayer es el jefe de una sociedad secreta de hoy, y la dactilógrafa aventurera una multimillonaria incógnito" (where the beggar of yesterday is the head of a secret society today, and the adventurous typist ends up as the multimillionaire).[19] As Glen S. Close observes, for both Erdosain and Barsut, cinema represents the possibility of a fantastical ascent to riches and stardom, bypassing the tedium of daily labor.[20] This, for Arlt's characters, is also the opportunity offered by crime. If, as I have argued, *Nueve reinas* inscribes itself within this tradition, *El aura* demonstrates the chasm between the clean choreography of imagined, fictional crime and the unpredictable, messy, dangerous nature of the real thing. Significantly, the plot ends inconclusively: we see the taxidermist back at work in Buenos Aires and can only speculate whether he managed to retrieve the stolen money from the locked ambulance or not; certainly, we are denied the satisfaction of seeing his enrichment. The nonchalance of the last sequence—very similar to the first—suggests that whether the robbery was eventually successful is irrelevant and that the film's truncated ending is a deliberate attempt to subvert the get-rich-quick narratives of crime and capitalism so commonly seen on cinematic screens.

It would not be unreasonable to attribute the contrast between *Nueve reinas* and *El aura* to the emergence of a post-Crisis sensibility in Bielinsky's filmmaking. While *El aura* is still clearly designed to fulfill the criteria of the crime thriller, and to be fully legible to an international audience, it stages the unwelcome and messy intrusion of reality into the neatness of fiction. While both films consciously educate us to see beneath the surfaces, in *Nueve reinas*, beneath the film's appearances lie only more illusions, deceptions, and performances; in *El aura* it is the gap between illusion and reality that becomes instructive, warning us of cinema's own complicity in producing aestheticized versions of acts that are, in reality, often more reckless, more foul, or grotesquely banal.

UN OSO ROJO: THE CONTESTED SPACES OF AN URBAN WESTERN

The western's depiction of a society organized around honor rather than the law, and around informal alliances rather than institutions, lends its conventions particular aptness for an exploration of the social context of Argentina at the beginning of the twenty-first century. Many of the motifs and structures of the western are exploited in Adrián Caetano's *Un oso rojo* (2001) to establish parallels between the lawless societies of the western, characterized by corruption, swindling, rough justice, and retribution, and the violence and anarchy rife in some of the most deprived neighborhoods in Greater Buenos Aires during the worst moments of the Crisis. These are contested spaces in which the law is absent or represented only by corrupt and prejudiced police officers whose heavy-handed actions often inflame conflict rather than diffuse it. Caetano's film explores the idea of the city as a frontier, a society in the making, or—perhaps more accurately—a society in dissolution. Like many westerns, the film explores the conflict between the law and a more informal, personal form of ethics that has to do with honor, love, vengeance, and survival in the toughest of environments.

Un oso rojo tells the story of Oso, a man imprisoned for seven years for murdering a policeman, who returns to his home to find it occupied by another man, living with Oso's wife and eight-year-old daughter. The film focuses on Oso's attempts to create a new life for himself outside of prison, to regain the love and trust of his daughter, and to secure a better future for her. As an ex-convict he is the victim of prejudice and finds it difficult to reenter society. Moreover, the country he discovers on his release from prison has been ravaged by economic collapse and social fragmentation. The streets of his old neighborhood are deserted, and the bars are populated by dropouts, gamblers, and criminals. The threat of unemployment and debt hangs over everyone. Crime and violence appear to offer the only ways out of a listless depression created by the enforced leisure of a postwork Argentina.

The film is set in Greater Buenos Aires, a sprawling urban desert surrounding the capital city. Its characters roam the hot, dusty streets of San Justo, an area west of the city that is explicitly described in the film as being as violent as the Far West. The film avails itself of several clichés associated with the western genre. When Oso walks into a bar, everyone falls silent,

13. A citation from *The Godfather* combines with several clichés and conventions borrowed from westerns and gangster movies in *Un oso rojo* to represent a lawless, violent Buenos Aires at the beginning of the twenty-first century.

and all heads turn to stare at the stranger; many of the characters have nicknames, like El Turco (the Turk) and El Chino (the Chinaman). At points the film also appears to be parodying the spectacular gun skills characteristic of the western. This is most obviously the case in the final shootout, when Oso kills his remaining two assailants with a single bullet, his last one, which passes through the heart of one man to lodge itself in the chest of another. Echoes of the gangster film are also present, as El Turco's hand is pinned to the bar with a knife (Figure 13) in a move which precisely reenacts Virgil "The Turk" Sollozzo's killing of Luca in *The Godfather* (Francis Ford Coppola, 1972). The depiction of Argentina as the frontier of civilization is enhanced by the repeated use of *cumbia* on the soundtrack, replacing the Argentine rock, tangos, or European styles of music prominent in recent Argentine productions. As a popular style of dance music associated with the Caribbean coast of Colombia (bearing African influences), the use of cumbia clearly situates the film's narrative within a broader Latin American context, associating the lawlessness we witness in Buenos Aires with the violent, mafia-controlled societies stereotypically associated with Colombia. Rather than modeling itself on European culture and "civilization," *Un oso rojo* presents us with an Argentina that is beginning to recognize its affinity with the "barbarism" of other Latin American countries.

What distinguishes *Un oso rojo* from the gangster movies from which it draws certain motifs, bringing the particular social context of the film sharply into focus, is the amateur nature of Caetano's criminals. Caetano's murderers are not calculating professionals but inexpert desperados who do not weigh the consequences of their actions. Typically, the final heist in *Un oso rojo* is botched, the frayed nerves of the gang members resulting in more deaths than strictly necessary to complete the job. Perhaps most poignant, we witness Oso's accomplice risking capture to cram the last remaining coins into his loot bag (under the contemptuous gaze of the security guard), an action that most clearly marks the criminals as amateurs in real need of cash rather than cool and professional thieves. One of the most heavily ironic moments in the film is created by superimposing the Argentine national anthem, being sung by schoolchildren to mark Independence Day, onto the violent scenes of the robbery. The strains of the anthem lend an epic quality to these scenes, and the final line, "Coronados de gloria vivamos, o juremos con gloria morir" (Let us live crowned with glory, or swear with glory to die), acquires a particular irony, juxtaposed with a shot of the street littered with bodies as the robbers make their desperate escape. There is glory neither in life nor in death in *Un oso rojo*.

Against his more amateur accomplices, the protagonist of *Un oso rojo* emerges as a clear-sighted individual with a well-developed sense of justice and responsibility. Caetano's success lies in his creation of an antihero whose personal sense of honor leaves us all the more troubled by his cold-blooded cruelty. As in many westerns, rough justice emerges as a more credible alternative than the blunt instruments of the law. However, *Un oso rojo* diverges significantly from many of the more conventional westerns in its moral ambivalence: it does not present a moral warning or draw clear cause-and-effect relationships between characters' actions and their consequences. The absence of a moralizing narrative in the film is thrown into relief by the presence of a story-within-the-story, Horacio Quiroga's "Las medias de los flamencos," a rather gory tale of vengeance in the animal kingdom that obeys the conventions of a fable, offering an ingenious explanation for a particular state of affairs in nature (the color or behavior of an animal, the movement of the sun, and so forth) in order to teach a moral lesson. Here it is the flamingo's pink legs and the birds' habit of standing in water that are "explained" in a tale that suggests the dangers of caring too much about one's appearance or wanting to impress others. Quiroga's tale, which enters the film at several points (the book is given to Alicia by her father) and whose ending becomes, significantly, the film's own, stands in marked contrast to Caetano's own approach to storytelling. Where the fable traces a clear cause-and-effect relationship between past action or attitude and resulting state, *Un oso rojo* refuses to speculate on the forces that originally drove Oso to crime, and it leaves the end of the story untold. Where the fable communicates an unequivocal moral message, *Un oso rojo* neither justifies nor excuses Oso's involvement in violent robbery. Like Robin Hood, he is somehow beyond the law and beyond conventional morality, capable of acts of sacrificial kindness yet impulsive and vindictive in his treatment of his enemies. He is a compromised hero in a turbulent world: Caetano offers us a very personal kind of heroism that bears no traces of idealism, yet it can form the basis of a political reading of the film suggested by the director himself: "me parece que está bueno tener un héroe en este tiempo en el que no lo hay, en el que ningún político es capaz de sacarse los zapatos para dárselos a otro" (it seems good to have a hero at a time when there aren't any, when no politician is capable of taking his own shoes off to give them to someone else).[21]

The political framework governing *Un oso rojo* emerges most clearly when the film is directly contrasted with the cinematic antecedents it readily acknowledges. Unlike many westerns, *Un oso rojo* does not betray any nostalgia for the courage and ambition of heroes of bygone days, nor does it settle into comfortable distinctions between good and evil, hero and villain, order and anarchy, or civilization and barbarism. Unlike many gangster films, it does not introduce a psychopathic loner into an otherwise law-abiding and decent community; instead it portrays a society riddled with violence and corruption. Indeed, the question of personal ethics becomes considerably complicated by its setting in a country facing economic ruin, and this marks *Un oso rojo* out from some of its cinematic predecessors. Jameson's analysis of *The Godfather* draws attention to "the ideological function of the Mafia paradigm," which represents an anxiety over "an organized conspiracy against the public"; this constitutes, Jameson argues, an act of displacement in which crime substitutes for the resentment that would be more accurately directed toward "American capitalism in its most systematized and computerized, dehumanized, 'multinational' and corporate form":

> The function of the Mafia narrative is indeed to encourage the conviction that the deterioration of the daily life in the United States today is an ethical rather than economic matter; connected, not with profit, but rather "merely" with dishonesty, and with some omnipresent moral corruption whose ultimate mythic source lies in the pure Evil of the Mafiosi themselves. For genuinely political insights into the economic realities of late capitalism, the myth of the Mafia strategically substitutes the vision of what is seen to be a criminal aberration from the norm, rather than the norm itself.[22]

In *Un oso rojo* personal ethics have become compromised by economic necessity and the brutality of the state in a rhetorical move that clearly suggests the real crime to be that of the system, not the individual. When Sergio hesitates before accepting the money Oso offers him (which he rightly suspects to have been stolen), Oso tells him, "Toda la guita es afanada" (All money is nicked), placing his own act of robbery within a broader context of corruption and exploitation. His participation in the crime—which will almost certainly lead to the sacrifice of his personal freedom—becomes an act of selflessness, in which he gives his rival the means to support the family he has appropriated in Oso's absence. Where the state has failed to protect a family on the brink of financial ruin through unemployment and debt, the aberration from the norm comes not in the form of a crime but in the form of a disregard for self in the desire to protect others. In a ruthless world Oso stands out, not for his honesty or his decency (he has neither) but for his motives, which, if they do lead to crime, are not governed by the greed that leads to corruption. Again, as with *Caballos salvajes* and *Nueve reinas*, the crime of the individual serves only to throw into relief the greater crimes of the state and its institutions.

SHADES OF NOIR IN *LA CRUZ DEL SUR*

If Hollywood genres typically focus on psychological explanations for the conflict of the individual with society, contemporary Argentine reworkings frequently displace these onto a more properly social framework or critically interrogate the relationship between the two. *La cruz del sur* (Pablo Reyero, 2003) obeys a similar dynamic, taking some of the themes and styles of psychologically motivated drama and imbuing them with concerns of a broader social nature. Several critics have attempted to convey the uncompromising bleakness of Reyero's production by describing it as a noir film, a term the director himself has used in discussing the production.[23] The association merits closer examination, as it provides some keys for an analysis of the film's portrayal of subjectivity in the context of Argentina's violent past. Any study citing film noir as an antecedent runs immediately into problems of definition. Noir is subject to more than the usual slipperiness of analytical categories, and the difficulties of deciding which films should be considered as belonging to the genre, whether noir is primarily a style or a mood, or, indeed, whether it can be described as a genre at all, have occupied critical attentions ever since the first studies published in the 1950s. Although it is not my purpose here to rehearse these arguments in depth, it is worth noting that they are not unrelated to noir's own internal contradictions, as the progeny of two unlikely bedfellows, German expressionism and Italian neorealism. It is around these internal contradictions that the analysis offered below will revolve, as I trace the rather different resolution attempted by *La cruz del sur* to an analogous set of representational challenges.

With a plot involving a heist, drugs, betrayals, and shootouts, *La cruz del sur* has many of the ingredients of the classic noir film of the late 1940s and 1950s in America. It follows a group of young criminals as they steal a large consignment of cocaine and are pursued to a bloody death. Many of the film's locations—docks, factory, sleazy nightclub—are stock noir settings. Lighting, too, bears traces of the chiaroscuro effects achieved by noir. A number of the sequences take place at night, with faces moving in and out of shadows created by low-key lighting. Even the shots taken in daylight create an ominous mood, with swaths of washed-out colors producing a monochrome effect. The film's bleak, rain-drenched landscapes recall the menacing compositions of noir; external shots at the family's *balneario* on the Atlantic coast, where the criminals hide from their pursuers, are overwhelmed by gloomy expanses of gray ocean or brown sand. If leaving the grim city for the safety and freedom of the country was a common narrative pattern in noir films, in *La cruz del sur* the cruelty of the city is only matched by the ferocity of nature. The natural environment is no less hostile than the city, and the shots of high winds and crashing waves that punctuate the film's sequences provide a fitting backdrop to the violence of its story. The sense of claustrophobia, persecution, and entrapment so pervasive in noir takes on even greater proportions as the characters are tracked down to the most remote locations; their isolation merely makes them easier to find and dispose of.

More than any of these elements, however, it is in the nihilism and fatalism of *La cruz del sur* that its noir antecedents are most clearly seen. As in many noir films, the characters' actions seem predetermined; individuals are compelled toward tragedy by forces greater than they, and many are indelibly marked by the violence of their past. Here, just as in films such as *Ossessione* (Luchino Visconti, 1943), characters' desires lead to their own destruction and that of others. Fatalism is emphasized by the use of a range of cinematographic techniques. Reyero's use of the alternating syntagm, a common technique used to create suspense, adds to the sense of inevitability as the protagonists, split up, are hunted down in turn. The high-angle shot often used in noir to create such a sense of fatalism is put to particular effect in the sequence showing the first capture made by the pursuing mafia. A high-angle long shot of the beach shows the tiny figures of Javier's parents making their escape; as spectators we see the approaching car enter the frame before the characters are aware they have been cornered, a device that also reinforces the inevitability of their fate. As if this fatalism had impregnated its very fabric, however, the film moves almost listlessly toward its conclusion, making only seldom use of the usual techniques to increase pace, such as rapid montage, and eschewing extradiegetic music altogether. The film's pace is thus contradictorily marked by the narrative inconsistencies implied by fatalism itself: the inexorable movement toward tragedy (narrative drive) is inescapable and therefore needs no propulsion (narrative lethargy and indifference). Its preference for a neorealist aesthetic over the more stylized compositions of many noir films also dictates a rejection of their most spectacular narrative twists and convoluted temporal sequences.

The frustration of the criminals' enterprise does not, in contrast to more conventional police dramas, result in narrative closure. Their deaths are brutal and hasty (Wendy's is accorded only one second of screen time) and imply no restitution of order. The identity of their pursuers remains unclear: they may be either corrupt police officers—a common theme in film noir, with *The Maltese Falcon* (John Huston, 1941) only one of a number of examples—or members of a drug-trafficking mafia; either way, the murder of the gang members is unwitnessed and the bodies simply dumped at sea, with their hands tied together, in a manner reminiscent of one of the military's favored methods for effecting disappearances during the dictatorship. As Javier had previously buried the booty, little or nothing is gained by the snuffing out of a few hopeless lives. The only survivor, Nora, is abandoned to find her own fate as the film comes to an inconclusive end: in the final scene, washed up on shore, she runs neither toward land (toward a new life) or into the sea (toward death) but enigmatically parallel to the line of waves. This absence of narrative closure enhances the film's nihilism, producing a similar sense to that achieved in the closing sequence of Orson Welles's *Touch of Evil* (1958), when Tana, pressed to say something positive about the corrupt detective Quinlan lying dead at her feet, says expressionlessly: "He was some kind of a man. What does it matter what you say about people?" Likewise, the swift and senseless dispatching of the criminals in *La cruz del sur* leaves us wondering what could be said about their lives and whether it would make any difference at all.

The narrative disruptions of film noir have been treated by several critics in parallel with disruptions to normative sexuality. Whether one wishes to accept the critical consensus that gender representation onscreen reflects

changing social identities in 1940s America (specifically, the more prominent role of women in the postwar economy),[24] or to follow David Reid and
Jayne L. Walker in rejecting the suggestion that the "hobgoblinization of
working women" was a particular hallmark of the period in question,[25] it is
nevertheless clear that noir stages categories of sexual identity and gender as
shifting and unreliable in a way that is consonant with the disorientation
and disruption of the noir world as a whole. In narrative terms fatalism
undermines stereotypical gender constructions at both ends of the spectrum as commonly imagined: by leaving no room for heroism, conventional
masculinity suffers emasculation; by removing hope in the possibility of
transforming love or redemption, conventionally female characteristics are
also thwarted. Frank Krutnik points to the extent to which the quest for
power and control in noir films often ends in failure, and he relates this
failure to achieve "masculine consolidation," together with "the prevalence
of traumatised or castrated males," to "a disjunction between, on the one
hand, the contemporary representational possibilities of the masculine self-
image and, on the other, the traditional cultural codifications of masculine
identity."[26] Arguably, of course, the instability of gender categories in noir
may reflect the broader pessimism expressed by its narrative disruptions
rather than the other way around.

The male characters of La cruz del sur enact a range of possible gendered
identities, from the macho Javier and his intolerant, wife-beating father to
the transvestite Wendy and the maternal attentions of his boy lover, who
treats him with infantilizing tenderness, mopping his fevered brow and
blowing on his soup to cool it before he eats. The film reinforces certain
stereotypes—"gay men are more caring"—and makes use of a rather pre-
dictable spectrum with, at one end, conventionally masculine attributes
equated with greater violence and social disintegration, and, at the other,
conventionally feminine attributes associated with nurture and sociability.
Unconditional love in the film is found only in the relationship between
mother and sons, yet the sons—in Freudian fashion—are cast out by the
father. Misogyny, however, which has often characterized noir's polarized
portrayal of women, is markedly absent: Nora is neither the woman-as-
redeemer nor the scheming temptress of classic noir films such as Double
Indemnity (Billy Wilder, 1944) and Laura (Otto Preminger, 1944). Moreover,
the film's use of gender categories—which includes, at least, some alternatives to "normative" identity—posits the availability of a number of different
alternatives, although they are all equally undesirable. Wendy—the most

communicative and compassionate of the main characters—is ill (probably suffering from AIDS) and unable to integrate into "normal" society, suffering prejudice at every turn.

This presentation in *La cruz del sur* of a range of possible gender performances, all of which lead to alienation and tragedy, is inseparable from its narrative fatalism. Drawing on the work of Dana Polan and J. P. Telotte, Jonathan Munby argues perceptively that the anxieties evident at thematic and formal levels of film noir are not so much the result of social instability as an attempt to convey "the disenfranchised feeling of trying to speak in a world that's already narrated, already patterned and ordered."[27] This uncertainty about the world—is destiny the product of chance and chaos or tragically foreclosed?—is poignantly represented in *La cruz del sur* through the characters' frequent use of talismans. As Nora places on the family "shrine" a wrought-iron cross found marking an unnamed grave nearby, solemnly cutting a lock of her own hair to accompany it, the camera pulls back to show a miscellany of candles, rosaries, and other objects of veneration, some with religious meaning and others invested with personal sentiment or memories. These icons and talismans help the characters cope with uncertainty; they also allow them to imagine themselves in some way connected to the events that happen to them or around them, providing the comfort that the presence of a devotional card, the reciting of a prayer, or the lighting of a candle might alter, in some small way, the destiny already marked out for them, or at least leave some mark of their passage through the world. They evoke both the fear of uncertainty and chaos and the terror of an implacable destiny.

Krutnik associates the frequent use of voice-overs and flashbacks in 1940s noir thrillers with the popularization of psychoanalysis, which began to gain momentum in the United States after the First World War. The darkness of noir stems at least in part from the overwhelming sense that "the protagonists of these films are not totally in control of their actions but are subject to darker, inner impulses."[28] For Telotte one of noir's defining characteristics is its experimentation with the subjective camera, a fitting technique for its exploration of the inner world. He argues that the extended point-of-view sequences employed in many noir films, while offering viewers a new, exhilarating cinematic experience and "promising some freedom from classical narrative's usual manipulations of the spectator position" (this point is highly debatable), also "opened up a potentially disturbing vision," revealing "how much of our lives always remains unseen, particularly how much of the self persistently eludes our vantage or understanding."[29] In *La cruz del sur* a similar effect is achieved but—paradoxically—not by means of the subjective camera so much as by the observational, semidocumentary one. Our knowledge as spectators is clearly limited to what we are able to see, which is often even less than the characters themselves: we are left to surmise facts that seem of crucial importance in the characters' lives, such as whether Nora's father was disappeared during the dictatorship, whether Nora is pregnant, or whether Wendy has AIDS (we see Nora looking at the medication he takes but can only guess the reason for her reaction because the camera does not show us what she is able to read). In place of the point-of-view shot, *La cruz del sur* makes frequent use of insert shots of a character's face, captured warily observing another character. Shot composition also reveals an emphasis on the interpersonal rather than the individual, with characters placed in the foreground or background looking on to the focus of action. Instead of focusing on the secrets of the individual psyche, *La cruz del sur* explores a different facet of subjectivity: the (im)possibility of solidarity among its human characters, who watch each other constantly but are unable to overcome the boundaries that isolate them from each other. Even their caresses—anguished and desperate—offer only fleeting respite from their alienation and misery; they merely throw into relief the mutual destructiveness of broken and hurting individuals who are rarely able to console each other for the damage they wreak on each others' lives.

This emphasis on the social experience of the individual is consistent with *La cruz del sur*'s appropriation of noir themes and techniques in the exploration of a set of concerns that are clearly anchored in the social as well as the psychological. Foster Hirsch contrasts noir's concentration on "private obsession" with the more specifically social crime films of the 1930s: "the gangster's rise and fall took place in a public arena, and the films (partly to placate the censors) assumed a propagandistic cast, claiming to be social documents aimed at eliminating public enemies," while noir's focus was "psychological rather than social."[30] Other critics, however, have emphasized noir's status as a social document, registering the anxieties of a specific historical moment. Of interest here is the perceived conflict between the two modes of meaning, a conflict explicitly recognized by Krutnik, who cites several critical arguments that posit noir's emphasis on psychoanalysis as a displacement technique, averting attention from social responsibility (in particular, the cruelty of war) by attributing behavior in a fatalistic way to inner forces greater than individual consciousness.[31] If the social referent of classic noir is not easily pinned down, it becomes rather more precise in *La cruz del sur*. Munby, drawing again on the analyses of Polan and Telotte, describes how these construct film noir as "part of a distinctively modern crisis in subject-power relations where individuals find themselves disenfranchised of any agency before the machinations of some abstract sense of fate."[32] In *La cruz del sur* this crisis is given a more specific historical meaning. The *balneario* is cursed, Javier's mother claims, and that comes from "haberles hecho favores a los milicos" (having done favors for the military); the trauma of the dictatorship lies only thinly buried under the surface of their lives, like the human bones his father finds buried only a couple of feet down in the sand. *La cruz del sur*'s social agenda necessarily interferes with the conventional narrative thrust of a crime thriller in the same way that Nora's obsession with finding her father's grave literally arrests the gang's advance toward the scene of the heist. If the plot loses momentum at the *balneario*, it is because it becomes clearly more concerned with exploring the trauma and the failed interactions of its characters than with adhering to more formulaic structures of narrative suspense.

If noir was concerned with disruptions and aberrations from normality, *La cruz del sur*'s neorealist techniques have the effect of normalizing the desperation of its characters, to the point that we understand their trauma to be part of a much broader social phenomenon. Hirsch considers that the inclusion of neorealist devices in some noir films detracts from their impact: "In its most provocative and absorbing form *noir* inhabits a twilight zone shakily suspended between reality and nightmare; it thrives on and indeed requires spatial as well as psychological dislocations, whereas the tendency of Neo-Realism is toward simplicity, directness, reportorial accuracy."[33] Such techniques in *La cruz del sur*, when interpreted in the light of the specific historical context in which the film is rooted, do not militate against the nightmarish quality of the film but actually work to enhance it. Reality, as presented in the film, is gruesome enough without need for flights into fantasy. The *balneario* used as a setting in the film, El Marquesado, was indeed carved out of the cliff face with dynamite by the military, and it was said to have been used as a mass grave during the dictatorship;[34] unnamed graves litter the countryside in *La cruz del sur* as an implicit reference to the disappeared. The sinister impact of the dock scene is generated not so much by artificial effects as by shots of rusting half-submerged wrecks looming out of the darkness, a phantasmal image that simply captures the present-day reality of the abandoned city dockyards of Buenos Aires (Figure 14).

La cruz del sur's mediations between nightmare and reality are lent greater significance by the noir styles and themes that echo within the text. The film draws on a recognizable set of generic conventions, not in order to suggest—

14. Noir meets neorealism in *La cruz del sur*, as rusting, abandoned wrecks in the old city docks barely need chiaroscuro lighting effects to lend them a sinister and phantasmal appearance.

as the original noir films did—that new cinematic techniques may more adequately portray the anxieties bound up in modern subjectivity but that life itself has taken on something of the terror and phantasmal nature of film noir. *La cruz del sur* contains nothing of the postmodern nostalgia or pastiche Jameson detects in neo-noir films such as *Body Heat* (Lawrence Kasdan, 1981), where intertextual resonances are used to connote a "pastness" in which "the history of aesthetic styles displaces 'real' history" as a series of dehistoricized citations of style divorced from their historical moment.[35] Instead, I would suggest, *La cruz del sur* acts to rehistoricize some of the central concerns and styles of film noir. In a sense it (re)inserts a sociohistorical referent that was arguably missing in the noir films of the 1940s and 1950s in North America. As Reid and Walker persuasively argue, "Rather than struggling with a depression, the post-war era lived in fear of one, wrestling with a shadow all the more minatory because it obstinately remained a shadow, a phantasm, not a state of affairs. . . . This complex mood of apprehension goes farther towards explaining the characteristic air of grim and baffled fatality in *film noir* than any passing downturn, as in 1947 or 1949, that actually occurred."[36] In contemporary Argentina the phantasm has become reality; the displacements of noir are wrested back into a more strictly realist frame of reference; style becomes inseparable from subject. Perhaps that which characterizes both noir and *La cruz del sur*—and therefore permits a "reinvention" of noir in the Argentine context—is a shared sense of loss, whether real or feared: a disillusionment in the 1940s and 1950s with the "American Dream," an analogous experience in some ways to the disillusionment occasioned by the economic and political collapse of Argentina at the threshold of the twenty-first century.

The relationships between the Argentine films analyzed in this chapter and the various genres from which they borrow suggest a series of deeper structures governing film's relationship with its local and global contexts. Jameson argues that "in the postmodern, autoreferentiality can be initially detected in the way in which culture acts out its own commodification. From the generic standpoint, what interests us here is the way in which the former genres (thrillers, spy films, social exposés, science fiction, and so on) now conflate in a movement that re-enacts the dedifferentiation of the social levels, and by way of their own allegorization: so that the new post-generic genre films are allegories of each other, and of the impossible representation of the social totality itself."[37]

Contemporary Argentine cinema's forays into genres associated with Hollywood—the crime thriller, the western, film noir, science fiction—have always been self-conscious appropriations from the periphery of the center's codes and formulae. Jameson's concept of "postgenre," developed in relation to North American cinema, can be adapted to express something of the temporal and spatial distance implied by these reworkings, as well as the even greater self-awareness with which "culture acts out its own commodification" at the periphery. Indeed, Argentine films have double reason to demonstrate the autoreferentiality Jameson identifies, by virtue not only of the décalage between the original development of the genre and its rearticulation in the present (some genre films in Argentina are consciously "retro" in style, in clear recognition both of the commodification of genre and of the out-of-phase condition of the periphery) but also of their position at the margin of the film-producing and film-distributing centers of North America and Europe, which have also historically been the centers of genre production. They become allegories, in Jameson's sense, of the commodification of the genres they adopt and (in some cases) subvert; if we understand genre as a distribution strategy as much as a set of narrative or stylistic formulae, they can also be read as allegories of the periphery's difficult access to global networks of distribution.

It is also clear that the postgeneric nature of these films allows us to glimpse the hybridizing potential of cultural texts at the periphery. Ana Amado characterizes contemporary Argentine cinema as "un cine de 'estilo,' de 'firma,' que coquetea con rasgos de género como recurso para contrariar la dirección de la fábula" (a cinema of "styles," of "signatures," which flirts with the characteristics of genres as a way to produce contrarian fables).[38] The reversal of the more conventional association between criminal and state in *Caballos salvajes*, among other films, is an example of the subversive reworking of genre codes to engage with rather different socio-political conditions. At a more sophisticated level the deliberately anachronistic use of genre signs and conventions in *Un oso rojo* (codes from 1950s depictions of the western frontier transported to twenty-first-century Argentina) bring into play a series of oppositions—between similarity and dissimilarity, there and here, then and now, global and local—which allegorize the production of difference and hybridity at the periphery.

Moving away from a simple center-periphery model, however, these films can be understood as postgeneric in another sense: that of revealing the workings of genre itself and the hybridized character of its original enunciation. This cinema of code-switches and shifting signifiers points to genre as a phenomenon that is itself neither original nor pure but is already a hybrid production, just as *La cruz del sur* explores the tensions inherent in noir in America of the 1940s and 1950s, which drew on multiple, often conflictive, existing traditions. It identifies the nature of genre itself as necessarily involving a play between repetition and innovation, similarity and dissimilarity, producing variations on a theme in order to secure its place within the market; genre itself is an allegory of commodification, even before the more self-conscious "post-generic" films Jameson identifies.

5

NATION, MIGRATION, AND GLOBALIZATION

One of the effects of the Crisis has been to promote changes in the imagined space of the nation. Contradictory trends have emerged in the representation of the nation in contemporary media and culture, which emphasize first the internal fragmentation of the nation and then the consolidating effect of a shared experience of crisis; first the apparent dissolution of national borders through migration and globalization and then the undeniably real and inflexible nature of frontiers that, as Alejandro Grimson points out, "continúan hoy marcando la línea en la cual el migrante se convierte en ilegal, así como el límite donde empieza y termina una crisis, donde cambian las dinámicas y, especialmente, los modos en que las crisis son vividas" (still today mark the line beyond which the migrant becomes illegal, as well as the boundary at which a crisis begins or ends, where dynamics change and, in particular, the ways in which crises are experienced).[1] The events of the Crisis were to mobilize a set of nationalist discourses around a common experience of economic disaster and against a set of common enemies: the World Bank, the IMF, and the multinational companies that took over many of Argentina's assets during Menem's program of privatization. The image emerged of an Argentina ransacked by multinationals and then abandoned by the international community to its fate. In this chapter I explore the conflicting images of the nation that have emerged in recent cinema, locating them within much older, historical discourses of nationhood in Argentina. While the growing separation between nation and state is a phenomenon common to many countries, it has received particularly dramatic expression in Argentina as a result of the near-breakdown of the state during the Crisis; some of the films analyzed here suggest a specific role for cinema in rebuilding national identity in the absence of a functioning state.

The Crisis was to shatter the illusion of "Argentine exceptionality" in the Latin American context that had prevailed throughout the twentieth century. The illusion was one of the nation's integration, with a more equitable distribution of wealth and fewer differences in development than neighboring Brazil, for example, a successful, modern nation orientated politically and socially toward Europe and one in which, as Beatriz Sarlo notes, "la miseria no era una mancha expansiva sino un estado transitorio, en vías de desaparición" (poverty was not a sprawling stain but a transitory state, on its way to disappearing).[2] The Crisis was to accentuate the deep divisions that had always existed between city and country and between *barrio* and *villa* in Argentina, making visible the enormity of the chasm between the nation's richest and its poorest. The reality of the nation's decline, with more than 57 percent of the population below the poverty line at the worst point in October 2002,[3] was powerfully expressed in photographs of starving children from northeastern provinces, photographs that resembled too closely the images of children dying in famine-stricken countries of Africa. These images have also been marshaled for compelling political effect in several documentary films, including Fernando Solanas's *Memoria del saqueo* (2003) and *La dignidad de los nadies* (2005), and Jorge Lanata's *Deuda* (2004). They have succeeded in exposing the fictions underpinning Argentina's First World aspirations and resituating the country within a Latin American context of underdevelopment and inequality.

The depiction of appalling poverty in the provinces does not, however, settle comfortably into the simple opposition between city and country that, in a variety of forms, has structured so many Argentine narratives since Independence. Contemporary representations of Buenos Aires as a fractured, heterogeneous space with internal divisions of its own undermines another discourse, that of the exceptionality of Buenos Aires as a cultured, First World capital set apart from the troubles of the rest of the country. It is a discourse that Adrián Gorelik refers to as "la figura de 'las dos Argentinas'" (the concept of "the two Argentinas"), a notion that has held considerable sway over nationalist thought at least since its powerful articulation in Juan Bautista Alberdi's *Grandes y pequeños hombres del Plata* (published posthumously at the end of the nineteenth century). Gorelik traces the evolution of the idea through the work of Eduardo Mallea, typical of nationalist imagery of the 1930s, in which the cosmopolitan city is contrasted with the "authentic" country, and through the left-wing versions that surfaced from the 1950s onward, in which the "two countries" figure is rearticulated within an urban, progressive imaginary: "gracias a la nueva representación de la villa miseria y de los migrantes internos, aquel interior profundo y auténtico podía verse ahora incrustado en el mismo corazón de la metrópoli, subvirtiéndola" (thanks to new representations of the shantytown and of internal migrants, those far-flung, authentic rural provinces could now see themselves embedded in the very heart of the metropolis, subverting it).[4] However, as Gorelik argues with reference to *Mala época* (Nicolás Saad, Mariano De Rosa, Salvador Roselli, and Rodrigo Moreno, 1998), here the "two countries" paradigm dissolves altogether: "No hay otra Argentina: la película no ofrece ninguna contrafigura salvadora a la miseria moral y social de la ciudad" (There is no other Argentina: the film offers no redemptive counterfigure to the moral and social poverty of the city).[5] In some cases, however (notably in more commercial films), an anticapitalist rhetoric has resulted in a clichéd (and historically regressive) depiction of the countryside as a place of authenticity and purity, constructed as "other" to the city's materialism; as will be shown, *Cleopatra* (Eduardo Mignogna, 2003) provides an excellent example of this paradigm. In contrast, the narrative structure of *El cielito* (María Victoria Menis, 2003) moves from the barbaric countryside to the equally barbaric city, refusing to permit the establishment of space external to, or in any way separate from, violence and degeneration. Carlos Sorín's *Historias mínimas* (2002) and *Bombón, el perro* (2004) provide an interesting counterpoint to *Cleopatra*, given their visions of a hybridized rural society, besieged almost to the same extent as the city by aggressive global trade practices. In the segregated city of many contemporary films, no spaces or social groups are set aside as liberating, revolutionary, or authentic, in the manner of earlier representations. The figuring of the migrant from the provinces (or from neighboring Latin American countries) and his or her reception in the city—a popular theme in early-twentieth-century Argentine film—clearly demonstrates the collapse of this particular paradigm, as neither migrant nor citizen carry any message of salvation, and both are equally embroiled in a hostile society divided not just along lines of race or provenance but also by class, socioeconomic position, gender, and sexuality. This vision is most devastatingly captured in *Bolivia* (Adrián Caetano, 2001), in which the fate of a migrant worker becomes indicative not just of the city's hostility toward foreigners but of a much broader disintegration of urban society.

Images of migration and globalization in contemporary films also demonstrate the extent to which some of the founding narratives of nationhood in Argentina have been delegitimized by recent events. If such images in other film industries have drawn attention to the increasing instability and permeability of the nation's borders in a globalized era, they receive more complex treatment in Argentine cinema. The Crisis intensified a wave of "reverse migration" in which Argentine citizens inverted the steps of their grandparents and great-grandparents to return to those countries (largely Spain and Italy) that had been the homeland of the largest number of Argentina's immigrants in the first half of the twentieth century. Images of people queuing outside European embassies, clutching papers to prove their European heritage, have become recurring motifs in post-Crisis films, among them *El abrazo partido* (Daniel Burman, 2003) and *Buena Vida Delivery* (Leonardo Di Cesare, 2003). We are reminded once again of the density of the nation's borders, separating destitution from opportunity, those with the means to escape from those without. But we are also given a glimpse of the social and symbolic impact of reverse migration in a nation founded on immigration, and Diego Gachassin's exploration of immigrant experience in *Vladimir en Buenos Aires* (2002) demonstrates, as I will show, the depths of Argentina's fall from a land of opportunity for immigrants to one of economic failure and desperation.

Grimson calls for a new framework for understanding national identity, one that moves beyond both essentialist and deconstructionist approaches. This last, he argues, has effectively and devastatingly revealed the nation as a construct, invented to bolster the sovereignty of the modern state. However, it cannot explain why certain constructions were successful and others not; neither can it take account of the persistence of ideas of national identity in the context of the demise of the state. Grimson proposes a third version, based on shared experience: "ese conjunto de personas socialmente de-siguales y culturalmente diferentes que se consideran miembros de una nación comparten experiencias históricas marcantes que son constitutivas de modos de imaginación, cognición y acción" (that group of socially un-equal and culturally different people who consider themselves members of a nation share historical experiences that mark them, and that are constitu-tive of forms of imagination, cognition, and action). Among the shared experiences Grimson identifies in Argentina are those of genocide, institu-tional instability, hyperinflation, and the *corralito*. While inequality and cul-tural difference ensure that these phenomena are not experienced identi-cally by all, they are experiences that "atravesaron al conjunto del cuerpo y tejido social" (penetrated the totality of the social body and fabric). If, as Grimson suggests, "la paradoja es que justamente un conjunto de personas que comparten básicamente experiencias disgregadoras tienen en común haber vivido esos procesos y estar atravesados por ellos" (the paradox is that a group of people who share experiences of disintegration do have in common the experience of living through those processes and being marked by them),[6] film creates a similarly paradoxical matrix of representations, able both to reveal the disintegration of society and, through that same act of representation, to reflect (and even create) a common experience.

The role of the media in creating imaginary forms of community becomes self-reflexively evident in *Una de dos* (Alejo Taube, 2004), which is set during a time of violent confrontations in the capital between demonstrators and police in December 2001, prior to the resignation of President Fernando De la Rúa. The opening shot of the film unites, with apparent incongruity, the sound of rioting on the audio track with long traveling shots of rural Argentina, filmed along the road to a small town near Luján, fifty miles from the capital in the province of Buenos Aires. The regular insertion of television footage of social unrest in Buenos Aires serves on one level to mark the contrast between the experience of the Crisis in the city and beyond it. In response to the news of financial catastrophe the townspeople mount their own protest, a rather halfhearted and beery affair, gathered around a bonfire near the road leading into the town. The crowd, drawing inspiration no doubt from the images of *piqueteros* and the *cacerolazo* shown incessantly on television, bang empty saucepans and recite the slogans of the Crisis—"Que se vayan" (They should all go)—together with other populist chants—"El pueblo unido jamás será vencido" (The people united will never be beaten). Although these protests are a distant echo of the riots taking place in the capital, ultimately the use of televised scenes of the Crisis acts to situate the local squarely within the national. The original televisual broadcasts link city with country in a relationship of synchronicity—the experience of synchronicity generated by "clocked, calendrical time" being, for Benedict Anderson, one of the catalysts for the imagined community of the nation[7]—and their citation in the film stages this relationship for the spectator, who is able to watch the unfolding of events in a small town parallel to those in the city and thereby to grasp the properly national dimension of the Crisis, uniting city and country in a shared experience of impoverishment and unrest. Film also plays a significant role in representing the nation to itself in times of crisis, and the role of reportage (more typically associated with broadcast television) has often been appropriated by contemporary cinema in order to position itself as the image-maker of the nation.

Contemporary cinema's interest in narratives of migration and globalization can frequently be read as reflexive meditations on the position of Argentine culture within the world, and this becomes the focus of the analyses of *Hoteles* (Aldo Paparella, 2003) and *Bar El Chino* (Daniel Burak, 2003), concluding this chapter, which treat cosmopolitanism and migration as the "essence" of Argentine identity, transcending a simplistic binary opposition between the local and global and producing a sense of place that does not center on "its separate or 'pure' internalized history, but rather its uniqueness as a point of intersection in a wider network of relations" (David Morley).[8] This understanding of place that emerges in films such as *Bar El Chino* and *Hoteles* owes much to their self-consciousness as products of the same global economic system on which they reflect.

IMAGES OF RURAL ARGENTINA

Alejandro Agresti's *El viento se llevó lo que* (1998) explores in a tragicomic vein the experience of life at the periphery of modernity, in a small town in Patagonia during the 1970s. Everything arrives late to Río Pico, including film reels (worn out, badly mended, and with sections missing after their passage through the cultural centers of the country), major inventions and theories of the twentieth century, and even news of the dictatorship. But Agresti's vision is essentially nostalgic, one in which a sense of genuine community is associated with an earlier, purer era: once television arrives in the town and the cinema falls into disuse, such social ties are atomized. There is no reason for the protagonist to stay, as "un pueblo con televisión se parece a cualquier pueblo" (one town with television is like any other town).

Other recent films have depicted the rural in rather more ambivalent terms that complicate the center-periphery model underpinning Agresti's film. The anticapitalist impetus of many films has certainly produced nostalgic images of a rural, lesser-developed Argentina, in which the country has retained a community spirit now unattainable in the city, where everything has been subsumed into economic relations. However, the overlaying of different imaginaries—such as European romanticism, the dichotomy between civilization and barbarism as traced by Sarmiento and then reformulated by other Argentine thinkers, together with neoliberal ideas of progress—has produced contradictory images of the country, in which it appears as authentic and the place of self-discovery but also as the site of barbarism, raped by industrialization but also as an economic resource for new forms of revenue, such as tourism. As I will show, the superimposition of two or more of these discourses creates complex images; in contrast to the rural cinema popular during the first couple of decades of the twentieth century in Argentina, a period of intense modernization and expansion in which the rural is often constructed as reassuringly "other" to the city, undisturbed by the upheavals of modernization,[9] recent cinema more often depicts a countryside significantly impacted by neoliberal and globalizing economic forces. A revived cinematic interest in the landscapes and societies of rural Argentina also reflects a broader, discursive repositioning of Argentine national identity in closer relation to regional underdevelopment than to European cosmopolitanism, as a result of the experience of the Crisis. Mario Rapoport gives as one of his recommendations for foreign policy following the Crisis "volver a instalar a la Argentina en su ámbito geográfico natural, América Latina, intensificando los intercambios, estableciendo políticas comunes con nuestros vecinos frente al resto del mundo, tanto en el terreno económico como en el político y estratégico, y afianzando la identidad regional" (to reestablish Argentina in her natural geographical sphere, Latin America, strengthening exchanges, forging common policies with our neighbors with respect to the rest of the world, in the field of economics as well as of politics and strategy, and consolidating regional identity).[10] What is shared among most films located in the "interior," and particularly Patagonia, is that the country, as in earlier narratives, becomes a testing ground once again—not just for individuals in search of adventure but for notions of national and regional identity and for new (and not-so-new) forms of nationalism in the early twenty-first century.

City and Country in *Cleopatra* and *El cielito:*
Civilization and Barbarism Revisited

Fantasies of precapitalist society are most clearly at work in Eduardo Mignogna's *Cleopatra* (2003), which takes the clichéd form of a road movie in which the city-dwelling protagonist flees from consumer society toward authenticity and self-discovery. The film rehearses a critique of materialism that has a long history in Argentine thought, perhaps most famously in the work of Ezequiel Martínez Estrada, who inverts Sarmiento's formulation in *Facundo* to associate urban centers not with liberal values and civilization but with barbarism. In the figure of the feisty Sandra, who rejects international stardom in order to discover herself and a new love in the interior of the country, *Cleopatra* merges anticapitalist rhetoric with nationalism, a frequent formula in contemporary cinema. Sandra's pushy producer, Francis, is delirious about the possibility of entering "el mercado latino" (the Latino market), which is opening up in the States; as he explains to Sandra, they now want a Latina actress, instead of Sandra Bullock, to star in a three-hundred-episode soap opera, and they also want to contract her face to be used for a doll and to turn her into a brand for a new perfume. Everything Sandra is or has belongs to Francis, she explains, including her "famous" cleavage (she removes gel pads from her bra): "Soy una marca registrada" (I am a registered brand). Her flight from the city represents not just a rejection of commodity culture in general but specifically of U.S. mediatizations of Latin America. Set for the most part in the stunning beauty of Argentina's northwestern provinces, *Cleopatra* constructs the countryside as a place of spiritual renewal and serendipity, where weary city dwellers may rediscover themselves or find a new passion. The plot, driven by the fickle desires of its protagonists, is antiteleological: Sandra and Cleopatra almost return to the city at various points in the narrative, but the final return never takes place. Sandra decides to stay indefinitely, and the final scene leaves Cleopatra sitting down "para pensar un poco" (to think a bit), having deliberately missed her coach back to Buenos Aires. The spatial elasticity of the road movie, in which chance and whim are the motors of narrative development, conflicts with the measured time and the organized itineraries of the metropolis.

Lest we should think that all is rosy in the provinces, however, a narrative tangent reveals a darker side to rural simplicity. If the countryside provides a liberal space for Cleopatra and Sandra to refuse a destiny programmed by career progression and fame (in Sandra's case) or one obedient to norms of conjugal respectability (in Cleopatra's), for its permanent residents it is a space of patriarchal conservatism in which the practice of domestic abuse goes unchallenged. Cleopatra scolds a husband for beating his pregnant wife and receives a bruise of her own for her efforts. Antimaterialist discourses come into sharp conflict with liberal ones, as the country is constructed contradictorily as the last bulwark of civilization in a barbaric, industrialized world, and also a place of unenlightened barbarism, untouched by liberal values.

The ugly scenario of domestic violence is given greater prominence in *El cielito* (María Victoria Menis, 2003), in which the portrayal of the country is also given ambivalent (but rather more coherent) treatment. Like many historical narratives of conquest and settlement in Argentina, the film suggests the existence of a fundamental disharmony between humans and their natural environment. By contrast to these earlier narratives, however, in which the inhospitality and brutality of nature resists the civilizing efforts of humans, here it is the brutality of humans that badly repays the fruitfulness of nature. This disjuncture is often given temporal expression in the film. The rhythms of day and night, planting and harvest, are evoked by establishing shots of the farm, land, and sky, inserted at intervals to mark the passing of days and lend a sense of order. The placidity of nature, obediently abundant and somnolent at harvest time, contrasts with the tempestuous events of the narrative. Surrounded by the open and lush riverine landscape of Entre Ríos, Roberto's wife, Mercedes, is nevertheless imprisoned in a claustrophobic relationship of abuse, reduced to performing just three roles: feeding the family by making and selling preserves, looking after her baby, and satisfying her drunken husband's sexual needs on demand. When the fragile loyalties holding the family home together finally erupt, the still shots of rotting fruit abandoned in half-filled baskets symbolize the extent to which the relationship between the productive land and its destructive inhabitants is ruinously out of phase.

El cielito's narrative of barbarism and degeneration shares certain images and forms with Borges's story "El evangelio según Marcos." In the film Mercedes introduces Félix to the farm's rudimentary preserves workshop with obvious pride, reverently showing him the "recetas muy antiguas" (very old recipes) handed down through generations of the family, originally brought from abroad. She marvels at the neat handwriting of her forebears, which she is able to read aloud only slowly, concentrating hard on each word. In Borges's story the Gutres, a farming family with Scottish antecedents, have descended after a few generations in Argentina into ignorance and moral depravity; their illiteracy prevents them even from reading their own family history. When Mercedes flees the farm, Roberto smashes up the workshop and its contents in a blind rage. The wanton destructiveness of an ignorant man obliterates the inherited wealth and skills of generations, signifying a profound rupture with a more illustrious past to which there can be no easy return. By evoking these absent forebears, of whose trials and successes so little now remains, *El cielito* inserts its own narrative into a broader discourse of failure, common to many contemporary Argentine narratives, which contrasts the dreams of yesterday's immigrants with the bankruptcy and disillusionment experienced by today's citizens. As in "El evangelio según Marcos," the effect of Argentina on its European immigrants is to submerge them in barbarism.

Crucially, the brutality of *El cielito* spans both the country and the city, to which Félix escapes with the baby he has saved from Roberto. The film's narrative of sacrifice and redemption is violently truncated, as the selfless love of one individual is powerless to prevail against a violence so endemic in society, whether in traditional rural communities or on the streets of the city, both scarred by poverty and unemployment. While in *Cleopatra* the rose-tinted vision of the country is marred only by an offense to the liberal sensibilities of the urban protagonists, in *El cielito* city and country truly mirror each other in their barbarism. "Lo que Sarmiento no vio," writes Martínez Estrada, "es que civilización y barbarie era una misma cosa, . . . que la ciudad era como el campo y que dentro de los cuerpos nuevos reencarnaban las almas de los muertos" (What Sarmiento did not see is that civilization and barbarism were the same thing, . . . that the city was like the countryside and that the souls of the dead lived on in new bodies).[11] Menis allows us no reassuring, utopian space exempt from violence and hopelessness.

Entrepreneurialism and the Rural in the Films of Carlos Sorín

City and country are continually brought together in the films of Carlos Sorín, in a series of encounters that emphasize the economic and cultural interdependency of the two. At first sight it is a nostalgia for another time or, more precisely, another place, which appears to be the driving force in *Historias mínimas* (2002), and this is the basis on which it has delighted audiences in Argentina and beyond. Sorín's Patagonia appears to be a place of dignity, authenticity, and humanity, whose inhabitants offer help and hospitality without thought of remuneration—a place where the stranger is welcomed into communities that nevertheless retain a distinctive cultural identity. The film would therefore epitomize the impulse Fredric Jameson identifies in all works of contemporary art, including those of mass culture, to express "our deepest fantasies about the nature of social life, both as we live it now, and as we feel in our bones it ought rather to be lived"; this "ineradicable drive towards collectivity" is contrasted here with our "privatized and psychologizing society, obsessed with commodities and bombarded by the ideological slogans of big business."[12] Like Roberto, an energetic traveling salesman armed with the latest psychocommerce self-help manual ("me cambió la vida" [it changed my life]) who is taken aback when a woman refuses payment for her cake-decorating services, the film's city-dwelling spectators are allowed to glimpse another way of life in which not everything is reducible to private economic gain.

The implicit contrasts marked in *Historias mínimas* between urban and rural practices would seem to inscribe the film within a recognizable set of nostalgic, conservative discourses. However, although Sorín occasionally returns to certain stock images of the Argentine countryside—including the *chacareros* who burst spontaneously into song around an *asado*—the vision of the country that ultimately emerges is hybridized rather than evocative of any originary essence or purity. Both in *Historias mínimas* and in Sorín's following film, *Bombón, el perro* (2004), the countryside does not represent the utopia initially promised but is instead an ambivalent space, crisscrossed by contesting paradigms of nationalism and modernization. Such images align these films with Sorín's earlier production *La película del rey* (1986), in which Patagonia is presented unromantically as a stark, windswept land of economic and social deprivation but a place that acquires surrealist and oneiric tones as the protagonists of both the film and the film-within-the-film verge on insanity. Sorín's films maintain an oblique relationship with traditional constructions of Patagonia in visual and literary texts. They retain some notion of the wilderness as a spiritual retreat for Argentina's city dwellers: more than one character in *Historias mínimas* attests to the pleasure of driving solo through the windswept Patagonian wilds, and Julia, the molecular biologist from Buenos Aires, has escaped from the city in order to think. Present on occasion, too, is a familiar dig at the lack of education and sophistication of rural inhabitants on the periphery of cosmopolitan modernity: in *Bombón, el perro*, for example, Juan mispronounces the French name of his dog's kennel, Le Chien, to form the hispanicized "Lechién." Little about the Patagonian landscape or ways of life that Sorín captures responds, however, to their aestheticized, mythical, or otherwise homogenized portrayals in earlier texts. His films consistently point to the spillages between city and country, such that the country can no longer be regarded as a counterpoint to the modernity of the city but is simply the place where the contradictions of Argentine modernization and the inequalities of global capital are most clearly seen.

Figuring among the recurring motifs of *Historias mínimas* are the incongruous, anachronistic interventions of television in the lives of the film's rural or small-town inhabitants. While they wait for the cake to be redecorated, Roberto and the baker's wife are gripped by a lover's fit of jealous pique in one of the day's *telenovelas*; in the doctor's waiting room banality intrudes in the form of a TV commercial gushing exaggerated praise for a cross-trainer machine; in his hotel room, after having seen the woman of his affections with another man, Roberto's glance is drawn toward the images of a pulsating heart benefiting from the latest advances in cardiovascular surgery. These images often appear as both out of time and out of place, enunciated at another conjunction of time and space (urban modernity) that differs from their point of reception. They evoke what Harvey refers to as the "disruptive spatiality" of globalized capital, which brings local and imported products into spaces of coexistence in the same way that "all the divergent spaces of the world are assembled nightly as a collage of images upon the television screen."[13] Television in *Historias mínimas* is thoroughly complicit with advertising; the culture of consumption it promotes is parodied through the juxtaposition of these images with those of the unsophisticated lifestyles of the film's characters, for whom most of the products advertised would be completely inaccessible. Even the local television channel, with its noticeably dated filming techniques and low-budget technology, is clearly dependent on advertising, albeit of a more parochial kind. Frequent cuts are made in Channel 12's game show to promote the show's commercial sponsor, whose name also appears plastered on every visible surface of the set.

In both films Patagonia is not so much an unspoiled haven of simplicity and traditional values as a place of hardship, in which the economic facts of underdevelopment are not fully integrated into a picturesque vision of rural life, just as the austere scenery filmed by Sorín is not readily packaged for tourist promotion. *Bombón, el perro* offers a stark image of a privatized Patagonia, whose few thriving businesses are now managed by multinational businesses with little regard for the social and economic welfare of the local residents. The protagonist, Juan Villegas, has been dismissed from the gas station where he worked for twenty years, which is now in the hands of a multinational company that has replaced the existing staff with younger and more attractive personnel. The farcical vision of Solanas's *El viaje* (1990), in which vast tracts of Patagonian land have been sold off to multinational companies, returns to the screen in a more realist mode to testify to the misery of unemployment in post-Menemist Argentina.

An undercurrent of violence and the inclusion of sequences of ambivalent meaning threaten these otherwise cheerful comedies. In a doctor's surgery in *Historias mínimas*, a woman is under police guard and a man bleeds from multiple wounds. That his brief presence on the screen is to be understood as a sinister intrusion into the main narrative is made clear by the addition of a low-pitched string ostinato on the soundtrack. A similar irruption occurs toward the very end of *Bombón*. Juan's search for his runaway dog leads him to a wretched cluster of shacks, deserted apart from the half-obscured face watching him silently through a rudimentary window, and then to a brickyard, enveloped in thick smoke, whose workers react with suspicion to his request for help. The ominous effect is not entirely dispelled by the happy discovery of the lost dog, which constitutes the film's abrupt and unsatisfactory ending. The import of these disturbing images is left unexplained, and the disorientation Juan experiences as he stumbles suddenly into unknown and rather frightening worlds translates for the spectator into a sensation of having taken the wrong turn, ending up backstage, and seeing what we weren't supposed to see.

What we are not supposed to see, as Sorín reveals in a series of glimpses, are the harsh realities of the Argentine countryside as the sweatshop of urban development; as the corral of the hopeless and destitute; as the dumping ground for consumer-goods surplus to First World requirements, such as the multifunction food processor María wins on the game show in *Historias mínimas* (her house has no electricity), the cheap plastic toys García sells (made in China), or the latest stock Roberto is trying to sell off, "Fat-Away," a weight-loss product from Sweden claiming extremely improbable results. Sorín stops short, however, of fashioning the countryside merely as the passive receptacle for urban and global waste. Roberto's advice to García, which effectively becomes the film's central theme, is that "en estos tiempos él que no tiene capacidad de improvisación, desaparece" (in these times anyone who can't improvise, disappears). His own capacity for such improvisation is clearly demonstrated by the transformations to which he subjects the birthday cake destined for the son of a young widow whose attention he is trying to attract. Suddenly unsure whether René, whom he has never seen, is the name of a boy or a girl, he has the cake, originally in the form of a football, retouched to become a tortoise. This same spirit of entrepreneurialism and adaptability is demonstrated by several of the country inhabitants. After the TV show the large and irrepressible Gladys drives a hard bargain with María to exchange the food processor she had wanted for a makeup set she has no use for; the young widow of Roberto's affections has exchanged her haberdashery for handmade regional crafts in the expectation of the arrival of more tourists. This business acumen and propensity for change presents the countryside as something more than the preserve of tradition and timelessness, and it does not allow us to posit the rural environment as the passive partner in a conflict of values and lifestyles.

Sorín's hybridized perspective is reflected in a certain heterogeneity, or ambivalence, of style. Both *Historias mínimas* and *Bombón, el perro* borrow techniques readily associated with neorealist or documentary filmmaking, including the use of nonprofessional actors and a minimalist approach to dialogue. The influence of neorealist styles is most evident in the opening sequences of *Bombón*, in which the clumsy pans and zooms of a handheld camera record Juan's attempt to sell some hand-carved knives to make a living. The whole film was shot with just two cameras and with extensive use of a Steadicam, which, as an alternative to dollies, has the effect of detracting from the fixity of the image, lending it fluidity and instability. Sorín refers to the influence of documentary filmmaking on his work, explaining that he aims for a neutral approach in which "nada esté puesto para la cámara, ella simplemente mira y pasa desapercibida. . . . Si el personaje no se mueve, yo no muevo la cámara. . . . Por eso, si alguien se mueve, la cámara también lo hace pero uno poco después, como en el documental" (nothing is deliberately placed for the camera, it simply observes and moves around unnoticed. . . . If the character doesn't move, I don't move the camera. . . . For the same reason, if someone moves, so does the camera, but a bit afterwards, as in a documentary).[14] The opening shots of *Bombón* quickly settle, however, into a more conventional narrative that draws heavily on the structures of classical cinema, including the use of music and close-ups to heighten identification at moments of intense emotion or pathos; in this way techniques associated with independent filmmaking are redesigned and packaged for box-office success.

In short, Sorín's films display the same appetite for hybridization and the same disregard for purity as Bombón himself, the pedigree *Dogo Argentino* who is impotent when asked to perform stud services to other champions of his breed but suddenly regains his libido in order to mount a nondescript stray bitch. The allegory is made rather obvious as the traditional national pedigree runs off to the *barrio "El Progreso,"* regarded with suspicion by more conservative elements of the country folk, and found gaily copulating with a mongrel. The themes of hybridization, adaptability, and exchangeability in Sorín's narratives can be read allegorically to reflect the entrepreneurial recycling of cultural forms in which the films themselves are so enthusiastically engaged. In the use of neorealist techniques in films with broad commercial appeal, we can perhaps detect a transformation similar to that identified by Vittorio Spinazzola as the emergence of "pink neorealism" in the context of postwar Italy.[15] As Angelo Restivo observes, films after 1954 "took the trappings of neorealism—everyday life among the poor, location shooting, and so on—and, stripping them of any political engagement, used them to make programmatic, bland comedies."[16] In some ways it could be argued that Sorín's films hold a similar relationship to the earlier neorealist films of New Argentine Cinema, recycling their themes and styles for use in a broader market. Restivo refers to "a period of aesthetic retrenchment," in which neorealism was often "diminished to a kind of populist celebration of local color";[17] this period, during which "pink neorealism" succeeded in consolidating its public, marks "the death knell of neorealism as political praxis linked to the transformation of the nation."[18] Sorín's films, while they certainly appropriate neorealist techniques for market purposes and occasionally veer toward such "populist celebration," cannot, however, be dismissed as apolitical. They take care to demonstrate ways in which myths and images of the rural are punctured by economic realities, while pointing self-reflexively to the potential that still remains for entrepreneurial development, this time of a lighter, cleaner industry: that of filmmaking.

Adrián Veaute extends the civilization/barbarism dichotomy to a discussion of the tensions between Hollywood-style and counterhegemonic cinema in Argentina. With reference to key films by some of the most celebrated Argentine directors of the 1950s, such as *Los tallos amargos* (Fernando Ayala, 1957), *La casa del ángel* (Leopoldo Torre Nilsson, 1957), and *Rosaura a las diez* (Mario Soffici, 1958), Veaute argues that an alternative line of filmmaking began to establish itself in opposition to industrial Hollywood models and conventions, laying the foundations for "un cine verdaderamente bárbaro y opuesto a las reglas de la civilización representacional" (a genuinely barbaric cinema, opposed to the rules of civilization in representation), which in the 1960s and early 1970s finally broke the power of the industry dominant from the 1930s to the 1950s, opening up "el camino de la barbarie, de lo 'otro,' de la alteridad cinematográfica" (the path of barbarism, of the "other," of cinematographic alterity).[19] In this sense Sorín's films can be seen not only as an attempt to bring city and country together in a national imaginary but also to "resolve" a historical divide between independent and commercial cinema in Argentina. *Nobleza gaucha* (Humberto Cairo, Ernesto Gunche, and Eduardo Martínez de la Pera, 1915), the first Argentine feature-length film to be commercially released, presents an opposition between country and city—one characterized by honesty and dignity, the other orientated around the value of money—in response, as Tranchini states, to "la necesidad de alcanzar la modernización preservando los viejos valores y modos criollistas aunque aceptando las diferencias" (the need to achieve modernization while preserving old values and Creole ways, although accepting difference).[20] Nearly a century later, in a neoliberal era that in many ways continues the liberal project that propelled Argentina through rapid modernization, Sorín's vision responds to much the same dilemma: although city and country are now not so easily disentangled, the question remains how to innovate and achieve commercial success while retaining a sense of cultural identity, which is also, paradoxically, key to cinema's entry into an international market. Sorín's success in this venture marks him out as one of very few directors whose careers have spanned from the 1980s to the present day and whose visual practices have undergone a process of adaptation, both in response to a changing socioeconomic climate and to paradigm shifts in ideological and aesthetic approaches to filmmaking in Argentina.

MIGRATION AND THE NARRATIVES OF NATIONHOOD

If the experience of the Crisis has, to some extent, fomented images of the nation as a heterogeneous whole, united in its suffering, some films have focused on the frontiers marking the nation's lines of internal fragmentation. Recent films focusing on immigrant experience have often used the violence and isolation of life in the interstices of the city to comment on the breakdown of the city's wider, more established, community, as well as the discourses of nationalism on which Argentina was founded. As Marc Augé suggests, "Perhaps the reason why immigrants worry settled people so much . . . is that they expose the relative nature of certainties inscribed in the soil."[21] The unflinching testimonies to the misery suffered by immigrants in current-day Argentina presented in films such as *Bolivia* and *Vladimir en Buenos Aires* give the lie to several fictions of Argentine nationhood. Among these is the fiction of the "país de la plata fácil" (country of easy money) held out to immigrants who, in the context of economic recession, are now more often condemned to live precarious lives and rarely to realize those dreams in a nation ill-placed to provide even for the basic needs of its own citizens.

Bolivia: The Liminal Spaces of a Divided Community

The sequences interspersed with the opening credits of *Bolivia* (Adrián Caetano, 2001)—footage of a superior Argentine soccer team scoring several goals against Bolivia, accompanied on the soundtrack by lively panpipe music—introduce in a humorous, almost frivolous, manner the theme of national rivalry that will culminate in tragedy. Through the experiences of Freddy, an illegal Bolivian immigrant forced to seek work in Buenos Aires when the coca fields he used to harvest at home were burned by the *yanquis*, the film evokes the fragility and misery of immigrant lives in an unwelcoming city where employment is scarce. It employs a distinctive set of styles and techniques to portray the heightening of tensions in a disintegrating community on the brink of financial ruin. As so often in recent Argentine cinema, financial exigencies mark the production process, as well as the film's themes. *Bolivia* is a paradigmatic case of the synergies that have emerged between budget constraints and aesthetic decisions. The grainy black-and-white Super 16-mm film used—significantly cheaper than color— lends an austerity to the production that is fully in keeping with its grim realism. The film was made by unpaid actors and technicians, using a small number of locations that were available at no cost and needed minimal lighting, and was shot only with equipment that could fit in a car. Filming was done mainly on weekends and nearly always with the bar open (a condition imposed by the owner).[22] The film took three years to shoot, and filming was sporadic, as and when funds became available. The result is an uncompromising study of a community in crisis, riven by a catalogue of prejudices: homophobia, misogyny, xenophobia, and racism.

Such divisions clearly undermine the fiction that maintains the imagined unity of the nation. Homi K. Bhabha draws attention to the intricate negotiations that characterize subject-formation in nations:

> It is in the emergence of the interstices—the overlap and displacement of domains of difference—that the intersubjective and collective experiences of *nationness*, community interest, or cultural value are negotiated. How are subjects formed "in-between," or in excess of, the sum of the "parts" of difference (usually intoned as race/class/gender, etc.)? How do strategies of representation or empowerment come to be formulated in the competing claims of communities where, despite shared histories of deprivation and discrimination, the exchange of values, meanings and priorities may not always be collaborative and dialogical, but may be profoundly antagonistic, conflictual and even incommensurable?[23]

The little neighborhood bar in *Bolivia* is an interstitial space in which we can clearly appreciate the complexity of negotiations between such overlapping and competing interests. The incommensurability of these competing subjects and communities reveals the extent to which "nationness" as a unifying concept has broken down, leaving only differences (of race, class, and gender). The financial difficulties the characters share—Héctor is forced to return to live with his mother in Córdoba because he can't find work in Buenos Aires; Enrique, the bar manager, works long hours to keep his head above water; Oso owes money to everyone and may lose his taxi and his livelihood—do not produce any sense of solidarity. In spite of, or because of, the characters' "shared histories of deprivation and discrimination," any sense of community has collapsed. The characters treat each other resentfully, turning the knife wherever possible; most loyalties are short-lived, formed only in the hope of economic advantage; records of wrongs are kept with the same assiduousness with which Enrique notches up Oso's credit at the bar. Frequent crosscutting between characters (the prevalence of montage techniques over camera movements) heightens difference, discontinuity, and division.

The idea of a national community is mobilized only in the name of personal survival: Héctor reproaches Enrique for taking on an employee from abroad and not thinking about his own country, a criticism echoed later by another bar customer. In his own tirade against Freddy, Oso accuses him bluntly to his face: "Te venís a sacar el hambre y dejás sin laburo a los pibes de acá" (You've come to get rid of your own hunger and you've taken work off kids from here). The arrival of immigrants like Freddy and Rosa (the Paraguayan-Argentine waitress), forced through hardship to abandon their own countries in search of work elsewhere, provides an easy target for the resentment of the Argentine characters. The success of the nation-state was founded—as Zygmunt Bauman reminds us—on "the *suppression* of self-asserting communities,"[24] on the erasure of its roots in violence and displacement. For Bhabha "the very idea of a pure, 'ethnically cleansed' national identity can only be achieved through the death, literal and figurative, of the complex interweavings of history, and the culturally contingent borderlines of modern nationhood."[25] If this is so, then the fragmentation of the community depicted in *Bolivia* inscribes a kind of double-forgetting, in which the xenophobic customers of the bar conveniently forget their own immigrant origins. National lines in Buenos Aires may be policed only by dint of forgetting its historical status as a colonial settlement and, later, as a city of mass immigration. Of course, there is a vital distinction to be made: Argentina's earlier immigrants were almost exclusively European, whereas economic migrants of more recent years have tended to cross the border from other Latin American countries. Racial prejudice is voiced repeatedly in the film through the use of the word "negro" in the most disparaging tone, with its local meaning of darker-skinned—therefore probably indigenous, therefore (as certain discourses in Argentina of racial purity and European heritage would have it) from elsewhere in Latin America, therefore not Argentine. With an ignorance bred of arrogance, the Argentine bar owner and customers continually misaddress Freddy as Peruvian or Paraguayan; Enrique mistakes Peru for a Central American country and assumes that Freddy won't know how to operate the television remote control.

The subtlety with which racial stereotypes are documented in *Bolivia*—a little assumption here, a dismissive remark there—reinforces the endemic nature of prejudice.

Hamid Naficy describes the way in which the "worldview, mise-en-scène, shot composition, and plot development" of many transnational films are pervaded by a "sense of claustrophobia":

> These are films of liminal panic, of retrenchment in the face of what is perceived to be a foreign, often hostile, host culture and media representation. This perceived (and at times very real) threat is dealt with by invoking confining but comforting claustrophobic spaces. A variety of strategies are used to create such spaces, including the following: closed shot compositions, tight physical spaces within the diegesis, barriers within the mise-en-scène and the shot that impede vision and access, and a lighting scheme that creates a mood of constriction and blocked vision.[26]

Although *Bolivia* is not a transnational film in the strictest sense, many of the strategies discussed by Naficy are relevant to the film's aesthetic treatment of tensions between immigrants and the host country.[27] The film is highly claustrophobic, although the spaces it creates are not "comforting" ones of protection but spaces of imprisonment that offer no refuge from hostile aggressors. The effect of claustrophobia is generated first by the mise-en-scène: few external shots liberate the spectator from the interior of the bar, a tiny theater in which the rancor of a suffering community plays out daily. It is also evoked by the homogeneity of filming styles employed and the simplicity of the form: the film follows a single narrative thread, building tension toward a spectacular climax, and suggesting a stultifying circularity. The placement of a sign in the bar window ("se necesita cocinero/parrillero" [cook needed]) after Freddy's death, very similar to the one shown at the beginning of the film, together with the repetition of the same signature music (of Andean origin), indicates the disposable nature of immigrant lives and the impossibility of escape from urban violence. Predators await Freddy in every space he enters: the owners of the illegal *locutorio* to which Enrique sends him to phone home cheat him of the few pesos he possesses, and wandering through the streets late at night without money for a hotel, he is easy prey for patrolling police cars. Freddy's death, together with the coverup we strongly suspect will ensue, indicate the extent to which illegal immigrants like him become lost in the interstices, unable to appeal to a justice system whose laws they have already contravened. He will

15. Freddy's fall across the threshold of the bar in *Bolivia* highlights the film's exploration of the demarcated territories and claustrophobic spaces of immigrant experience.

simply disappear, like the many others the *pensión* owner complains about, who vanish without a trace, leaving behind their few possessions as a sign of the desperation of their flight from the city or—as in Freddy's case—a more permanent elimination.

The "liminal panic" to which Naficy refers receives particular expression in *Bolivia*'s attention to thresholds. The drawing and redrawing of discursive boundaries between the self and other is mirrored in the careful policing of spaces and, particularly, their borders. When Freddy presumes to see Oso off the premises himself and then to stand guard at the threshold of the bar, making sure that Enrique's orders to leave are fully obeyed, he physically assumes control over a space in which—in the eyes of Oso—he is but an intruder. As Oso gets into the taxi, nursing a bloodied nose, the camera returns twice to a shot of Freddy standing in the doorway. The third time we see Freddy framed at the threshold, his back is turned, but his return to the bar is prevented by a fatal shot fired by Oso from the moving car. In slow motion, soundlessly, Freddy's body falls over the doorstep: half inside, half outside, over the border of the space he inhabited as an employee but into which he was never fully allowed to assimilate (Figure 15). That the initial reaction of Enrique and Héctor is to pull the body quickly back into the privacy of the bar, the latter looking over his shoulder repeatedly in an attempt to determine whether they are being watched, reinforces the film's construction of the threshold as a place of anxiety, this time of a different sort. Freddy's body is reclaimed into the bar only out of fear of reprisal from the law: the street becomes suddenly a place of danger for all. Only the punitive state, a common enemy, brings the characters to a point of cooperation, momentarily allowing them to forget their differences.

Deconstructing National and Migrant Identities
in *Vladimir en Buenos Aires*

Like *Bolivia*, *Vladimir en Buenos Aires* (Diego Gachassin, 2002) revisits the topos of the immigrant dream and, with it, questions of cultural identity left unresolved in the nation's foundational fictions. The film explores the often-difficult lives of immigrants living in small *pensiones* across the city, here focusing particularly on the large number of immigrants from the former USSR and Eastern Europe who arrived in Argentina during the 1990s. Pasha is an engineer from the former Soviet Union; he has brought with him carefully elaborated plans for a housing project that is to be built and owned by a cooperative. The project is met with superficial interest from various politicians and officials, but in the middle of a recession no one has the time or inclination to support its implementation. When Pasha finally finds employment as a private security guard (one of the few areas of employment growth at the turn of the century in Argentina), he observes the irony of his situation: he is being paid to do the opposite of what he set out to do, contracted to guard an empty building from being inhabited by homeless people. His friend is unable to get his Russian medical qualification validated and faces the prospect of studying for years to retake it. Both lie to their families back home about their circumstances, perpetuating the myth of the "tierra de oportunidades"; the truth, of course, is that the hopes of skilled and educated immigrants are more likely to founder than flourish in the hostile environment of an Argentine nation in the midst of economic crisis.

If the immigrant dream is here subject to rupture and frustration, the film does reveal an important continuity with the discourses surrounding immigration in previous periods in Argentina's history. In the opening scene, which depicts Pasha's journey from the airport to the center of the city, the taxi driver's monologue locates the film's explorations of migrant identities within broader discourses of Argentine nationalism. He differentiates between European immigrants, whose social integration is generally made easier in Argentina, and those from neighboring South American countries, who are often the victims of racialized prejudice, claiming that "acá hace falta más de los tuyos, sabés, y menos bolitas. Está llena de bolitas" (we need more of your type here, you know, and not so many Bolivians. We're stuffed full of Bolivians).[28] His personal "theory" about the hardworking nature of citizens of colder countries strongly echoes Sarmiento's preference for hardworking northern European immigrants over those from southern Europe. The latter, Sarmiento writes, had much in common with indigenous American races, which were "incapaces, aun por medio de la compulsión, para dedicarse a un trabajo duro y seguido" (incapable, even under compulsion, of dedicating themselves to sustained hard work).[29] As is well known, Argentina failed to attract the kind of immigrants Sarmiento and Alberdi had prescribed for the country's economic development (skilled workers from the urban centers of northern Europe), and instead its population was swelled by thousands of Italian peasants; more recent immigration has typically come from Bolivia, Peru, and Paraguay in the form of cheap, unregulated labor. Despite significant shifts in migratory patterns, however, the film shows the persistence of certain ideas about immigration dating from Sarmiento's era: first, a predilection for attributing the current problems of the nation to its racial and cultural makeup and, second, the imaginary axis between *europeísta* and *americanista* policies that continues to haunt present-day constructions of Argentine identity, poised between its Latin American and European heritages.

In the face of these two particularly tenacious ideas of nationhood, *Vladimir en Buenos Aires* posits cultural identity as an imaginary construction rather than an essence (racial or otherwise) and proposes cultural difference as something irreducible to binary oppositions. It does so largely through an exploration of the distance between enunciation and reception in exile and the imaginary and constructed nature of place and identity. Naficy has drawn attention to the play of presence and absence in this process of enunciation and reception in his examination of the frequent use of epistolary forms in exilic filmmaking: "Exile and epistolarity necessitate one another, for distance and absence drive them both. However, by addressing someone in an epistle, an illusion of presence is created that hovers in the text's interstices. As a result, address is not just a problem but the problematic of these films."[30] *Vladimir en Buenos Aires* draws attention to the deferral and postponement of meaning in exile in the form of the letters Pasha writes home but fails to commit to the postbox. His addressee is never shown in the film; even when we see him call home by telephone, sound is restricted to his own voice, with that of his interlocutor silenced. Naficy differentiates between the use of letters in exilic filmmaking and their use in classical realist cinema, in which they often perform functions relating to the film's plot; for example, "they may complicate or clarify the plot's trajectory or the characters' motivations and psychology; they may mislead, be mislaid, or be misdelivered." In the case of what Naficy calls "accented films," however, "epistolarity appears to be less a function of plot formation and character motivation than an expression and inscription of exilic displacement, split subjectivity, and multifocalism."[31] While the voice-overs that represent Pasha's letters in *Vladimir en Buenos Aires* do give us a privileged insight into his perceptions, they are clearly intended to question the "presence" of speech and language in Derrida's sense. The play of presence and absence positions us ambiguously as spectators, as (on an extradiegetic level) the intended recipients of Pasha's letters and voice-overs but (on a diegetic level) as unintended recipients, a fact made clear by the use of Russian dialogue and Spanish subtitles. Heteroglossia, as Naficy points out, produces slippages of its own and is often used to locate transnational or exilic films as "texts of cultural and temporal difference."[32]

Pasha, pursuing a romance with a prostitute living in the same *pensión*, writes of his difficulty in interpreting social codes, which are culturally determined: he cannot yet tell if she is interested in him because "here [he reflects in Russian], everyone kisses everyone and it doesn't mean anything." The film's emphasis on the slippages between enunciation and interpretation is also achieved through formal devices, principally the overlaying of citations from *Crime and Punishment*. As Pasha wanders through the streets of Buenos Aires, we hear his voice reading a passage from the opening of Dostoevsky's novel, in which Raskolnikov registers his impressions of St. Petersburg on his way to the house of the pawnbroker he will later murder. Several displacements mark this scene: the use of nonsynchronous sound, the use of third-person narrative voice in a subjective voice-over, the use of subtitles, and the use of a citation that—for the majority of spectators—will only be recognized as such when the camera shows Pasha reading *Crime and Punishment* in his room at the *pensión* (before or after he walks the streets?). The anachronisms and slippages produced by bringing a classic Russian text to bear on an individual's first impressions of Buenos Aires point to the traces of texts and images in all constructions of place. The superimposition of the citation, which describes how the heat, bustle, and smell of the streets "all worked painfully upon the young man's already overwrought nerves,"[33] conditions us to "read" the images we see in a certain way, just as Pasha's first experiences of Buenos Aires appear to be overlaid with images and meanings from another source. It points to the potency of imagined experiences that overlay the real experiences of the immigrant.

The superimposition also points to the nature of the text as already multiple, bearing traces of other texts that are both present and absent in meaning and interpretation. *Crime and Punishment* effectively hijacks the film text: although no further reference is explicitly made to the novel, at several points Pasha's rather unusual actions create parallels between the two texts on which the filmmaker draws or, more evocatively, suggest Pasha's own unconscious attempt to write himself into Dostoevsky's narrative. Like Raskolnikov, Pasha lives in cramped quarters and is being pursued by his landlady for unpaid rent; his social conscience propels him to save disadvantaged girls from abuse; he commits a murder to which he eventually confesses and for which he is imprisoned at the end of the narrative. This process of "mapping-on," or the search for narrativity more generally, allows the director to explore the disjunctions between aspiration and reality. Pasha's attempts to insert his existence in Buenos Aires into a coherent narrative are often frustrated. He tries to "save" his new friend María from prostitution, but she doesn't want to be saved. Most importantly, the confession scene is utterly derailed: as Pasha tries to give himself up for the murder of a politician and his prostitute, he realizes that a coverup has been orchestrated to save the reputation of the politician, with the story of a fire fabricated to explain the deaths. There is therefore no crime to which he might confess, as it has been effectively erased by corruption at a higher level. Eventually, he is imprisoned for the "wrong" crime, the lesser offense of renting out rooms in an unoccupied house to Russian immigrants, but accepts his penalty as punishment for the murders. The use of *Crime and Punishment* as a parallel text that guides the film's story constructs both immigrant experience and cultural identities in general as marked by *différance*, being signifiers that bear the traces of other signifiers; these derailings of the plot also enact the ruptures and disjunctures that characterize the narratives of immigrant experience.

To emphasize the constructedness of identity, its reliance on difference rather than essence, is not to deny the psychological and social importance of the narratives with which we construct cultural identities. Naficy notes that "the epistolaries are also driven by epistephilia, which often involves a burning desire to know and to tell about the causes, experiences, and consequences of disrupted personal and national histories."[34] *Vladimir en Buenos Aires* shows the very real personal cost of the shattering of a narrative: Argentina as the land of opportunity for immigrants. It is only through crime and punishment that Pasha can attain a kind of closure (only from prison that he is eventually able to finish the letter home he has been trying to write); like Arlt's protagonist, Silvio, in *El juguete rabioso*, also inhabiting a cruel world of few opportunities, an act against humanity lends his life the kind of transcendence and meaning he yearns for. At every turn, a hostile Argentina thwarts Pasha's attempt to write his own story or to give him a role in the nation's own.

Both Freddy in *Bolivia* and Pasha in *Vladimir en Buenos Aires* are exploited and cheated by individuals around them, as well as by authorities and institutions; while particular venom is often directed against them as immigrants, it is notable that in both films mutual exploitation characterizes the wider community of Argentine citizens. They chart both the breakdown of the state and the collapse of civil society. The state in both films signally fails to nurture either its immigrants or its own citizens, punishing where it should protect and vice versa. The vision that emerges is one of a breakdown in the social contract that underpins civil society: the contract between the state and its citizens. As Sarlo observes, drawing on Hobbes's premise that citizens choose to cede their autonomy to the state in order to avoid civil war, modern nations were established on the basis of a promise: belonging to a nation guaranteed certain rights, among them peace and security. In contemporary Argentina the state has failed to guarantee those rights and is therefore in a position of debt toward its citizens.[35] Sarlo argues elsewhere that in circumstances of extreme hardship, "no hay ciudadanía" (there is no citizenship).[36] While to be Argentine in the first sixty years of the twentieth century meant to be literate and to have secure employment, "cuando ser argentino no significa ni trabajo, ni comida, ni tiempo, *vale poco ser argentino. La nacionalidad no es sólo imaginaria. Se arraiga en su inscripción material sobre los cuerpos*" (when being Argentinian does not mean work, or food, or time, *it is worth little to be Argentine. Nationality is not only imaginary. It is rooted in its material inscription on bodies).[37] Films such as *Bolivia* and *Vladimir en Buenos Aires* testify to the material impact of the collapse of liberal discourses of nationhood. Here, national identity is defined only in purely negative terms: to be Argentine is not to be a foreigner.

POSTNATIONAL IDENTITIES AND STRATEGIES OF RETERRITORIALIZATION

In recent years the plots of international coproductions—such as *Martín (Hache)* (Adolfo Aristarain, 1997) and *Un día de suerte* (Sandra Gugliotta, 2002)—have often mimicked the migratory paths of middle-class Argentine citizens, returning to European locations in search of greater economic prospects. The transnationality of these productions, which frequently cast one or more European actors in order to fulfill coproduction requirements, is given a thematic corollary in their depiction of the erosion of the state's sovereignty under neoliberalism and globalization. Neither the recourse to international coproduction nor the theme of vulnerability to encroaching neocolonial forces is, of course, particularly new in Argentine cinema. What is of most interest in contemporary films is a persistent concern with constructing the national in the face of the growing impact of globalized identities and, above all, the self-consciousness with which many films negotiate between local and global meanings. While appearing to emphasize the dissolution of the nation in globalized frameworks, many recent Argentine films have reappropriated discourses of transnationalism for the purpose of reasserting contemporary forms of national identity.

Marvin D'Lugo, drawing on García Canclini's discussion of the twin processes of deterritorialization and reterritorialization in Latin American media,[38] suggests that "while seeming to exploit or promote the cultural capital of their respective national cinemas as globally marketable commodities, some Latin American film auteurs have over the last decade sought to resist mere standardization of global film patterns by channeling some of the reterritorial dynamics of which García Canclini speaks into a new form of identity politics." D'Lugo identifies Argentina as "the most highly developed area for such reterritorialized film industries." However, his analyses of *Camila* (María Luisa Bemberg, 1984), *La historia oficial* (Luis Puenzo, 1985), and *Un muro de silencio* (Lita Stantic, 1993)—all coproductions—do not uncover any strategies more sophisticated than an attempt "to compensate foreign audiences for their ignorance of local culture or history." The maneuvers he describes displace the local onto the universal with the aim of gaining access to an international market. Only in his powerful reading of a more recent coproduction between Spain and Argentina, *Martín (Hache)*, does D'Lugo locate strategies that can properly be described as reterritorializing. While appearing to undermine a national framework by emphasizing multinational business relationships between Latin America and Europe, and by "'Americanizing'" the narrative by employing devices and characters belonging to Hollywood action genre films, *Martín (Hache)*, as D'Lugo shows, ultimately rejects a "'borderless' global position," affirming the importance of cultural roots and placing the questions of identity it raises squarely within an Argentine narrative of migrancy and exile.[39]

This subversive reappropriation of the transnational and the global for national uses is discernible in several contemporary Argentine films. To demonstrate the significance of transnational and migratory discourses in the construction of the national, I analyze two films produced within Argentina and whose aesthetic and thematic choices were not circumscribed by the demands of international coproduction agreements. The first is *Hoteles*, which appears to travel the world but was largely shot in home territory; the second is *Bar El Chino*, a film produced by two Argentine companies that retraces the narrative movements between Spain and Argentina typical of coproductions between those two countries and even incorporates the guest appearance of a renowned Spanish actor, José Sacristán. Both films reveal, through their different constructions of the local and the global, the complexity of notions of place and identity at the beginning of the twenty-first century: they attest to the urgency of challenging fixed notions of the national while betraying an anxiety concerning cultural transmission in a postnational world.

The Simulation of Global Space in *Hoteles*

As an extremely experimental film, *Hoteles* (Aldo Paparella, 2003) occupies an anomalous place in contemporary Argentine cinema, much of which adopts a broadly realist framework in its narration of social crisis. In fact, the film was deliberately constructed to go against the trend in national film-making.[40] If the film appears entirely committed to inserting itself into a globalized frame of reference, I will argue that it may also be read as reinscribing the nationality it is so keen to erase, both at a discursive level and in relation to the material conditions of its production and distribution. In its exploration of place and identity under globalization, *Hoteles* raises a series of hermeneutical questions concerning its own interpretation and the relevance of national and transnational frameworks in relation to the analysis of film.

Hoteles has achieved a certain notoriety by virtue of its extensive and explicit sex scenes, which are—unusually in cinema, with the exception of the pornographic industry—not simulated but real. One of the functions of this unexpected intrusion of the real into an act that is conventionally feigned, cut, and embellished (either at the service of euphemism or of romance) is to throw into relief the simulated status of nearly everything else in the film. *Hoteles* is composed of five chapters, labeled with intertitles giving the names of five cities: Shanghai, Asunción, New York, Buenos Aires, and Chernobyl. The majority of these places are very obviously not filmed on location, which draws immediate attention to the fact that the film's apparent transnationalism is only really the effect of a series of simulations. I will suggest that through experimentation with mise-en-scène and perspective, the film signals within its own cinematic language the complex

16. Black-and-white stills of Manhattan are used to evoke "New York" as part of a series of meditations on the meaning of place in *Hoteles*.

17. Later shots reveal the images of Manhattan to be full-frame photographs of photographs: *Hoteles* disorients the viewer by playing with perspective and context to blur the boundaries between real and simulated place.

relationship it maintains both with its cultural context and with a globalized film industry.

While *Hoteles* ostensibly travels the world, it is almost entirely filmed at home. Visual representations such as photographs and paintings are used to construct a sense of location, treating place as a set of signifiers rather than a geographical territory and emphasizing its mediated quality over any idea of origin or authenticity. "Shanghai" is brought to us by shots of Chinese paintings with drums and a tam-tam on the soundtrack. In a similar vein "New York" is conjured up by means of a series of shots of postcards of Manhattan, even though it was the only sequence other than Buenos Aires actually to be filmed on location. Indeed, "New York" exemplifies a set of techniques used in the film to make the real appear simulated and the simulated appear real. The black-and-white shots of the city are not external to the apartment depicted but (as we discover later) full-frame shots of photographs stuck to one of the inside walls of the apartment. Figure 16 shows one of these photographs, which by taking up the entire frame appears to be simply a photograph of a real city; Figure 17, part of a later sequence, reveals the image to be a photograph of a photograph. Interior and exterior space are folded together in the film, with the external world reduced to the four walls of the film set and frames removed in order to disorient the spectator. As will become evident, the representation of context as essentially unstable in this way is key to the film's aesthetic.

The place of production, Argentina, is not accorded any kind of privileged status within the film. When the film "comes home" to Buenos Aires, the expected shots of the city are replaced with those of the nearby Tigre

Delta, a lush counterpoint to the urban sprawl of the capital. With the exception of one or two external shots, showing the buildings and surroundings of Hotel El Tropezón, made famous as the site of Lugones's suicide in 1938, the images we are shown could well have been shot in other locations. The relative absence of local color in the very place that might easily have been constructed with more reference to reality than representation is indicative of the film's attempt to collapse distinctions between the local and the global. The specificity of place is undermined in several ways. Each chapter of the film, for example, is introduced in the same manner, with an aerial shot of a city by night, taken at a distance too remote to allow its identification. But perhaps most strikingly, the mise-en-scène of each location is carefully constructed to include a series of repeated objects that effectively circulate through the spaces of the film, in and out of context. These are an ephemeral collection of objects of supposed sentimental value that lose much of their meaning outside their original context, like postcards, ornaments, and old books. The objects that appear and reappear with greatest persistence include a large piece of coral, a plastic ornament in the shape of a deer, a red dressing gown embroidered with a Chinese pattern, and a badge bearing a hammer and sickle.

The unfeasible reappearance of many of these same objects in different locations, scattered across the world, draws attention to the ever-longer reaches of global flows. These circulations are ultimately given a rather negative significance in the film. When we first see the dressing gown in Shanghai, it appears to belong to its context, but it later appears rather incongruously in Buenos Aires and Chernobyl. When we see the hammer and sickle insignia in New York, it does not acquire the same resonance as it does when it is inserted into the later Chernobyl sequence. The deliberate wrenching of these objects away from their contexts suggests an extreme form of commodity fetishism, as they wash up like flotsam and jetsam on the tides of globalization, far from the contexts of their production or even those of their consumption. They represent neither production nor consumption but simply global circulation itself, acquiring an existence of their own, which survives and transcends that of their human owners. As the director comments,

La película trabaja en dos grandes vías. Opone el camino de las personas y el camino de los objetos. . . . El mundo como lo inalterable, que se opone a la finitud de las personas. Los objetos van pasando de una historia a otra. El mundo continúa y nosotros como hombres, llegamos y pasamos, en cambio el mundo pervive. Y esa especie de fetichismo vuelve la atención sobre las personas, funciona como una pantalla reflectora.

[The film explores two major avenues. It contrasts the journey of people with the journey of objects. . . . The world as something unchangeable, which contrasts with the finite nature of people. The objects pass from one story to another. The world continues and we, as humans, come and go, while the world remains. And that kind of fetishism returns our gaze to people, it functions like a reflective screen.][41]

This contrast between the transcendence accorded to objects and the transience of human existence is signaled in the photographic treatment given to both objects and humans in the film. Diego Lerer comments, without elaboration, that "la cámara de Paparella trata a los objetos como sujetos y a los sujetos como objetos" (Paparella's camera treats objects like subjects, and subjects like objects).[42] This dynamic can be seen at work in the film with the use of close-ups much more frequently for objects than for humans; where close-ups are used for human subjects, faces are much less often the focus than other parts of the body. Sex is filmed with the same mixture of detached indifference or scientific curiosity that one might accord to the observation of animal behavior. Indeed, Paparella claims that the effect on the spectator is intended to be that of watching animals on a Discovery Channel nature program. Sex becomes an anonymous, mechanical exercise, entirely devoid of the romantic significations often given to it in cinema.

The reification to which humans become subject is suggested at a textual level by means of particular montage techniques: many of the film's sequences are dominated by the use of single shots of a short duration, often even a series of freeze frames. The film's characters do not create the objects around them so much as take on many of their characteristics, in a reversal of the conventional relationship of priority between reality and representation. For example, the closing sequence of "Chernobyl" (Figure 18) depicts the woman holding the man she is torturing in a pose reminiscent of a Pietà and recalling the precise form of a statue (Figure 19) seen earlier in the chapter. As the director comments, "Terminamos hechos a imagen y semejanza de los objetos que tenemos, y no viceversa" (We end up being created in the image and likeness of the objects we possess, not the other way around).[43]

Other techniques enhance our sense of the disconnection of both objects and humans with their context. The ill-fitting, anachronous quality of these

18–19. Reality copies representation in *Hoteles*. The director comments: "We end up being created in the image and likeness of the objects we possess, not the other way around."

objects, the lack of any coherent relationship between object and context, is emphasized throughout *Hoteles* by unprepared cuts between long shots of the room and extreme close-ups of an object: the absence of match cuts (and of many other rules of continuity editing) disorientates the spectator, who remains unsure of the relative size of the object, its position in the wider frame, or its relation to previous and subsequent images. The unusual use of perspective ensures we cannot easily grasp the spatial relationships between character, objects, and environment: their position or relative proportions. In "New York," for example, a still of the girl's face is immediately followed by one of a girl's face from a comic book: the similar perspective, size, and cinematic treatment of each suggests an equality of status, as both the real and the represented occupy the same plane of signification within the film.

This play with perspective and context is mirrored, I propose, in the film's underlying anxiety concerning its own context: the context of production, of its circulation as a commodity within the global market, and of its critical interpretation. In many ways it is a film that is conscious of being out of place, and out of sync, with its own context. This reading is suggested both by extrafilmic discourse (the director's own appraisals of the film and its relationship with national cinema) and by the textual operations of the film itself. *Hoteles* was intended to draw attention to the inclusion of certain Argentine cultural products for global distribution and the exclusion of others, specifically the First World demand that Third World cinema be primarily concerned with social issues and re-create a strong sense of local place. Paparella refers to this process of selection, by which only gritty, socially committed films are given international funding, as a subtle form of colonialism.[44] By contrast, *Hoteles* appears to erase all sense of local place or social meaning. It inscribes itself within a global context through its emphasis on intersubjectivity, the common world we all share, regardless of language or culture. Many of the images of *Hoteles* re-create a kind of global imaginary. Sci-fi comics and postcards strewn around the film's five interiors draw on anxieties with specifically global dimensions, such as nuclear catastrophe, alien invasion, and other forms of apocalypse. The iconography of major world religions and political movements, such as crucifixes and Soviet insignias, also refers to a set of shared discourses, a jumbled collection of artifacts that might be assembled to form a beginners' guide to world history. These images are juxtaposed with more recent but equally familiar products of global trade, such as Haribo candies. Sex enters here as one of the most fundamental instances of human intersubjectivity, crossing all borders, and this is one of the reasons that it is reduced in the film to its biological essentials and stripped of all cultural resonances.

However, the circulation of these objects of religious or political significance outside of their proper context also exposes the amnesia of the present, a present in which historical ruins like Chernobyl have become playgrounds for the young, who have no memory of the momentous events of the past. A certain tendency toward degeneration is evident in the film, which gives rise to disturbing, almost sacrilegious, images, such as that of a lesbian provocatively passing her tongue over a monument to Leopoldo Lugones, Argentina's most revered poet, or a laboratory assistant practicing sadistic sex amid the contaminated debris of a Russian nuclear disaster. The circulation of signs becomes a rather insidious process in which cultural meaning is irrevocably lost. Thus, while the film appears to deny the importance of place and to shun local color in favor of discourses of intersubjectivity, it also registers a crisis of meaning that arises from the circulation of signs out of context. The most persuasive reading of *Hoteles* may turn out to be one that retains a strong sense of the specificity of the film's context. I will suggest three ways in which the film's visual rhetoric, despite its appeal to intersubjectivity and global discourses, can be more convincingly read in a national, rather than a transnational, context.

First, the simulation of place in *Hoteles* has a clear economic referent: by such means, even the most low-budget productions can appear to travel the world. At the same time at which its imagery appears to claim a kind of universality and to erase the boundaries between the local and the global, this act of simulation confirms the perspective of the film as being grounded firmly at the periphery, from which such distant places can only be imagined. Although it appears to be about the unrestricted free flow of commodities across national boundaries, analyzed in the national context, the film actually becomes a protest against the asymmetries and the inequalities of such flows and can be read as an allegory of Argentina's difficult insertion into the global economy. The question of finance always inscribes a hermeneutical uncertainty into the analysis of independent films from impoverished countries, which often owe their aesthetic choices to the availability or unavailability of certain resources. For example, the stills used in the "New York" scene are filmed photographs rather than frozen frames, as this reduced the wastage of expensive film stock.[45]

Second, a postcolonial reading of the film, one that imbues the subjugated margins with something of the power of the dominant center, can be developed further in relation to the exploration of power in the text itself. The gendered power struggles of *Hoteles* take up the theme of unexpected reversals in the balance of power, with the apparently submissive females often turning out to dominate the men who are violent toward them. We initially assume that the male partners are dominant: in "Asunción" the man appears to have tied up a woman clad in black PVC, but we later realize that he is the one in the submissive role, and in "Chernobyl" the woman captured and kept as a sex slave manages to break free and wreak horrible revenge on her captor. Our expectations are continually overturned in a film that repeatedly challenges our assumptions about the dynamics of power and representation.

Third, the film's pretensions toward the global reflect a desire for universal culture that is, of course, a particularly Argentine one. Again, this reading is suggested in part by the director himself, who condemns the dominant place given in recent cinema to social unrest and poverty, to the exclusion of the more cosmopolitan heritage of Argentine culture:

> Somos un país cosmopolita, con gente que ha venido de todo el mundo. Consumimos cultura de todo el mundo. No tiene sentido que nos limitemos a hacer películas como si viviéramos en un país que lo único que tiene son los conflictos sociales y la pobreza.

> [We are a cosmopolitan country, with people who have come from all over the world. We consume culture from all over the world. It would be senseless to limit ourselves to making films as if we were living in a country where social conflicts and poverty were the only thing we had.][46]

Hoteles explores the tensions between cosmopolitanism and peripherality that characterize so many cultural discourses in Argentina. Paradoxically, then, the film's deliberate eschewing of local color brings into sharp relief the precariousness of Argentine film within the global culture industry and the importance of the national context in our reading of the film. Within this framework, however, it does much to demonstrate the instability of concepts of the local and the global. It lends support to critics such as Charles R. Acland, who reject the "unfortunate dichotomy between the local and the global" on which much research on global film culture is premised, arguing that the association of the local, on one hand, with "the immediate, the concrete, the real, the political, and the site of agency" and the global, on the other hand, with "the distant, the abstract, the ethereal, the corporate, and the site of containment" leads to "a rather rapid, and mistaken, critical closure around the local as the site of politicized difference and the global as the ideological production of homogeneity."[47] *Hoteles* empties the local of any sense of immediacy, politics, or realism in order to insert itself fully within the global, but in doing so, it reminds us of its grounding both in local discourses and in the material conditions of its production and distribution. By deconstructing the local in this way the film effectively resists the appropriation of the local as a place of purity or premodernity, rejecting a rhetorical move that—as I will explore further below—could ultimately be argued to serve the purposes of global capitalism.

Reterritorialization and Reflexivity in *Bar El Chino*

Bar El Chino (Daniel Burak, 2003) interweaves documentary sequences focusing on El Chino, a tango singer who died in 2001, with a fictional narrative in the form of a love story between Jorge and Martina, both professionals in audiovisual production who become involved in the making of the documentary. As a film about the making of a film based on a film that hasn't yet been finished, *Bar El Chino* is a highly reflexive production that brings a strong element of self-referentiality to bear on its exploration of the status of the national in contemporary globalized frameworks.

The film is set during the Crisis and touches on the civil unrest that accompanied it. With particular economy, reference is made to a number of stock images of poverty and instability in Argentina at the end of the twentieth century, used here as ciphers for a whole series of social and political problems: the unemployed rummage through rubbish for food and recyclable items, young boys wash the windshields of cars momentarily held up at red traffic lights, and demonstrators bang empty pots and pans in protest. As the Crisis comes to a head in the *corralito* of December 2001, Jorge and Martina are working day and night to meet a production deadline for a promotional video commissioned by a Spanish company planning to invest in Argentine highways. The key events of the Crisis are almost entirely mediated for the viewer through news bulletins shown on Jorge's television set. This device—which, one suspects, provided an economic solution to the filming of social protests—allows the director to exploit the full irony of juxtaposing these images with those of the promotional video being edited by Jorge and Martina. The calm and complacent tones that predict the prosperous future of a modernized Argentina, together with the clean digital graphics that assemble a virtual network of highways crisscrossing the country, contrast sharply with the footage of food riots in Buenos Aires. In one sequence the audio track of the highway video is superimposed onto the visual track of the television footage; as the voice-over, in a markedly Peninsular accent, presents the business opportunities available in an Argentina ripe for market expansion and modernization, the scenes of starving crowds being subjected to bloody police repression depict a very different country.

That the paternalistic Spanish rhetoric of modernization thinly disguises a neocolonial opportunism is not left to doubt. The video extols the Spanish company's "espíritu de liderazgo" (spirit of leadership) in Argentina, claiming that the two countries will be "más unidos que nunca a través de Autopistas Argentinas" (more united than ever by Argentine Highways). The Spanish interest, we may surmise, is in the expansion of the Argentine market through improved transport systems. In the next scene, with the first whiff of trouble, the company reneges on its investment deal. As the risks begin to outweigh potential profits, it simply pulls out of the country, like so many other financial institutions and businesses in the weeks following the Crisis. Throughout, the film draws attention to the inequality of the relationships that link Argentina with its foreign business partners, who operate at arm's length from the impact of corporate decisions on individuals on the ground, like Jorge, who is not paid for his work on the video, and Martina, who is fired from her job in TV production on the basis of a list faxed through anonymously from the parent company in the United States.

Bar El Chino dwells on the shattering, as a result of the Crisis, not just of Argentina's capitalist dreams but of another powerful illusion: the embedding of the nation in those relationships of equality, mutual benefit, and reciprocity that underpin the rhetoric of globalization. Popular consensus since the Crisis has formed around the image of an Argentina exploited by its foreign creditors and abandoned in its hour of greatest need. The political scientist Daniel García Delgado finds that in Argentina, in contrast with recent crises suffered elsewhere in the world, "una crisis esperada por el mundo (y no sorpresiva, como las otras) no recibió ayuda externa, más bien todo lo contrario. . . . La vivimos abandonados a nuestras propias fuerzas, en soledad y aislamiento" (a crisis anticipated by the world—and not a surprise, like the others—did not receive external help, rather the reverse. . . . We lived through it left to our own resources, alone and isolated).[48] Prior to the Crisis, the multinational banks operating in Argentina had won the confidence of their depositors by emphasizing the security of a global network, implying that the parent institution would act as a "lender of last resort." In fact, Argentina's foreign banks were not branches but subsidiaries, and there existed no legal requirement for the parent companies to bail them out when they ran out of money. The Crisis revealed the fundamental fragility of finance capitalism, which, since the dematerialization of money, is now further and further removed from raw materials and labor, depending heavily on the confidence of individual bank users and gambling on the improbability of a nationwide run on banks; it revealed, too, the fragility of relationships of mutual dependency with which nations are ostensibly bound together in a globalized economic system. The IMF, often considered to play the role of an international lender of last resort, provided no funds during the Crisis or in the year that followed (2002).[49] It is unsurprising that many Argentine analysts concur with the view of French regulationist Robert Boyer, for whom the Crisis demonstrates the deception at the heart of this system: "La globalización es el discurso que inventaron las multinacionales norteamericanas para hacerse abrir todos los mercados de los países emergentes. . . . La globalización es una falsa convergencia" (Globalization is the discourse invented by North American multinationals in order to open up the markets of developing countries. . . . Globalization is a false convergence).[50] Even those accounts that are more sympathetic to neoliberal aims—such as that offered by Mauricio Rojas, who blames state interventionism for making Argentina's industries vulnerable to global fluctuations[51]—concur that the problem rests in the complexity of Argentina's economic relationship with the external world: too open, or too closed, to world markets; borrowing too much, or abandoned by its creditors. The Argentine Crisis represents, as much as an internal political crisis of legitimization, the crisis of Argentina's position in the world.

In the context of Argentina's economic misadventures on the global stage, the discourse of *Bar El Chino* appears to be mobilized by a nostalgic intent to denounce the impact of modernization and commercialization in favor of localism and of traditional values of friendship, solidarity, spontaneity, and authenticity. Certainly, nostalgia provides a key theme for the marketing of the film, as is evident in this excerpt from the film's Web site:

> El único lugar en el mundo en donde se canta el tango como hace 60 años atrás. En Buenos Aires, una enorme ciudad compenetrada con los nuevos tiempos, existe un barrio que se conserva como en los viejos tiempos. Sin maquillaje. Auténtico como ninguno. Es Pompeya, uno de los lugares en donde nació el tango. Existe un Bar. Un lugar único: Bar El Chino.

> [The only place in the world where tango is sung as it was sung sixty years ago. In Buenos Aires, a huge, modern city, there exists a neighborhood where time has stood still. Without makeup. More authentic than any other. It is Pompeya, one of the birthplaces of tango. There is a bar. A unique place: Bar El Chino.][52]

The version of tango performed at the bar is not the flashy show aimed at international tourists but a pastime to be shared among friends, in a dilapidated bar in a city suburb. In Marx's formulation *Bar El Chino* consistently emphasizes use value (social benefits) over exchange value (price and profitability). Or to borrow Pierre Bourdieu's terms for a use not too remote from his own, in the absence of economic capital, the appeal is made to social capital (the community centered on the bar) and cultural capital (traditional and contemporary skills such as tango and filmmaking competence). José Sacristán sends a message to Jorge expressing his hope that the El Chino documentary will be completed, for the benefit of future generations to appreciate that "más allá del folclorismo, más allá de las tradiciones, más allá del significado musical o no, que hubo unos seres humanos en un momento determinado en esto puto planeta que entendieron lo de la amistad, la solidaridad, la lealtad y el afecto como lo entiende la gente que habita y pasa por el boliche del Chino" (beyond folklore, beyond traditions, and beyond whatever significance they hold musically, there were some human beings at a certain point on this fucking planet who understood friendship, solidarity, loyalty and affection in the way it is understood by the people who live in, and pass through, El Chino's bar). When Martina and her colleague Beto set off to find the bar, the last on a list of tango venues that will be featured in a television program, Martina confidently predicts that a taxi driver will be able to find it without any difficulty: "los tacheros conocen todos los lugares para turistas" (the cabbies know all the tourist spots). The confusion of the driver—who struggles even to recognize the names of the streets they give as the address—reinforces our understanding of the bar as a place patronized by locals, rather than tourists, located on the margins of the city proper (close to the Riachuelo River, which divides the capital from Gran Buenos Aires, the urbanized province that surrounds it). Once Martina and Beto are inside, it is clear that the bar has been entirely overlooked by modernizing forces, having remained largely untouched since the 1950s and with fading decor mercilessly exposed by harsh strip lights. In one of the interviews that make up the documentary strand of the film's narrative, El Chino reinforces the authentic nature of tango performance in this setting: without a microphone or a stage, "either you can sing or you can't." The prominence given to authenticity and origins is also replicated at points in the film's exploration of national identity. At first sight, at least, *Bar El Chino* seems to appeal to a certain set of stereotypes—chief among them the Argentine triumph of gastronomy, "un buen bife de chorizo"—which coalesce into a rather impoverished, nostalgic concept of national identity.

This reading is at least partially undermined, however, by the film's ironic treatment of questions of nationalism and national identity and its self-consciousness of its own status as a cultural product for export. Notions of cultural authenticity become the object of comedy as Jorge's ex-wife in Spain is said still to be having cosmetic surgery, "para no perder lo que le queda de su argentinidad" (so as not to lose what she has left of her Argentineness); insistently, the film points to Jorge and Martina's ignorance of tango (even Jorge, who is older, identifies more with rock 'n' roll), thus detracting from tango as a cultural phenomenon around which a sense of national identity could credibly be formed. Argentine identity is constructed more frequently with respect to images of artificiality than those of authenticity. Most importantly, *Bar El Chino* is acutely conscious of its positioning as a cultural product attractive to a European market. Near the beginning of the film, Beto tells Martina that he has heard through a contact in Europe that "allá en Francia siempre están necesitando material nuevo, siempre" (over there in France they are always looking for new material). As the camera pauses briefly to show a group of *cartoneros* rifling through sacks of rubbish on the pavement, Beto muses: "¿Y una nota sobre la pobreza y los chicos que comen de la basura? Eso vende allá en Europa" (What about a report on poverty and kids eating from garbage sacks? That sells well in Europe). If the power of colonial discourse, as Stuart Hall argues, resides in "the power to make us see and experience ourselves as 'Other,' "[53] this film produces a series of refractions of the cinematic gaze, in which viewers from both

Europe and Argentina see themselves seeing the Other see themselves. This self-consciousness effectively places under erasure the film's use of tango as cultural capital in order to appeal to European spectators, or perhaps to the growing number of Argentines resident in Spain and other European countries who, like Martina at the end of the film, earn their salaries in euros but are still nostalgic for the sights and sounds of home.

Like many other recent Argentine films, *Bar El Chino* constructs ideas of national identity not so much around essentialist notions as around ideas of cultural hybridity and the experience of migration. This emphasis is evident in the film's treatment of tango, which—like cinema itself—is a cultural icon in which ideas of the national are invested, but which is, and has been, very much subject to transnational exchange. The *desarraigo* of tango and the disjunctures in time and space implied by nostalgia are reappropriated as an essentially Argentine condition, by means of which identity is always exiled from itself. The description of this condition in the film, given first by one of the bar's singers (of Italian origin) and echoed later by Jorge, is that his heart beats once in Europe, once in Argentina—"tic aquí, tac allá"—as he is destined always to be a foreigner in either country.

These migrations are not merely symptomatic here of increasing cross-border movements in a globalized era but, crucially, a foundational element of national identity, speaking to the difficult partings, the insecurity and the transitoriness that characterize Argentine experience as much for contemporary citizens as for European immigrants of past decades. The immigrant culture of tango finds a contemporary echo in the recent migration of Argentines to Europe. The oily Jesús, Jorge's agent, succeeds in luring Martina to work in Spain, not by the tenacious exercise of his personal charms (Martina's colleague remarks caustically: "los españoles . . . siempre tratando de conquistar América" [Spaniards . . . always trying to conquer America]) but by the promise of a stable job paid in euros. Martina thus joins the many in her generation who are seeking better prospects abroad in the wave of "reverse migration," which bears testimony to the impact of economic crises at home. To read these migrations as just so many instances of the deterritorialized flows of globalization, in which people, goods, and money constantly cross national borders, would be to strip them of the particular meaning they are given in the Argentine context. Reading the film in this way allows us to understand its migratory trajectories as an appropriating strategy in which the transnational becomes renationalized and reterritorialized.

Ironically, of course, strategies of renationalization may also be programmed by globalization itself, which emphasizes the importance of the nation while eroding its borders in what Harvey refers to as "the central paradox" of space under capitalism: "the less important the spatial barriers, the greater the sensitivity to the variations of place within space, and the greater the incentive for places to be differentiated in ways attractive to capital."[54] Place-bound identity, of crucial importance to many social movements, is also of interest to capitalism; as Harvey laments, "the irony is that tradition is now often preserved by being commodified and marketed as such."[55] Although for Harvey such strategies of differentiation ultimately serve the interests of capitalism, what remains to be contested, of course, is *which* places are to attract that capital, and *which* traditions will be preserved through such marketing. *Bar El Chino* engages in this struggle for visibility, at the same time encoding anticapitalist messages. Burak's framing of the documentary within a romantic fiction, shot with regard for the usual narrative conventions of a love story, provides a kind of allegory for the embedding of counterhegemonic messages within a Hollywood-dominated, global film industry.

Furthermore, the definition of place and identity that emerges in both *Hoteles* and *Bar El Chino* is not inward-looking but "extroverted" in Doreen Massey's terms, in the sense that it "includes a consciousness of its links to the wider world." Massey proposes a dynamic, open concept of place that is not rigidly fixed or bounded, arguing that place does not have to be defined "through simple counterposition to the outside" but can, in part, be suggested "precisely through the particularity of linkage *to* that 'outside' which is therefore part of what constitutes the place."[56] The reflexivity of both films is key to their depiction of identity as a nexus of social and cultural relations, in constant flux but still positioned in a geopolitical sense at a unique juncture of these crisscrossing relations and interactions. In *Bar El Chino* this concept of place keeps in check the more essentializing forces of nostalgia. As John Durham Peters suggests, "To see self, home, homeland, world as works we collectively author liberates us, in the view of both cosmopolitans and poststructuralists, from other-denying dreams of communion and homogeneity. Here the nostalgia for a home in exile and diaspora is directly attacked."[57] These films' understanding of cultural identity as always already the product of cultural mixture allows them to move beyond a simple dichotomy between the local and the global.

What is more, *Bar El Chino*'s self-reflexive exploration of film as economic commodity, as well as cultural expression, subject to the ebbs and flows of a global industry yet rooted in national experience, goes some way

20. *Bar El Chino* takes a reflexive approach to the recycling and repackaging of traditional art and values within contemporary culture and technology.

to exposing (if not derailing) the process Harvey describes, by which the local is commodified for the purposes of the global system. One of the ways Argentine cinema has sought to negotiate a market for its own films is precisely by drawing attention to the circulation of film as commodity both within the nation and in international distribution flows. This self-reflexivity operates in contrast to First World industry films, which typically obscure the social and economic relations that lie behind their production. In Burak's film the aura belonging to El Chino as an authentic, unique performer is undermined by the film's thorough demystification of the filmmaking process, in which artistic inspiration often takes second place to the hard graft of production schedules, and the whole project depends greatly on the availability of funds. Jorge is forced to interrupt his shooting of the El Chino film because the advance that would have paid for the hiring of assistants and equipment has been retained by the bank; more is not forthcoming from Jesús, who shouts: "Esto es un negocio, no un fondo de cultura" (This is a business, not a cultural fund). *Bar El Chino* testifies to the dogged survival of Argentine cinema during the Crisis. Jorge and Martina are not career film directors who direct a large team of technicians; they are simply individuals with a knowledge of shooting and editing, gained through television production and commercial advertising, who decide to lend their skills to a more personal project. They do all their own filming, on borrowed equipment, and edit sequences at home on a desktop computer. The film is to Hollywood blockbusters what the bar itself is to ostentatious tango shows in high-tech Buenos Aires auditoriums: with some know-how, talent, dedication, and "feeling," the result (we are encouraged to suspect) may be much more "authentic." This discourse—of dignity in the face of poverty, of the survival of culture in the midst of economic collapse—has a nationalist end but is equally appealing to European consciences. It provides a space for a utopian belief that (as Sacristán, one of the film's Spanish voices, expresses it) there is, or could be, somewhere out there, a group of people who do things differently.

Shots of Jorge and Martina's onscreen editing of interviews carried out with the bar's singers (Figure 20) draw attention to the ways in which traditional culture and values may be captured, framed, recycled, and promoted for contemporary uses. Tango, cinema, and culture more generally—rather than beef—may well be Argentina's most successful products for export in times of crisis. If—in a very Argentine discursive formula—cultural success maintains a kind of compensatory relationship with economic failure, it is also worth pointing out, with Bourdieu, the convertibility of cultural capital with other forms of capital.[58] With the threat of eviction hanging over El Chino's family at the time of filming, the project acquired a strongly conservationist agenda;[59] the bar is now firmly on the tourist map, recommended among others by the travel section of *The Economist* Web site, whose writer complains, however, that the place "has lost some of its authenticity since tourists woke up to it."[60] Films such as *Bar El Chino* and *Hoteles* demonstrate a consciousness of cinema's synecdochic relationship with the nation, being on the one hand positioned in geopolitical terms and, on the other, caught up in the ebbs and flows of international distribution networks. It is unsurprising, therefore, that film should play such a critical role in debates on cultural legitimacy and economic dependence that have long been significant in Argentine constructions of national identity and to demonstrate the politicization of culture under globalization.

6

MEMORY AND SUBJECTIVITY

Recent economic and political crises in Argentina have not displaced debates over postdictatorship memory, which appear to have lost none of their urgency since the early days of redemocratization following the regime's demise in 1983. The twenty-fifth anniversary of the military coup gave impetus to a critical reappraisal of those discourses that had been responsible for shaping collective memory: a number of prominent intellectuals (including Hugo Vezzetti, Beatriz Sarlo, Héctor Schmucler, Oscar Terán, and others associated with Argentina's premier cultural journal, *Punto de vista*) called for a greater depth of engagement and a diversification of voices to challenge the sins of omission and repetition into which memory had lapsed. This renewed interest in the legacies of the dictatorship was not unrelated to the social context of its expression during the worst years of the Crisis (2001–2). In the rise of anticapitalist fervor in Argentina it has often been recalled that one of the military regime's legacies for the present was the ushering in of an era of neoliberalism. Idelber Avelar goes as far as to argue that the dictatorship's "central role," while ostensibly focused on eliminating enemies at home, was "to purge the social body of all elements that could offer some resistance to a generalized opening to multinational capital";[1] the regime's association with the neoliberal policies largely blamed for the Crisis thus provides yet another, more contemporary, reason for censure (external debt, for example, rose from $13 billion to $46 billion during the dictatorship period of 1976 to 1983).[2] For María Teresa Gramuglio, writing in 2002, the question of the dictatorship's lasting impact on the network of relationships between politics and society remains urgent, "aun en situaciones de extrema penuria económica y miseria política como las actuales, o quizá justamente a causa de ellas" (even in situations of extreme economic poverty and political ruin like the present, or perhaps precisely because of them).[3]

What links the two films analyzed in this chapter with the others explored in this book, more directly related to the experience of the Crisis, is first and foremost an awareness of shifts in subjectivity in an era when the demise of simplistic, hegemonic discourses of nationhood opens the door for new and diverse voices, which threaten the integrity of such discourses and expose their founding on myth and fiction. "For every image memory produces"—Marita Sturken claims—"something is forgotten."[4] *Potestad* (Luis César D'Angiolillo, 2002) and *Los rubios* (Albertina Carri, 2003) challenge the orthodoxies of postdictatorship memory, in which the remembering of certain events has entailed the forgetting of others. Both films depart from the theme of justice and the testimonial impetus that have governed the majority of postdictatorship films such as *La historia oficial* (Luis Puenzo, 1985), *Un muro de silencio* (Lita Stantic, 1993), and *Garage Olimpo* (Marco Bechis, 1999). Instead, they explore shifts in the meanings assigned to the past by the present, historicizing memory in a manner that parallels—and informs—directions in theoretical debates of the time. In both films the conscious subversion of cinematic conventions, and in particular their play with processes of identification, is central to their exploration of memory and subjectivity. The ruptures and continuities they establish with the canonical narratives of memory find a parallel in the critical dialogue they maintain with the conventions of cinematic realism.

MEMORY AND SPECTATORSHIP IN *POTESTAD*

Luis César D'Angiolillo's *Potestad* is an anomalous contribution to postdictatorship memory in Argentina. Ideologically and aesthetically at odds with many earlier cinematic explorations of the most recent military dictatorship and its legacies, the film's primary intent is not to testify against the regime's violent repression of civilians, which resulted in the death and disappearance of thousands between 1976 and 1983. D'Angiolillo turns our attention instead to the politics of the act of remembering itself, as the film lays bare the often-insidious mechanisms of collective memory, revealing ways in which memory crystallizes around certain stereotypes, becoming rigid and opaque. *Potestad* brings to the fore processes of meaning-production in film and the role played by the spectator in these operations. While it initially leads us to expect a psychoanalytical interpretation of the events it narrates, the film eventually points to the inadequacy of such a reading and, ultimately, to the insufficiency of psychoanalytical models of spectatorship to explain how meaning is constructed in film. As I will argue, such theoretical considerations become fully associated with the film's attempt to initiate fresh debates within the context of postdictatorship memory in Argentina and to open up new spaces to permit the circulation of countermemories.

Potestad is a free adaptation of the play of the same title by Eduardo Pavlovsky, first performed in Argentina in 1985.[5] Pavlovsky's play involves just two characters in a single setting and is almost entirely in the form of a monologue. Given such constraints, it is unsurprising that taking the play to the screen was a challenge that took D'Angiolillo and his cowriter, Ariel Roli Sienra, a number of years. Rather than a simple textual adaptation, theirs is a complex and powerful translation of the subjective, paranoid vision of Pavlovsky's protagonist into the medium of film and one in which D'Angiolillo's experience in montage is used to particular effect.[6] Perhaps in part due to its classification as an adaptation, or to the fact that its director belongs neither to the younger generation of filmmakers who have shaped Argentine cinema since the mid-1990s nor to a generation of children of disappeared militants whose visual texts (films and photographs) have taken center stage in recent years, *Potestad* has not received the critical attention merited by its aesthetic innovation and its significance for current theories of memory and of spectatorship. As an independent production, it was given only a brief—if reasonably successful—commercial release at home; its modest clutch of film-festival prizes abroad possibly reflects the difficulty of the film's translation beyond its immediate cultural context. My reading of the film places it squarely within recent shifts in critical debates on memory in Argentina. While forging entirely different aesthetic strategies, *Potestad* shares some ground with the much more widely recognized *Los rubios*, pointing to the crucial absence in postdictatorship memory of a critique of left-wing militant violence in the 1970s and reflecting on the role of memory in obscuring, as well as revealing, the past.

In his portrayal of the mental disorientation and psychological distress suffered by the protagonist on the loss of his child, Adriana, D'Angiolillo eschews the conventions of realism in favor of a more subjective logic: the displacements, denials, uncertainties, and repetitions characteristic of the experience of intense grief. The time of the film appears to be condensed into a single trip on the subway, lasting three hours on a Saturday afternoon and spanning several lines and connections within the city of Buenos Aires. The labyrinth of tunnels and platforms becomes a metaphor for the complex network of mental digressions of the protagonist, as his journey is frequently interrupted by a series of fragmented and interlocking flashbacks. D'Angiolillo uses a range of devices to portray the confusion and paranoia experienced by Eduardo. One technique, used to heighten a sense of the ominous throughout the film, is the use of extreme close-ups of a series of objects. Commonly, the use of such shots in a film ascribes a symbolic value to the objects shown; in *Potestad* these shots generate a sense of insecurity because the precise meaning of such symbolism remains unclear for most of the narrative. Insistent rhythms and percussive bass notes are interspersed with periods of silence to represent Eduardo's shifting in and out of engagement with his immediate environment and resulting aporias in time; the familiar sounds of the subway train, such as doors opening and closing and the screech of metal against metal tracks, are enhanced and denaturalized to sinister effect. Slow-motion sequences are used on occasion to defamiliarize actions that do not belong to the film's present or to its "reality" but correspond to Eduardo's memories or projections. But it is the work of montage—suggesting links, exposing certain things and hiding others—which emerges as the most powerful tool in the film's exploration of memory, its intricate play of suspense and revelation, and (as we will see) its investigation into how meaning is produced in film.

In particular, *Potestad*'s experimentation with the flashback reveals a number of significant departures from convention, all of which announce the ineradicable presence of the present in representations of the past. A number of different time frames irrupt into the present of the film's narrative. Some of these provide recognizable historical referents, such as the Malvinas (Falklands) conflict of 1982 or Argentina's victory at the World Cup in 1978; others belong to Eduardo's childhood and the early period of his relationship with his wife, Ana María. Transitions between such sequences and the present are often triggered by a shot of one of a number of everyday items, prominent among which are a whirring fan, a dripping shower head, and a spinning toy carousel. Thus, for example, we move from a shot of Eduardo washing his face under the shower in the rugby club to another shower, this time in the film's present and in Eduardo's house (Figure 21). The cut is almost seamless, and we are alerted to the shift in time and place only by a variation in lighting and the change in color of the background tiles. The end of the film's first flashback—the beginning of

21. Matched shots mark the almost imperceptible transitions between past and present in *Potestad*, in which the direction of the narrative is governed by memory's subjective associations.

which is entirely unannounced—is signaled not by any conventional means, such as a dissolve or a fade accompanied by a voice-over, but by very rapid crosscutting between two views of Eduardo sitting in a subway carriage. In one he is responding in alarm to the activity of the raucous Malvinas demonstrators who have just boarded the train; in the other he is sitting passively in a quiet carriage in the film's present. The intersection of sequences here and elsewhere in the film effectively portrays psychological disorientation and the associative work of memory but also signals the imbrication of past and present in the production of memories.

During flashbacks, Eduardo consistently appears to be the same age, that of the film's present. As Maureen Turim argues with reference to *La prima Angélica* (Carlos Saura, 1974), in which the protagonist also remains identical in appearance across cuts to the past, this technique has the effect of masking the shift between flashback and present in such a manner that the audience experiences each transition with uncertainty;[7] this hesitation between past and present is paralleled by the overlapping of time within the unconscious that both Saura and D'Angiolillo seek to highlight. Turim refers to "the sense of irony and the uncanny" produced in Saura's film by the incongruous sight of an adult entering the world of childhood. In *Potestad* this is experienced with particular impact when Eduardo is dragged off to play rugby with the friends of his childhood—who evidently do not see the sixty-year-old body we see, criticizing him for his poor performance on the field—and also during Eduardo's encounter with his father, noticeably younger in appearance than his son.

While Eduardo retains his present appearance throughout the film, Ana

María is played by three different women, with no attempt to make them appear younger or older versions of each other. The youngest Ana María (Denise Dumas) is blonde and quite possibly—given the idealized and fantasy-like nature of the shower scene "flashback"—not a real person but merely the projection of Eduardo's desire. She resembles neither the dark-haired Ana María (Noemí Frenkel), with whom Eduardo brings up Adriana, nor the older, grief-stricken Ana María (Susy Evans) of the film's present. The presence of multiple Ana Marías is suggestive of the extent to which memory is contaminated by desire; that fear also becomes a filter in this way is evident in the use of the "reverse" technique, in which multiple characters are played by the same person. Thus the same waitress appears in two different cafés and the Malvinas war supporter chanting slogans on the train is also the man sitting next to Eduardo in the film's present and, yet again, the chauffeur who drives Eduardo and his associate, Colombres, at a later point in the film. Eduardo's paranoia is fed by (or produces) duplicate images of characters that effectively stalk him through the film.

By such means *Potestad* radically undermines the truth value traditionally assigned to the flashback in realist film as a motor of autobiographical explanation. Moreover, the sequence of flashbacks cannot be sorted into a consistently logical order. During the scene in which Eduardo awakes to find himself in a hospital bed, displaying the disorientation that we have learned to equate with his grief at Adriana's loss and talking about Ana María's inability to overcome hers, Adriana's godfather shows him a necklace he intends to give the little girl for her birthday. Our attention is later drawn to this necklace around Adriana's neck during the party captured on Eduardo's cine camera. A number of *Potestad*'s sequences do not logically belong entirely to the present or to identifiable moments in the past. The film's use of, and deviation from, flashback convention becomes a significant element in what I will argue is a flirtation with, but ultimately a destabilization of, the explanatory narrative of psychoanalysis.

An ambivalent use of psychoanalysis can also be detected in the film's conscious exploitation of the processes of cinematic identification. *Potestad* is constructed in the manner of a jigsaw puzzle that is gradually assembled and in which the last piece, once placed, dramatically alters our perception of the whole picture. Murray Smith's refashioning of the psychoanalytical concept of identification illuminates the devices used here to encourage the viewer to adopt a particular hypothesis before it is shattered by the film's crucial revelation. In Smith's "structure of sympathy," which attempts to combine cognitive and emotive engagement with film, "alignment" describes "the process by which spectators are placed in relation to characters in terms of access to their actions, and to what they know and feel."[8] The frequent use of a first-person voice-over expressing Eduardo's feelings of despair and fear establishes a relationship of confidentiality and complicity with the spectator. At many points his vision is literally ours, as in the many traveling shots with a camera placed at the front of a subway train or on a boat moving across the water; in wildly panning point-of-view shots that implicate us in his own sense of paranoia; in our view of Adriana at her birthday party through the lens of a handheld video camera operated by Eduardo. We watch Eduardo's growing terror and his suspicions of conspiracy with no overlaying of irony: for the major part of the film we are afforded no alternative viewpoint from which to analyze the events we witness.

For Smith "alignment" precedes "allegiance," which represents "the moral evaluation of characters by the spectator," a kind of identification that has "both cognitive and affective dimensions."[9] In *Potestad* alignment is followed quickly and uncritically by allegiance because the context of the dictatorship—and particularly, the discourse of the postdictatorship film—is a familiar one to the spectator versed in Argentine culture. Eduardo's loss and fear of reprisal encourage us to associate his experience with that of the many victims of state violence whose testimonies resonate in our ears. The discourse of the dictatorship's abuses and their legacies for the present era is present right from the film's opening sequence, in which Eduardo reflects on the experience of coming face to face with evil and torture: "Aunque yo sabía que existía la maldad, la imaginaba como una cosa más abstracta, teórica. Pero cuando uno la ve encarnada en personas que se mueven, hablan, gritan, insultan y persiguen a inocentes, la maldad se vuelve más humana, más real, y por eso más temible" (Although I knew that evil existed, I imagined it to be something more abstract, theoretical. But when you see it incarnated in people who move, speak, shout, insult, and pursue innocent people, evil becomes more human, more real, and therefore more terrifying). The misplaced bravura of the Malvinas supporters, references to Argentina's victory in the World Cup, the undiscovered mass grave with piles of human bones, and the sticker on the subway train bearing the slogan "Los argentinos somos derechos y humanos" (Argentines are just and humane) are codes that an Argentine audience would have no difficulty reading for military brutalities that, despite the success of the regime's propaganda campaigns, were eventually exposed to the world. The viewer strongly suspects, therefore, that Adriana's unexplained disappearance has something to do with the dictatorship; Eduardo's sense of persecution and estrangement from society initially suggests that he has been a victim of military repression and that his daughter may have been abducted by the armed forces.

This reading of events becomes increasingly difficult to sustain, however, as details are gradually revealed that conflict with it. Adriana is still with Eduardo and Ana María after the demise of the dictatorship; an old acquaintance accuses Eduardo of hiding a guilty secret; and, perhaps most telling of all, we see Ana María bathing a baby, who is clearly not newborn, for the first time. Many of the recurring images in the film—the fan, the toy carousel, the showerhead—properly belong to, and presage, one scene of vital importance that we see only near the end of the film. These images correspond to Freud's concept of the "screen memory": the remembering of trivial details that substitute for a memory too traumatic to retrieve. For Freud the screen memory "owes its value as a memory not to its own content but to the relations existing between that content and some other, that has been suppressed."[10] The suppressed, in this case, is revealed in a flashback in which Eduardo, as a doctor collaborating with the military regime during the dictatorship, discovers Adriana as a baby in the apartment of two young activists recently murdered by soldiers and takes her home as his own child. The appropriation by military personnel of the children of murdered dissidents was a widespread practice during the Argentine dictatorship. Doctors played an important role in the covering up of the activities of the regime, reviving victims between torture sessions, delivering babies in detention centers or prison hospitals, who were often given to childless military couples to bring up as their own, or (as in Eduardo's case) providing false death certificates.

In the light of our knowledge of the truth of Adriana's origins, we are able to reinterpret Eduardo's disorientation as not simply the product of grief but also of the displacements and repressions associated with guilt. We understand, too late for our sympathies to be wrenched away, that Eduardo's talk of the terror wreaked during the 1970s does not refer to the actions of the military but to left-wing activists. Eduardo uses the familiar language of denunciation but, as we discover later, directs his accusations toward the opposing side in the "Dirty War": "Eran tiempos de mierda. Una época violenta, irracional. Había que estar allí. Todos los días un enfrentamiento, un ataque por la espalda. Los subversivos habían trastocado todo. No era fácil enfrentar ese odio asesino. Pero hubo que hacerlo" (They were hellish times. A violent, irrational period. You had to be there. Clashes and attacks from behind every day. The subversives had disrupted everything. It wasn't easy to confront that murderous hate. But it had to be done). As the bodies of Adriana's parents are thrown unceremoniously into the back of a truck, we hear Eduardo's self-justifications in a voice-over: "Fue injusto. Le dimos tanto amor y me la quitaron. . . . Los padres de Adrianita eran fanáticos capaces de volarte la casa. Y yo la salvé" (It was unfair. We gave her so much love and she was taken away from me. . . . Adrianita's parents were fanatics capable of blowing up your house. And I saved her).

The film's rhetoric works on the basis of setting up a series of ideological and psychological symmetries. Its impact is entirely predicated on our erroneous assumption that a loving father and a doctor must belong to a different category from a murder accomplice and an abductor and that the two opposite terms could not be manifested in the same person. We cannot merely dismiss Eduardo as a monster: he is too human, too like us. D'Angiolillo insists of Eduardo that "Este personaje es parecido a nosotros . . . porque si no tenemos una pauta ética o moral o religiosa que nos dé un marco de contención y si, además, tenemos la impunidad de nuestro lado (como ocurrió con la dictadura militar) podemos convertirnos en monstruos" (This character is similar to us . . . because if we do not have a set of ethical, moral, or religious guidelines to keep us in check and if, in addition, we have impunity on our side—as happened with the military dictatorship—we can turn into monsters).[11] The theme of child abduction during the military regime had previously been explored in *La historia oficial* (Luis Puenzo, 1985), one of the first and best-known fictional explorations of the experience of dictatorship in Argentine cinema. In marked contrast to Eduardo in *Potestad*, the military father in Puenzo's film is a terrifying character, incapable of compassion, who hits his wife and is complicit in the torture and rape of her best friend.

As I have suggested, many conventions employed in *Potestad* dupe the viewer into looking for a psychoanalytical interpretation of the film's events. These conventions include, as discussed, the flashback structure of the film, the disorientation of the protagonist, his problematic relationship with his father, the predominance of first-person voice-overs, and themes of bereavement, paranoia, and—later—guilt. We understand at an early stage of the film that the flashbacks represent repressed elements that return to haunt the protagonist, and we assume the role of the analyst, discovering what the patient is trying to remember by interpreting a series of free associations. Furthermore, Eduardo's behavior appears to conform to Freud's description of "acting out" as a compulsive repetition that replaces remembering.[12] Adriana's disappearance, for example, is "acted out" three times and in different ways within the narrative of the film. On the day of her christening

Eduardo leaves her in her mother's arms momentarily and receives a present from Colombres; when he turns back, the street is empty. She also disappears from a carousel in a playground while her father is talking to an acquaintance and from the doorway of a bakery from which she is watching an antidictatorship demonstration. Eventually we discover that the circumstances of her disappearance are rather more mundane: after questioning Eduardo, Ana María, and Adriana herself, an official removes her from their care. Similar acts of displacement are associated with the scene of Adriana's kidnapping. In one of the film's most surreal scenes, Eduardo fails to save a patient who has been shot in the chest. As Eduardo attempts to extract the bullet, the patient hemorrhages and dies as a result of negligence and incompetence on the doctor's part, in another "acting out" of his repressed memory of guilt and complicity with the military regime. Two duplications link this scene with the one that takes place in the apartment of Adriana's parents: first, the limp arm of the patient hanging down from the operating table, along which a trickle of blood is flowing and forming a puddle on the floor, becomes the arm of Adriana's mother as she lies lifeless on the bed; second, Eduardo in the theater hears the words "¿En qúe mejores manos podría estar, no, doctor?" (What better hands could she be in, don't you agree, doctor?), which are later uttered to him by Colombres in the apartment when they discover the baby crying in the bath.

Yet the film ultimately insists on a political reading rather than a psychological one; psychoanalysis becomes associated instead with sinister acts of displacement in *Potestad*. Something of the significance of the film's rhetorical operations and the relationship of the psychological and the political can be grasped by comparing *Potestad* with Robert Wiene's 1920 classic of German expressionism, *The Cabinet of Dr. Caligari*. Both films contain flashbacks that prove to be delusionary in nature; both are concerned with the abuse of authority and psychic disturbance and portray a doctor complicit in serial killings; both attempt to subvert narrative linearity by means of duplication, displacement, ellipsis, and redundancy. However, since the publication in 1947 of Siegfried Kracauer's *From Caligari to Hitler*, many critics have agreed that the framing narrative of Wiene's film effectively neutralizes the film's political meaning by discrediting the version we are offered of the doctor's guilt: at the end of the film the storyteller is revealed as a psychiatric patient with paranoid delusions centered on the director of the institution to which he is confined. The presence of the frame story gives credence to a psychoanalytical reading of the film in preference to a political one. This has the effect of sanitizing the film's critique, which would otherwise, according to Kracauer, have offered an uncompromising vision of the institutionalized insanity of public life in Germany between the wars. In *Potestad* a reversal of this narrative process is discernible. Whereas Wiene's film starts with the crimes, only later suggesting their author to be a doctor, D'Angiolillo's presents us first with a doctor and then much later with his crimes, which remain largely hidden from society owing to the guarantee of moral impeccability he possesses: his white coat. In *The Cabinet of Dr. Caligari* order is eventually restored (the doctor is found not guilty of the crimes of which he is accused); in *Potestad* the ending exposes new and unbridgeable chasms in the society it portrays. It is the *political* that emerges here as a stubborn remainder, one that cannot be reduced to psychology.

Quite offensively, the film appears to suggest that postdictatorship memory operates rather like screen memory, with left-wing violence in the 1970s as the suppressed event. *Potestad* in no way excuses the exercise of large-scale institutional violence by the military regime; nor does it deny the enormity of the terror that regime wreaked. But it forces us to see the symmetries of violence at both ends of the political spectrum. If, just like his activist victims, the torturer loves his children and believes that his efforts will bring about a better society, and if both left-wing militants and the armed forces are involved in indiscriminate violence, the equation appears— at least momentarily and precariously—to be balanced. *Potestad*'s insistence on civilian complicity marks its distance from the "teoría de los dos demonios" (theory of the two demons), which has been criticized by Vezzetti and others for positing an innocent civilian society caught between two violent forces.[13] It also takes issue with another paradigmatic narrative of postdictatorship memory, referred to by Pilar Calveiro as the theory of "un único demonio" (a single demon),[14] according to which left-wing terrorism in the 1970s is whitewashed and society as a whole becomes the innocent victim of military repression. Adriana's parents, seen only in brief shots of their assassinated bodies (we are touched by their obvious youth), are not simply massacred victims, according to the image of the disappeared that has gained significant currency in the postdictatorship era, but militants whose acts played a part in the violence of the 1970s. As Calveiro reminds us,

> Los desaparecidos eran, en su inmensa mayoría, militantes. Negar esto, negarles esa condición es otra de las formas de ejercicio de la amnesia, es una manera más de desaparecerlos, ahora en sentido político. La corrección o incorrección de sus concepciones políticas es otra cuestión, pero lo cierto es que el fenómeno de los desaparecidos no es el de la masacre de

"víctimas inocentes" sino el del asesinato y el intento de desaparición y desintegración total de una forma de resistencia y oposición: la lucha armada y las concepciones populistas radicales dentro del peronismo y la izquierda.

[The disappeared were, in the vast majority, militants. To deny this, to deny them this identity is another way of practicing amnesia, another way of disappearing them, in a political sense this time. The correctness or incorrectness of their political beliefs is another question, but what is certain is that the phenomenon of the disappeared is not the massacre of "innocent victims" but the assassination and attempt to effect the disappearance and total destruction of a form of resistance and opposition: the armed struggle and radical populist convictions operating within Peronism and the left.][15]

Potestad thus challenges some of the most powerful discourses of postdictatorship memory, insisting that, as Vezzetti puts it, "el conflicto no se reduce a una oposición simple entre memoria y olvido sino más bien entre diversas 'memorias'" (the conflict does not reduce down to a simple opposition between memory and forgetting, but between different "memories").[16] When the credits roll and the lights come up, we are left with the question— largely ignored by postdictatorship memory—of how to negotiate a shared existence with the Other whose ideological convictions are not our own. It is also the question of how to remember without reinventing those same structures of alterity that produced the conditions for the original traumatic event. In *Potestad* the spectator becomes disturbingly complicit in processes of othering and prejudice through which even countermemories may adopt the monologic discourse of authoritarianism. Uneasily, we understand that our readiness to demonize the enemy has landed us in the wrong camp, and this process enables us to perceive the rather insidious, Manichean operations that lie beneath all kinds of memory, and to comprehend that historical reality is always much richer and more complex than its distillations in memory may allow us to glimpse.

Postdictatorship memory in Argentina has yet to grapple adequately with some of these issues, as has recently been emphasized by a number of theorists. Beatriz Sarlo argues that

todavía falta colocar a la dictadura militar en la perspectiva de los años que la precedieron. La dictadura fue excepcional en un sentido, el de su extremismo. Pero, en otro sentido, es un capítulo que se abre en los años setenta, antes del golpe militar. Precisamente será necesario reinterpretar los hechos e ideas hegemónicas de las últimas décadas.

[we have not yet properly placed the military dictatorship in the context of the years that preceded it. The dictatorship was exceptional in one sense, in its extremism. But in another sense, it is a chapter that begins in the 1970s, before the military coup. It will be necessary to reinterpret the events and the hegemonic ideas of the last few decades.][17]

Héctor Schmucler reminds us of the violence and the divisions that characterized predictatorship Argentina: "El 23 de marzo de 1976 [the eve of the coup] la palabra 'aniquilamiento' no era ajena al vocabulario corriente. . . . En medio del estrépito no se oyó el gemido de la desmesura" (On March 23, 1976, the word "annihilation" was not unknown in the common lexicon. . . . In the midst of the racket the cry of excess could not be heard). He argues that "deberíamos arriesgarnos a reconocer las condiciones que propiciaron el golpe de estado de 1976 y a registrar que fue bienvenido por gran parte de la población" (we should face up to the conditions that brought about the coup d'état of 1976 and admit that it was welcomed by a large proportion of the population).[18] Similarly, Hugo Vezzetti claims that, while the brutality of the dictatorship was unprecedented in Argentine history and therefore to some extent represents "una irrupción" (an irruption), it was also "un desenlace, a partir de una larga crisis política, incluso de una guerra civil larvada" (a climax, resulting from a lengthy political crisis, and even a latent civil war). Reflecting on the twenty-fifth anniversary of the coup, commemorated on March 24, 2001, Vezzetti claims that public debate in Argentina concerning that period of its history is "sumamente limitado y casi estereotipado" (extremely limited and almost stereotyped), and he calls for important work to be carried out in order to construct "una *memoria de las memorias*" (a *memory of memories*): to analyze the way in which memory's narrative operations stylize and simplify representations of the past.[19] *Potestad* representa a serious attempt to reopen space for public debate in this manner, to problematize stereotyped representations of the past and to place the crimes of the dictatorship in the context of the militarist ideological conflicts of the 1970s.

Perhaps most importantly in relation to this new imperative, *Potestad* leads us to understand that the memory of a nation divided cannot be other than a space of conflict. As briefly outlined above, recent debates have called for a new heterogeneity and greater sophistication in postdictatorship memory; this greater appreciation of difference should balance the obligation to rebuild a sense of national unity around collective memory. Some form of collective memory is, as Schmucler reminds us, essential to the concept of nation; this remains a difficult task in contemporary Argentina, which must accept that "pueden reconocerse diversas memorias" (different memories exist) and that "el 'clima de la época' pesa de manera distinta en cada una de ellos" (the "climate of the times" weighs differently on each of them).[20] Such differences should not, according to Oscar Terán, be buried in the name of constructing collective memory. Referring to the particular rupture in history and identity represented by the disappearance of persons and the appropriation of babies during the dictatorship, he argues against "el intento por embalsamar los hechos del pasado para construir un panteón reconciliado" (the attempt to embalm the events of the past in order to build a pantheon of reconciliation),[21] suggesting that without an active, intellectual, and moral recuperation of the past ("un revivir" [a reliving]), "los sujetos se sumen en la anomia, en el relativismo perezoso, en el nihilismo, que es el espejo del flujo veloz, incesante y sin sentido de las mercancías en el ámbito del mercado" (subjects join the forces of anomie, lazy relativism, and nihilism, which is the corollary of the rapid, incessant, and meaningless flow of goods in the market).[22]

The argument I have advanced for the revisionist character of *Potestad*, based on its manipulation of cinematic convention, has broader implications for our understanding of the role of the spectator in constructing meaning in film. Just as *Potestad* suggests a certain analytical framework (psychoanalysis) only to destabilize it, an examination of the ways in which the spectator is positioned by the film—or positions him- or herself in relation to it—leads us away from psychoanalytical models of spectatorship. If psychoanalytic film theory places the spectator in the position of analyst examining the dream-text of the film, *Potestad* shows us what poor analysts we are and how much we are governed by prejudice and misplaced empathy. Any illusion of dominance over the world afforded by the all-seeing, all-knowing cinematic perspective is destroyed: our perception of both the film's events and the real events to which it refers is thoroughly undermined.

We cannot dismiss such failure as a simple misreading. There exists no possible "ideal" spectator for *Potestad*: the film is not constructed in such a way that might allow even the most astute spectator to glimpse the full truth from the beginning or even by the end of a first viewing. In the narrative structure of the film, the memory or flashback frequently precedes the context or original event that would enable us to understand what we are seeing or what causes such alarm in Eduardo. Several shots of Adriana walking in a crowd, hand-in-hand with an adult, are inserted into the film before Adriana appears in such a way that she can be identified as Eduardo's daughter. Similarly, shots of Adriana's murdered parents and of one of the soldiers at their apartment are introduced into the narrative before we are able to understand these characters' significance to the film's plot. Nor is it possible to imagine an ideal spectator without knowledge of the film's social context who might, therefore, be able to avoid an erroneous interpretation based on familiarity with postdictatorship discourse: my own informal research suggests that such viewers are unable to construct any early hypotheses about the narrative and are therefore likely to experience the film's shifting time frames as disorientating in the extreme and meaningless.

The spectator of *Potestad* is not the passive object of Lacanian-Althusserian suture or interpellation but rather an active participant in constructing the text, aided and constrained in his or her interpretation not so much by unconscious processes as by his or her extrafilmic knowledge and experience. *Potestad* reminds us that meanings are produced by complex relationships between spectator, film, and sociocultural context, and exploring the spectator's response to this film becomes a more productive exercise if it is carried out with recourse to cognitive approaches to understanding how spectators make sense of films. If—as David Bordwell argues—viewers approach the task of making hypotheses with already established interpretative "schemata," or "organized clusters of knowledge," the viewer's relationship with the film implies a series of *preconscious*, rather than *unconscious*, operations.[23] Bordwell does not deny the "usefulness" of psychoanalytic theories of spectatorship but considers that film theory has often privileged subconscious explanations where the work of the conscious and preconscious has greater relevance. Indeed, he points out that "study of narrative cognition may in fact be a prelude to psychoanalytic inquiry for the same reason that Freud was at pains to show that psychoanalytic theory finds its best application when cognitive explanations fall short."[24] This emphasis on the conscious and the preconscious makes all the difference in political terms: if the operations of ideology and memory take place in these spheres of the mind, then there exists the potential for these to be opened up as spaces for contest, resistance, and negotiation. Such are the political implications of the rather more flexible theories of film spectatorship arising from cognitive analysis and cultural studies, both of which assume a greater degree of exchange between subjectivity and cultural representations. As Bordwell argues, psychoanalytic film theory provides "no satisfactory account of how social actors could criticize and resist ideology," there being "no room for 'agency' in a framework in which ideological representations so thoroughly determined subjectivity."[25] To the cognitivists' rather universalist examination of the abstract processes of constructing stories, Robert Stam would wish to add "a notion of a social vantage point, of spectatorial *investments* in representation, notions of ideological grids and cultural narcissisms that reflect the social channeling of emotional engagement."[26] *Potestad* insists in this way on the historically, socially, and culturally conditioned nature of spectatorship, drawing attention toward the politics of location in the construction of meaning in film and away from what Stephen Prince has termed the "missing" spectator of psychoanalytic theory and the abstract, positionless spectator of cognitive theory.[27]

The crucial impact of *Potestad* is to transform us, as spectators, into the object of our own gaze to the extent that we recognize our inability to read the film correctly not as an intellectual failing but as a "memory mistake." *Potestad*'s interrogations into spectatorship are intimately associated with its contribution to postdictatorship memory. Like all representations, memory betrays its object, obliterating reality while preserving it; the condensations, associations, and displacements of memory are mirrored in the construction and interpretation of film. Ultimately, it would appear, we want our memories to give us the same narrative pleasure as our films: to make our heroes heroic and our villains the embodiment of pure evil, to establish clear relationships of causality, and to tie all the ends together neatly. In opposition to such falsifications *Potestad* emerges as a truly countercultural film, joining its voice with those who recognize the difficulty of remembering differently and who are beginning to call for a greater heterogeneity, divergence, and opposition within postdictatorship memory.

LOS RUBIOS AND THE POLITICS OF TESTIMONY

If the significance of *Potestad* has hardly been registered in cultural debates on memory, that of *Los rubios* (Albertina Carri, 2003) has been exhaustively mined. The film is an experimental and often ludic reflection on the loss of the director's parents, Roberto Carri and Ana María Caruso, left-wing militants who were tortured and disappeared in 1977 when Albertina was just three years old. It combines interviews with family members, friends, and neighbors with "making of" sequences showing rehearsals and the activities of the technical crew; these two main narrative strands are punctuated on occasion by a third, in which small, plastic Playmobil figures, filmed in stop-motion animation, are depicted *en famille* at home or in the garden. Although critics have attempted to compass the film's self-referential complexities by using terms such as "un meta-documental" (a meta-documentary),[28] "una *road movie* sobre el cine" (a road movie about cinema),[29] and even "un *reality show* sobre la memoria" (a reality show about memory),[30] it would be more accurate to describe the film as a reflexive or performative documentary in line with the definition provided by Stella Bruzzi, for whom the use of performance within a nonfiction context "draw[s] attention to the impossibilities of authentic documentary representation," being "an alienating, distancing device, not one which actively promotes identification and a straightforward response to the film's content."[31] Carri's choice of this mode of filmmaking is startling: both political urgency and autobiographical investment might have dictated a more realist framework.

The film has provoked vehement debate, with detractors complaining about the frivolity of its tone and the intensely personal nature of its approach, which, it is argued, depoliticizes the violence of the 1970s. For Martín Kohan the film is "un juego de poses y un ensayo de levedad" (a game of poses and an essay in frivolity);[32] for Sarlo it is "un ejemplo casi demasiado pleno de la fuerte subjetividad de la posmemoria" (an almost-too-good example of the strong subjectivity of postmemory), given its deliberate exclusion of the public and the political in a very personal account of loss that makes no effort to understand the motives of the disappeared militant parents.[33] Cecilia Macón, mounting a defense, accuses Kohan of trying to dictate "cómo debe recordar" (how we should remember).[34] Carri's status as one of the children of the disappeared might seem to guarantee the legitimacy of her work as testimony, based on blood ties and firsthand experience. The ensuing debates have challenged that legitimacy, not by negating her experience but by contextualizing her work and—paradoxically—by decontextualizing it: by embedding its approach within a broader turn toward the subjective in contemporary culture and, at the same time, by differentiating Carri's text from those of other *hijos* (children of the disappeared).[35] Sarlo's response in *Tiempo pasado* is not to police the ideological purity of memory but to read *Los rubios* as fully governed by "este espíritu [subjetivo] de época" (the [subjective] spirit of this age),[36] through the prism of which the motives and actions of the previous generation become obscured. Intrinsic to these debates is the question of how collective memory is generated and particularly the role of individual testimony in shaping collective memory. Carri's critics evidently appreciate the performative nature of memory, which *creates* a state of affairs rather than merely describing them. Hence the anxiety that her film has occasioned: what is at stake is nothing less than the past, always occluded and unveiled in different ways according to the exigencies of the present.

I would argue, however, that Carri's film does not simply participate in this "espíritu de época" but, through its reflexivity, makes a significant contribution itself to the understanding of how collective memory is constructed. The text of *Los rubios* already presents the relationship between individual and collective memory as problematic and signals its own divergence from other accounts. Its principal concern is the fictions that memory creates in order to paper over the gaps of history, and its experiments with film form reveal an acute awareness of how visual rhetoric may be employed to produce a sense of veracity and coherence that is at odds with a properly historical perspective on the past. *Los rubios* exposes the complicity of film— whether documentary or fiction—in providing illusions of coherence, of closure, and even of experience, stitching the spectator into a narrative that produces easy emotional identification but ultimately results in political complacency. Through a series of self-reflexive devices the film disrupts identification, refusing to indulge in catharsis and mourning simply the impossibility of mourning, the absence of history and of experience, and the effect of these absences on identity and agency in the present.

Carri's exploration of the relationship between individual and collective memory allows a series of fissures and contaminations to emerge. As I will show, these are also signaled in the film's subversion of cinematic conventions. Relationships between individual and collective, private and public, past and present become problematic in *Los rubios*, subjected to unwanted transgressions across the frontiers that separate them or, alternatively, separated by unbridgeable divides. Carri emphasizes the mediated quality of memory and the difficulty of distinguishing individual recollection from collective memory. With every step that is intended to take her closer to the truth, she feels farther from it, unable to distinguish between her own personal memories and those of her sisters: "lo único que tengo es mi recuerdo difuso, contaminado por todas estas versiones" (the only thing I have is a vague memory, contaminated by all these versions). Collective memory becomes a constraining framework for individual recollection, which survives—as Maurice Halbwachs has argued—only "to the extent that it is connected with the thoughts that come to us from the social milieu."[37] These mediations are not exclusively part of a second generation's relationship with a past trauma that they have not directly experienced. Indeed, Sarlo questions Marianne Hirsch's elaboration of a theory of "postmemory" (often cited in critical work on *Los rubios*)[38] to account for a "temporal and qualitative difference from survivor memory, its secondary or second-generation memory quality, its basis in displacement, its belatedness,"[39] arguing that "*toda experiencia del pasado es vicaria*" (*every experience of the past is vicarious*) and that all constructions of the past are saturated by the mediatized images of contemporary society.[40] In fact, *Los rubios* moves beyond an association of mediation with second-generation experience, claiming that the memories of her parents' contemporaries are equally marked by the ideology of their time. Family members remember "de una manera en que mamá y papá se convierten en dos seres excepcionales, lindos, inteligentes" (in such a way that Mum and Dad turn into two exceptional, beautiful, intelligent beings)— constructing them as worthy bearers of their tragic/epic destiny—and contemporaries structure their remembrances in such a way that "todo se convierte en un análisis político" (everything turns into political analysis).

All memory in *Los rubios* is subject to intrusions and derailments. The screening of the film's "real" material is persistently disrupted. With very few exceptions all material in the film that represents or reflects on the past is viewed in the stubborn presence of the film crew and its equipment; our access to many of the interviews is limited to scenes in which Analía, in the foreground, edits film notes on a laptop and replays recordings of interviews on a television screen placed firmly in the background, sometimes even obscured by her own body (Figure 22). We are rarely given a direct, frontal shot of the interviewees, which according to cinematic convention would tend to ascribe truth value to the testimony given. Instead, what we are shown is partial, fragmented, and displaced, often with a disjunction between the soundtrack, containing testimony material, and the visual track, which focuses on Analía moving around the studio. The progress of Albertina's investigation, carried out in the film's present, is reported rather than filmed live or directly reenacted. The abduction of Carri's parents is enacted in a ludic displacement, by the jerky hovering of a model spaceship over two Playmobil figures, who are seized from their car seats and disappear from sight (Figure 23). All historical knowledge in the film is secondhand, provisional, fragmentary. Analía redraws on a piece of paper a sketch of the cells drawn by a survivor of "El Sheraton," nickname of the detention center where the parents were held, which had been shown to Albertina during an interview. The resulting sketch we see, as Analía presents "mi recuerdo de lo que ella dibujó en su recuerdo" (my memory of what she drew from memory) is a representation three times removed and a series of meaningless boxes that tells us nothing about the cells or of life inside them.

22. The documentary material of *Los rubios* is displaced, fragmented, or mediated: here recorded interviews are relegated to the background while in the foreground the actress playing Albertina makes notes and reflects on the difficulty of making *Los rubios*.

23. *Los rubios* often approaches the disappearance of Carri's parents in a playful manner, mediated through the imagination of a child: in one of the film's stop-motion animation sequences, a toy spaceship abducts two Playmobil figures.

Whereas the narrative of Albertina's investigation, containing interviews with family members, friends, and neighbors, and including a visit to the detention center where her parents were tortured, is for the most part shot in color and on 16-mm film, the scenes showing rehearsals and the activity of the technical crew are often in black-and-white video; however, the blurring of these distinctions, which are not always respected, serves to demonstrate the contamination of narrative by metanarrative or the encroachment of collective memory on the individual. Carri's film reveals in this way the fragility of memory: false; vulnerable; porous to ideology, nostalgia, and desire; and overlaid with official memory and the recollections of others.

In the context of Holocaust memory, Dominick LaCapra reminds us that "with respect to trauma, memory is always secondary since what occurs is not integrated into experience or directly remembered, and the event must be reconstructed from its effects and traces. In this sense there is no fully immediate access to the experience itself even for the original witness, much less for the secondary witness and historian."[41] *Los rubios*'s lack of narrative coherence remains faithful to the gaps and absences that arise from traumatic experience. The film's rigor lies in its refusal to spin us a tale or to position its director as a privileged witness. In this way it attempts to counter the operations of collective memory, which, as Vezzetti argues, "simplifica y tiende a ver los acontecimientos desde una perspectiva única que rechaza la ambigüedad y hasta reduce los acontecimientos a arquetipos fijados" (simplifies and tends to see events from a single perspective that rejects ambiguity and even reduces events to fixed archetypes).[42] Carri's conscious interruption of processes of cinematic identification, together with the film's multiplication of possible perspectives, can be read as an effort to disrupt the process by which events or the memories of individuals are assimilated and simplified in collective memory. The sequences set in the country, where Albertina and her sisters spent their childhood after the disappearance of their parents, present a catalogue of possible camera movements and montage effects: rapidly alternating jump cuts, 360-degree pans, and tracking shots of a figure spliced together to create the illusion of multiple "doubles." By exposing the tools of the trade and insisting on the materiality of film, these scenes (which have no clear meaning in narrative terms) inhibit emotional engagement with the film's story, continually bringing the viewer back to that place of reflection in the present. Such is also the effect generated by sequences focusing on the camera crew: these often consist of a series of stills, literally cutting up the forward progression of the narrative and suggesting a kind of stasis, a place of reflection and thought outside the narrative time of the film.

Cinematic identification is deliberately disrupted by the film's doubling (and tripling) devices. The intervention of the filmmaker in a documentary invariably signals the constructed nature of documentary representation by drawing attention to the presence of the "objective" witness and his or her interaction with the subject(s) of the film. But here *Los rubios* moves a step beyond many other performative documentaries, holding up a further mirror to distort and refract the relationship between director and performer. Carri's intervention is both as filmmaker and as the protagonist of her own documentary, yet her presence in the film is further supplemented and refracted by the introduction of an actress, Analía Couceyro, who introduces herself near the beginning of the film and explains clearly, in front of the camera, that she will be playing the part of Albertina. At least three Albertinas emerge, therefore, in the text of the film: the "real" Albertina, the subject of the film who initiates a search to discover more about her disappeared parents; Albertina the director, who appears as herself, shooting and editing the results of that investigation; and Analía-Albertina, the actress. The repetition of the actress's lines, the inclusion of Carri's direction during rehearsals, and the visible apparatus of filmmaking (Figure 24) consistently detract from the emotive value of what is recounted onscreen. Analía does not attempt to portray emotion or experience with any realism: even the scene in which she howls, wordlessly, alone in the woods, appears forced and rehearsed, a mere representation of emotional pain into which the spectator is not drawn.

24. The visible apparatus of filmmaking and the repetition of takes shatter any simple emotional identification with the protagonist of *Los rubios*.

At the heart of all representation in *Los rubios* is an absence that presents an insurmountable obstacle to representation. Carri states that the film's utter failure to reveal anything of any significance about her parents represents a conscious refusal to indulge the expectations of the viewer. We cannot come to "know" her parents through the film because, simply and crucially, *they are not there*:

> Quería impedir que los diversos elementos como los testimonios, las fotos y las cartas dejen esa sensación tranquilizadora, ese ya está, conozco a Roberto y a Ana María y me voy a mi casa. Lo que yo planteo es precisamente que no los vamos a conocer, que no hay reconstrucción posible. Son inaprehensibles porque no están.

> [I wanted to make sure that the various elements like the testimonies, the photos, and the letters didn't provide that reassuring feeling of "that's it, I've gotten to know Roberto and Ana María and now I'm going home." What I am suggesting is precisely that we can't get to know them, that there is no possible reconstruction. They are inaccessible because they aren't there.][43]

Los rubios presents absence and loss as irreducible experiences that may not be eased through the process of "making a film about it"; nor are they experiences that may be generated through cinematic identification for the benefit of the spectator seeking a cathartic experience or some kind of illusory closure to a troubled past. The film's refusal to "tell a story" is an essential element of its resistance to what Carri terms "la memoria de supermercado" (supermarket memory).[44] Unlike conventional documentaries, Carri's refuses to supply in the viewer the "sense of plenitude or self-sufficiency" that Bill Nichols identifies as the result of knowledge conferred on him or her ("a source of pleasure that is far from innocent").[45]

In many ways, then, Carri's film attempts to carve out a space for individual memory that is not immediately caught up in the simplifying, self-sufficient narratives of collective memory. It often eschews the privileged position accorded to the testimonial voice. This move can only be, of course, a rhetorical one, and much suggests that the film has been received precisely as the testimony of a primary witness whose legitimacy cannot therefore be questioned. Gonzalo Aguilar cites a response made to the film in the Facultad de Ciencias Sociales: "si la directora no se llamara Carri de apellido, a esa película ya le hubiéramos hecho un escrache" (if the director hadn't had the surname Carri, we'd have organized a public shaming of that film).[46] The bloodline that links Carri to her parents has provided at least some level of immunity to criticism. Elizabeth Jelin cautions, however:

> Existe el peligro . . . de anclar la legitimidad de quienes expresan la VERDAD en una visión esencializadora de la biología y del cuerpo. El sufrimiento personal (especialmente cuando se vivió en "carne" propia o a partir de vínculos de parentesco sanguíneo) puede llegar a convertirse para muchos en el determinante básico de la legitimidad y de la verdad. Paradójicamente, si la legitimidad social para expresar la memoria colectiva es socialmente asignada a aquellos que tuvieron una experiencia personal de sufrimiento corporal, esta autoridad simbólica puede fácilmente deslizarse (consciente o inconsciente/mente) a un reclamo monopólico del sentido y del contenido de la memoria y de la verdad.

> [There is a danger . . . in anchoring the authority of those who express the TRUTH in an essentializing vision of biology and the body. Suffering experienced personally—especially when experienced in one's own flesh or that of blood-relations—can become for many the determining factor with respect to authority and truth. Paradoxically, if the social authority to express collective memory is assigned to those who experienced bodily suffering, this symbolic authority can easily slide—consciously or unconsciously—into monopolies over meaning and over the content of memory and truth.][47]

Los rubios represents an effort to deconstruct that "autoridad simbólica" and to challenge existing monopolies of meaning. In one scene Analía and Albertina visit the Centro de Antropología Forense and have blood samples taken. Far from reinforcing a sense of biological continuity, however, the analysis of Albertina's DNA (Analía's blood is also taken, in strict accordance with the film's displacements of narratorial identity) points to the absurdity and the inevitable failure of such quests for identity, as there are no parental records with which her own might be compared. While, as Ana Amado notes, the visual texts of children of the disappeared attempt in a variety of ways to "recuperar lazos entre lo que es y lo que fue" (reestablish links between what one is and what one was)[48] and consistently underline "el carácter decisivo de la filiación biológica . . . como germen de la identidad personal" (the decisive factor of biological connection . . . as the core of personal identity),[49] Carri prefers to emphasize the absence of those links. Rather than claiming authority on the basis of blood-ties, *Los rubios* does what it can to insist on the rupture of the family line.

Carri's work, which nevertheless remains imbued with the power that attends autobiography, has provoked metadiscursive questions concerning the critical analysis of testimony. Sarlo observes: "La confianza en los testimonios de las víctimas es necesaria para la instalación de regímenes democráticos y el arraigo de un principio de reparación y justicia" (Confidence in the testimonies of victims is necessary for the institution of democratic regimes and the establishing of a principle of reparation and justice).[50] However, those testimonial discourses can, and should, be subjected to critical examination *as discourses*: "no deberían quedar encerrados en una cristalización inabordable" (they should not remain locked in an incontestable crystallization).[51] Sarlo's critique of the discourse of *Los rubios* laments the suppression of the political identities of Carri's parents. As is well known, this objection is explicitly countered within the text of the film itself, as the letter rejecting Carri's application for financial support from the INCAA is read and discussed by the film crew in front of the cameras. The writer of the letter describes Carri's project as "valioso" (worthy) but considers that "pide ser revisado con un mayor rigor documental" (it needs to be revised with greater documentary rigor) in order to do justice to the lives of her disappeared parents. Carri's intention in making the film was not, she claims, primarily to tell her family's history but to offer a very different perspective on the dictatorship period:

Nunca me sentí representada por las voces anteriores. Me parece que se ha tocado el tema de forma historicista o con demasiada vehemencia. Mi sensación es que nadie ha metido la mano en ese agujero negro que es la ausencia. Por lo general, las películas que han hecho sobre el tema surgen desde lo público (los desaparecidos, los jóvenes de la generación de los 70, la lucha, etcétera) para llegar a veces a una cosa íntima o más privada como el relato de una abuela o una madre. Yo quise hacer el camino opuesto.

[I never felt represented by those other voices. It seemed to me that they dealt with the issue in a historicist way or with too much vehemence. My feeling is that no one has reached deep into that black hole that is absence. Mostly, the films made on this theme start from public and political issues (the disappeared, the youth of the '70s, the struggle, etc.) and occasionally move toward something more intimate or private like the story of a grandmother or a mother. I wanted to do it the other way around.][52]

Recent work on postdictatorship memory in Argentina has called for a reemphasis on the subjectivity and agency of the militants, which have frequently been obscured by their casting as victims in testimonial discourses that seek to establish the regime's guilt.[53] Although we—and Carri—learn very little about her parents during the course of *Los rubios*, and it is clear that their militancy remains largely unexplored, it would be an error to assume that Carri's text does not therefore contribute to this particular task of memory. Although it remains suspicious of all attempts to reconstruct past identity, it does suggest another, more intimate, dimension to the subjectivity of the militants, a dimension that has become obscured by the political function of memory. If, as Sarlo argues, the political lives of Carri's parents disappear from view, it is equally true that the private individual, the parent, has become lost in the emphasis on the public significance of their death. Personal, intimate loss becomes difficult to articulate under the weight of the discourses that overlay the bodies of the militants. Moreover, Carri's parents emerge in the film as subjects who were the agents of their own demise, making deliberate choices, however difficult these are to comprehend. "Me cuesta entender la elección de mamá," recites Analía: "¿Por qué no se fue del país? me pregunto una y otra vez" (I find it difficult to understand Mum's decision. Why didn't she leave the country? I ask myself again and again). A similar sentiment is voiced by María Inés Roqué, the daughter of another disappeared militant, in her film *Papá Iván* (2003): "Digo mi nombre y me ven como la hija del héroe. A mí, que siempre dije que prefería tener un padre vivo antes que un héroe muerto" (When I say my name, people see me as the daughter of a hero. Me, who always said that I would have preferred a live father to a dead hero). These intensely personal expressions of loss do not depoliticize the disappeared but bear witness to the omissions and the

falsities created by memory itself and the work of excavation always necessary to penetrate at least some of the layers of discourse that mediate historical truth, as well as present identity. They do return a form of subjectivity
and agency to their parents, who chose a life of militancy and possible death,
thereby risking the security and integrity of their families.

Carri is charged with indifference, perhaps even hostility,[54] to the political
motives of her parents' militant action. For Aguilar, the inclusion of the
interview with one of the neighbors is evidence of the director's "afán de
demostrar que la lucha de sus padres estaba errada" (eagerness to show that
her parents' struggle was misguided):[55] the unreflective, mendacious, self-
seeking representative of the "pueblo" (people) is an entirely unworthy
receptacle for the latent political consciousness and capacity for resistance
ascribed to the people by the intellectual militants of the 1970s. In a sense
the question that arises here is whether the militants' actions should be
judged according to their own understanding of the value of such action or
with the hindsight of our knowledge of the failure of their efforts to bring
about societal change. A historical perspective would favor the first; Carri,
however, cannot but weigh up her parents' sacrifice with the personal impact of their absence. What child could truly accept abandonment of this
kind? Are the testimonies of those children who do explore the political
commitment of their militant parents genuinely more objective, or have
they found solace in constructing a political significance for the absurdity
and the pain of lives cut short? Carri's testimony may not have the objectivity
of history, but it reminds us, as nothing else could, of the persistent psychological legacies of the political violence of the 1970s, and the complex ethical
questions raised by shifting conceptions of the relationship between the
personal and the political.

At the heart of the debate over *Los rubios*, and particularly of Sarlo's
intervention, is a growing sense of the chasm that separates the contemporary generation's configuration (actual or imagined) of the relationship between the personal and the political from that of the previous generation,
and the obstacles that chasm presents for understanding the past. While we
should always be alert to the anachronisms produced by viewing the past
from the present, there is a specific sense in which a contemporary perspective might uncover important questions about the militancy of the 1970s,
which would otherwise lie undetected under the rhetoric of the era. Aguilar
contends that, far from being a depoliticizing technique, the film's use of
the child's perspective is a strategic one that

hace una de las críticas políticas más contundentes de la militancia de los años setenta: la que sostiene que al politizar todas las esferas de la vida social la militancia termina por poner en riesgo ámbitos que deberían quedar a resguardo. Hasta el epígrafe del libro del padre (*Isidro Velázquez* de Roberto Carri) que lee Couceyro habla de la desaparición del "ego-ismo" y el "interés privado" en favor de una "voluntad general," tema rousseauniano que adquiere otros matices cuando se considera desde el punto de vista de aquellos (los niños) que no forman parte de esa volun-tad. Al comprometer toda su vida con la militancia política, arrastraron a sus hijos, que no estaban en condiciones de elegir ni de comprender ese compromiso.

[produces one of the most resounding political critiques of the 1970s: one which sustains that by politicizing all spheres of social life, the mili-tary put at risk spheres that should have been protected. Even the epi-graph of the father's book—*Isidro Velázquez*, by Roberto Carri—which Couceyro reads, speaks of the disappearance of "egoism" and "private interest" in favor of a "general will," a Rousseauist idea that takes on other nuances when considered from the perspective of those (the chil-dren) who did not form part of that will. By committing the whole of their lives to political militancy, they dragged along their children, who were neither in a position to choose nor to understand that commitment.][56]

This critique of the militants' wholesale subsumption of private and fam-ily spheres within the political, disregarding their children's wishes in the quest for a "greater good," is a political one, but it is one that is, of course, most effectively mounted from the private and the individual. To revere the militants' political commitment without critically examining their actions in the light of the texts that informed their thinking—the study of which, Sarlo suggests, would provide an important historical corrective to the contempo-rary emphasis on memory[57]—is to commit the same historical error of which *Los rubios* is accused. More important, it is to ignore the considerable shaping power of a seductive contemporary discourse: a utopian construc-tion of the 1960s and 1970s that expresses nostalgia for a moment at which the personal and the political seemed, unlike now, to converge in the actions of "disinterested" activists prepared to sacrifice their lives for the greater good. For *whose* good, and in *whose* interest?—doubts Carri. If for this per-spective alone, her project should not be understood as antithetical to the kind of historicization of memory proposed by Sarlo and others but as an important contribution to the questioning of memory's lapses into rigid paradigms that impede a properly historical perspective. If it is certainly the case, as Sarlo claims, that the discourse of human rights is an anachronistic filter through which to view the events of the 1970s,[58] it is also true that our perspective on militant violence in the 1970s is colored by a contemporary nostalgia for an all-consuming political commitment that, it is imagined, remains untouched by the egotism and individualism of today's society. Deconstructing that particular myth, as *Los rubios* begins to do, is surely an important corrective to some of the erasures produced by acts of memory in postdictatorship Argentina.

7

THE POLITICS
OF PRIVATE SPACE

Growing social segregation in Buenos Aires receives perhaps its most telling expression in the absence of films dealing with class conflict. Subiela's
films of the 1980s and 1990s had often revolved around an encounter
between representatives of two different social classes, usually for the benefit of the middle-class characters, whose contact with the "earthiness" of life
at the city's margins restored a vitality they had lost and provided the inspiration they were seeking.[1] Such encounters are extremely rare in more recent
films, which portray a city increasingly divided along class lines. As Beatriz
Sarlo notes, the rise in crime, which has accompanied large-scale unemployment, has sent citizens back into their own homes to defend their
property; this has resulted in a significant reduction in mobility around the
city. With travel for leisure purposes reduced, citizens are "condenados al
aislamiento en viviendas donde el equipamiento cultural es mínimo" (condemned to confinement in homes with minimal access to culture); with
cultural impoverishment also comes greater social segregation: "también se
achican las posibilidades de contacto con otros niveles y consumos sociales"
(also reduced are the possibilities of contact with other social classes).[2] The
confined spaces of many contemporary films bear witness to this segregation. In Ezequiel Acuña's *Nadar solo* (2003), for example, the majority of the
action takes place within two or three blocks of the protagonist's home in
the wealthy Recoleta district. The film's insistence on precise addresses
marks a deliberate retreat into the knowable and the familiar for the direc-

tor and for middle-class Buenos Aires audiences.³ Other films, such as *El cumple* (Gustavo Postiglione, 2002) and *Ana y los otros* (Celina Murga, 2003), enact a similar return or retrenchment in their portrayal of the closed middle-class circles of a professional thirty-something-year-old's birthday party and a high school reunion.⁴

If the working classes become the protagonists of films by Adrián Caetano, Pablo Trapero, and Lisandro Alonso, the "othering" gaze constructed in these texts can be argued to articulate class difference. Another series of films, dealing exclusively with the middle classes, represent a turning-in to the private and domestic space of the family. Albertina Carri's exploration of incest in *Géminis* (2005) can be read as an allegory of such a movement. In the context of ever-greater divisions between rich and poor and the visible increase in fortifications protecting the private property of the rich, Carri's film explores what happens when the enemy is discovered within rather than without. The threat of scandal is always present in the film's bourgeois household but always imagined to take place beyond its boundaries. When her maid's daughter falls pregnant again, Lucía (baselessly) suspects the father, explaining to her new Spanish daughter-in-law, "Acá, en las clases bajas, eso es muy común, ¿sabés?" (Here, among the lower classes, that is very common, you know?). The discovery of incest in her own family is sufficient to drive Lucía to insanity. Carri's film delivers a stinging critique of a bourgeois obsession with image and the maintenance of a veneer of respectability. The film's self-conscious stylization underscores its central concern with artificiality: the insistent use of mirror reflections, duplicating and even triplicating their subjects, symbolizes duplicity and artifice. The repeated opening and shutting of doors also draws attention to what is seen and unseen, publicly known or remaining private, suggestive also of the desperate policing of boundaries between outside and inside, acceptable and taboo.

Such concerns are also central to the work of Lucrecia Martel, which focuses squarely on the middle-class family and also hints (with much greater delicacy) at the possibility of incest. While her films perform a retreat into bourgeois domestic spheres, I will argue that they do so in order to explore the boundaries between the public and the private and to suggest new ways of understanding the political significance of contemporary Argentine films, often erroneously labeled apolitical in their eschewal of explicit representations of class conflict or their refusal to organize their narratives around an identifiable program for social or economic change.

Contrasted with the radical politics and aesthetics of 1960s filmmaking in Latin America, with the didacticism of early postdictatorship cinema in Argentina, or even with the raw immediacy of contemporary documentary production associated with *cine piquetero*, the minimalist, intimate styles of contemporary fiction film can appear wholly resistant to political analysis. I will argue, however, that this retreat into private spaces does not primarily reflect a shying away from politics but is symptomatic of certain shifts *within* politics that demand a revision of the critical categories we use when discussing political cinema. My discussion will focus on two films directed by Martel, one of the key figures in the recent renaissance of Argentine cinema. In *La ciénaga* (2001) and *La niña santa* (2004) a reflexive staging of the breakdown of allegory suggests a broader collapse of distinctions between public and private spheres in contemporary society. This collapse can be theorized with reference to European thinkers such as Hannah Arendt and Giorgio Agamben, but it also pertains to certain experiences and perceptions proper to the Argentine Crisis.

Allegory was frequently the chosen form of Argentina's renowned auteurs of the 1980s and early 1990s, such as Eliseo Subiela, María Luisa Bemberg, and Fernando Solanas. Allegory—from the Greek, *allos*, "other," and *agoreuein*, "to speak in public"—figuratively unites two orders, one of which is shown and the other of which is kept out of view, establishing relationships of resemblance between them such that the reader or spectator may construe meaning over and above the literal. Allegory stages the relationship between personal and political, private and public, which is often central to the production of political meaning in art. If allegory was indispensable to artistic production under the censorship of the military regime, it has also been extensively used as a representational tool in the postdictatorship era. The violence of Argentina's most recent dictatorship has been treated allegorically with reference to repression in a psychiatric institution (*Hombre mirando al sudeste*, Subiela, 1986) or to the brutal excesses of Manuel Rosas's nineteenth-century regime (*Camila*, Bemberg, 1984); in a more ludic vein, the image of a city flooded with sewage has evoked the submerging of the nation under neocolonialist demands in Menemist Argentina (*El viaje*, Solanas, 1990).[5] In more recent cinema, however, little room is left for allegory between the dominant mode of naturalism, heavily influenced by the documentary tradition, and the more experimental styles of other filmmakers whose projects vigorously resist the imposition of any fixed meaning.

The problematic status of Martel's films as allegories is immediately obvious from early critical reviews. *La ciénaga* and *La niña santa* are intimate, minimalist explorations of family life in a northwestern province of Argentina. One of the questions that continues to tax critics is the extent to which we can interpret the indolence and parochialism of the middle-class families depicted, together with the suggestion of incest, as symbolic of a broader social decline in Argentina. Luciano Monteagudo, for example, states clearly that "no hay nada simbólico en *La ciénaga*" (there is nothing symbolic in *La ciénaga*), but he immediately goes on to find parallels between Mecha's drunken fall in the opening scene of the film and the collapse of the middle class in Argentina.[6] Martel herself at times rejects the symbolic interpretation of incest and claims not to be offering any kind of reflection on Argentine reality, but at other times she locates her own work squarely within an Argentine tradition of political filmmaking and specifically encourages political readings of *La ciénaga* as a post-1960s or a post-dictatorship film.[7] Although she professes a fear that the title of the film will give rise to symbolic interpretations, "que estaba muy lejos de mí" (which were far from my intentions),[8] on other occasions she uses the image of the swamp to explain the impulse behind her work and the difficulty of emerging from the collective experience of Argentina's recent history.[9] These inconsistencies reflect, of course, the inevitably complex relationships among a film's director, its critics, and its public. However, they are ultimately generated, as I will propose, by ambiguities embedded in the films themselves.

The films suggest symbolic readings while refusing to ground potential tropes within a defined frame of reference. The foreboding presence of nature in *La ciénaga*—oppressive heat, overcast skies, the frequent rumble of thunder—invites us to read the mundane activities of the film's characters within a mythical context. Images of entropy in nature seem to parallel a kind of social disintegration or moral degradation that marks the lives of the two families. The eponymous swamp is a source of fascination for the children, who watch a cow become mired in its mud and return later to find its stinking corpse attracting flies. Everything in the film tends inexorably toward inertia, stagnation, and disorder. Even the name of the ranch, La Mandrágora, suggests the numb stupor in which its residents stumble through life, given the mandrake plant's traditional use as a sedative. Such references encourage us to understand the film to signify beyond its literal content and to read the vicissitudes of the two families depicted as symbolic of a wider social decline. In the case of *La niña santa* an allegorical framework is also suggested by the decision to shoot the film in the famous Hotel Termas, which was built at the end of the nineteenth century as a retreat for Argentina's elite and foreign dignitaries. In Martel's film few traces of the hotel's original glamour are visible: the place is in a state of disrepair, with flaking paint and plumbing problems. The hotel metonymically represents, therefore, the sharp decline of Argentina from the turn of the century, when it took its place among the richest countries of the world, to the economic ruin of the film's present. As in *La ciénaga*, the world of *La niña santa* turns on those fragile appearances that keep chaos just at bay. The fear of contamination or catastrophe mobilizes the few remaining energies of the provincial middle class: scalps are treated to kill lice, hotel rooms are subjected to the vigorous application of air fresheners, Amalia is told not to cry "porque te llena los ojos de microbios" (because it fills your eyes with microbes), and Josefina looks for a way to preserve her virginal purity, respecting the letter of the law if nothing of its spirit.

Neither film provides sufficient grounding, however, for a fully allegorical interpretation that would allow us to read it straightforwardly as a political or social commentary. The camera, like its subjects, moves lethargically and myopically through a few chosen locations; the claustrophobia of these settings and the banality of the characters' lives do not permit any allusion to political events beyond the frame of the camera. In fact, I would argue that allegorical readings are deliberately disrupted through a series of devices that draw attention to the fracturing of relationships of reference between the literal and the symbolic, the material and the transcendent, and the private and the public, and that these disruptions provide a key to a political reading of Martel's films.

Most of these rupturing devices are associated with minimalist cinema, which often features open-ended narratives, a pseudodocumentary approach to camerawork, and the use of nonprofessional actors. The absence of a linear narrative in *La ciénaga* both impairs its ability to function allegorically and, paradoxically, encourages us to look for symbolic meaning to make up for a deficit of literal meaning. At the service of uncompromising naturalism the film replaces a conventional plot with a series of disjunctures in cause-and-effect relationships. Establishing shots are rarely used, conventional transitions between scenes are often omitted, and dialogue is not a motor for plot advancement. Montage techniques emphasize instead the unresolved, the truncated, and the elliptical. A child aims a rifle at the head of a cow stuck in a swamp, and Luchi is in the line of fire; we hear a shot, but a cut has already been made to a long shot of the hills. The action shifts immediately to an interior, where Mecha and Tali are discussing stationery and uniforms for the beginning of the school year. The cut is typically introduced at a crucial moment, and the narrative simply continues with no further reference to the danger alluded to. Characters who appear to be at risk of death, or at the very least serious disfigurement, simply turn up in the background in later scenes, as if nothing had happened. For us, as viewers, the experience of such narrative fragmentation is often disorientating: we are left uncertain about what is significant and what is not. The anxiety produced by the concealment of information is not later alleviated by revelation.

Martel explains that what she calls a "loosening" of the plot represents a deliberate attempt to reproduce in the viewer the same feelings of abandonment and disorientation experienced by her characters.[10] Events extraneous or tangential to the story routinely punctuate Martel's narratives, occasionally suggestive of the absurd, such as the sudden appearance in *La niña santa* of a naked neighbor who has inexplicably fallen from his balcony and appears to be unharmed. The banal and the irrational always threaten to destroy the last remaining illusions of stability, order, and meaning. The ominous threat of death or disfigurement hangs over *La ciénaga*: underage children drive cars, handle loaded rifles, horse around with machetes, and play at holding their breath under water while their parents are interested only in getting drunk on cheap wine and trying to keep cool in the summer heat. When tragedy does strike at the end of the film, it comes in the form of an accident, simple and meaningless. In both films we are ultimately denied narrative satisfaction in the form of closure. *La ciénaga* ends abruptly with a series of shots of the empty house—poignant images of stasis and silence—after the unwitnessed fall of Luchi, the youngest child, but before the discovery of his probable death. Likewise, *La niña santa* closes with a long take of Amalia and Josefina, floating serenely in the pool, oblivious to the devastation that will be wreaked, only a few feet away, by the public disclosure of sexual scandal.

Allegorical readings of the film are also disrupted by the extreme naturalism of dialogue and acting and the sheer materiality of its bodies. The suspense of a linear narrative is replaced by an intense sensuality, an eroticism that builds with every look or brush of skin between the characters. These are bodies that seem too robustly visceral to carry an abstract message. In any case Martel's vision is not a moralizing one: the theme of incest, for example, is carefully voided of denunciation.

The moral ambiguity of Martel's films rests largely on their challenge to depictions of childhood as a state of innocence. Her work shares a number of affinities here with that of the mid-twentieth-century Argentine writer Silvina Ocampo, whose short stories debunk myths of childhood as an idyllic time, drawing attention instead to the many fears, anxieties, and disappointments that characterize the child's experience of the world. In particular, Ocampo's focus on the subterranean power struggles between parents, children, and servants finds an echo in the daily frictions and repressions of Martel's films. Martel's documentary on Silvina Ocampo, *Las dependencias* (screened on Argentine television in 1999), makes much of the writer's predilection for the servants' quarters of the mansion in which she was brought up, as expressed in the poem "La casa natal":

> Yo huía de las salas, de la gran escalera,
> del comedor severo con oro en la dulcera,
> del mueble, de los cuadros, de orgullosas presencias
> porque a mí me gustaban sólo las dependencias
> que estaban destinadas para la servidumbre.

> [I fled from the salons, the great staircase,
> from the stern dining room with gold on the jampot,
> from the furniture, the paintings, the proud presences
> because I only liked the quarters
> that were assigned to the servants.][11]

In *La ciénaga*, likewise, the children form alliances and share intimacies with the servants in a reaction against the bourgeois formality of social conduct. In a broadly feminist vein both Ocampo and Martel portray the domestic sphere as a sinister environment rather than a safe haven. In *La ciénaga* and *La niña santa* the home is a place of disturbing passions, abuse, and neglect, where children suffer accidents, servants are victims of racial abuse, and adults parade their bitterness and contempt for each other in front of watching children. As in Ocampo's fiction, however, Martel's children are never simply innocent victims of abuse but often enter into complicit relationships, fueled by their desire to explore new sensations and even attain a degree of subversive power over adults. The ambiguity of her films militates against the moral clarity most often associated with socially committed cinema.

We are left, then, with texts in which much is potentially allegorical but nothing actually is. How can we locate the political in relation to these films? Would it not be a critical imposition to do so? While these texts are too unstable to be read as allegories, they do demonstrate a self-reflexive concern with questions of perception, meaning, and interpretation, which, as I will argue, address precisely the anxiety arising from critical readings.

Perception, and particularly its distortion, becomes a significant theme in both films, in which the children carry out a series of experiments with sound and vision. Luchi peers at the patio through the refracting Perspex of a set square; the youngest girls in *La ciénaga* recite lines into an electric fan that fragments the sound of their voices, lending it an automatized quality; in *La niña santa* Josefina and Amalia discover how their eyes readjust to vision after being pressed shut. Martel repeatedly brings questions of perception to the fore by insisting on the failure or the excess of vision, sound, or touch. What is seen or not seen? In *La ciénaga* one of the children has lost an eye in an accident, a local girl has been rocketed to stardom because of her vision of the Virgin (a sighting no one else is able to confirm), and Luchi's fall to almost certain death at the end of the film is not seen by anyone. In *La niña santa* the emphasis is more on what is heard or not heard. Inaudible or imagined calls (the call of God) are answered, while audible calls (from one character to another, or phone calls) often go unheard or unanswered. In general, characters see, hear, or touch more—or less—than they should. In one of the scenes in which Dr. Jano touches Amalia sexually, both are listening to the ethereal music of a theremin played in the street, producing notes by creating sound waves that are modified simply by the movement of a hand through the air. Dr. Jano's touching of Amalia in the crowd has its counterpart in the *absence* of touch, represented by the playing of the theremin. Dr. Vesalio, also present, reinforces the contrast between touching and not touching: "no toca nada, nada" (he's touching nothing, nothing at all), he exclaims, with reference to the theremin player and with unwitting irony, as Dr. Jano flees with embarrassment from the scene.

If sound is accorded meticulous attention in both films—Martel replaces the music that might feature on the soundtrack of a more conventional film with an extensive range of sound effects, all strictly diegetic—in *La niña santa* it also takes on thematic significance. In this film the particular symbolism acquired by sound and hearing is signaled in the insistent placing of the ear in the center of the frame, displacing the face or the back of the head to one side. Some examples may be seen in Figure 25, although the reproduction of stills does not capture how deliberately the camera moves in several of these cases to position the ear in the center of the frame and pauses to draw attention to the symbolism of these unnatural framings. The

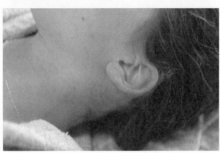

25. The camera often moves deliberately in *La niña santa* to frame an ear, drawing attention to the importance of sound and hearing in the film, as part of its broader exploration of perception and interpretation.

conference Dr. Jano is attending at the hotel is a gathering of ear specialists, and its closing ceremony will stage a "real" consultation between a doctor and a patient with hearing difficulties. As Dr. Vesalio explains with enthusiasm, "Es lo de siempre: ¿cómo interpretar correctamente lo que el paciente nos quiere decir?" (It's the same old question: how to interpret correctly what the patient wants to tell us). Indeed, the concern voiced by many of the film's characters—whether they are searching for a vocation, aiming for professional improvement, or negotiating complex emotions—is how to interpret correctly, or how to read symptoms. Our attention is continually drawn to what is misheard and misunderstood. What Amalia hears—and misinterprets—about the call of God and the nature of salvation at the Catholic group she attends ironically fans into flame her growing fascination with Dr. Jano. When Dr. Jano goes to confess all to Amalia's mother, Helena misreads his patent confusion as a sign of passion, silencing him in an ardent embrace. Helena is chosen to participate in the staged consultation because of her ear and hearing difficulties; under test conditions, she repeats wrongly words that have been read to her. In the rising tension of the last couple of days of the conference, both Dr. Jano and Helena mishear and misunderstand as Freddy's voice reaches them distorted by their own emotions and obsessions. As spectators we are also drawn to wrong interpretations. When we hear, for example, that there has been an incident in the hotel between a doctor and a girl, we initially assume (incorrectly) that the reference is to the one we have witnessed ourselves. In both films the dramatic climax is presaged more than once before it actually occurs. We become aware of our propensity to jump to conclusions, to scan signs for hidden meanings, and to read for narrative fulfillment.

Thus Martel's films can be seen to allude, not to an external set of referents but self-reflexively to the process of interpretation itself. Allegory marks a gap between representation and referent, the essential otherness of two planes of signification that is precisely the quality that permits them to be aligned in the production of meaning. Reflexivity, on the other hand, enacts a conflation of the two and a collapse of possible distinctions between them. This pattern of relationship between the literal and symbolic is repeated in *La niña santa* in the relationship between the profane and the sacred, another set of distinctions that traditional allegories have relied on, often drawing as they did on biblical typologies.

Martel problematizes distinctions between the profane and the sacred, or the material and the spiritual, as the girls in *La niña santa* try to relate the religious instruction they receive to their own experience, struggling to separate body from soul and unite them again in a coherent view of the world. The simple faith the girls are taught is found inadequate for the purposes of negotiating a path through the moral ambiguities they encounter every day. One girl, confused by references to the call of God, wonders how she might distinguish this voice from that of the Devil. For the untroubled Inés, leader of the Catholic girls' group, these are childish "tonterías" (foolish remarks): "No creo que alguien pueda confundirse algo feo con algo lindo, algo que te llena de felicidad con algo horripilante, ¿no?" (I don't believe that anyone can confuse something ugly with something beautiful, something which fills you with happiness with something terrifying). Martel, however, is interested precisely in those areas of experience that are difficult to define as either "feo" (ugly) or "lindo" (beautiful): the disquieting discoveries of sexual awakening, an experience at once so mystical and so mundane. To pursue the parallels suggested earlier between Martel and Ocampo, a similar dynamic can be seen at work in "El pecado mortal," Ocampo's subtle story of child abuse. As the narrator reflects, the little girl invited to watch her male minder through the keyhole mimics the stance of Pyramus and Thisbe whispering their love through a wall, and thus "lo horrible imita lo hermoso" (the horrible imitates the beautiful) with chilling accuracy.[12]

Martel asks us to consider parallels between spiritual experience and sexual awakening and to appreciate the human dignity evident in the girls' various attempts—comic, desperate, naive, or dangerous—to harmonize and integrate everything they are discovering about body and soul. Inés teaches the girls that their calling is to identify their vocation and to save others. As she explains that "todos los medios son buenos en las manos de Dios para llamarnos" (all means are good if they are used by God to call us), we see Amalia receive confirmation from these words of her divine mission to pursue Dr. Jano. Her anarchic and profane misinterpretations of the nature of salvation and vocation threaten the sacred authority of Inés's words, hybridizing them and creating subversive meanings unprogrammed by the Church. The lovesick Amalia, in the best tradition of young romantic heroines, is struck down with a fever. As Martel explains, "la fiebre se relaciona con el deseo y el éxtasis religioso, es el cuerpo caliente" (fever is related to desire and to religious ecstasy, it is the hot body),[13] becoming another means of demonstrating the convergence of spirituality and carnal desire. In Ocampo's words, from the opening of "El pecado mortal," "Los símbolos de la pureza y del misticismo son a veces más afrodisíacos que las fotografías o que los cuentos pornográficos" (The symbols of purity and mysticism sometimes make better aphrodisiacs than photographs or pornographic stories).[14]

In the fragility of a world marked by "el desamparo divino" (divine neglect), Martel suggests, "el cuerpo es la única certeza que uno tiene" (the body is the only certainty we have).[15] Her emphasis on the material conveys a sense of a scandalous divine neglect—hence perhaps the abundance of cuts and illnesses in her films as her characters are left to fend for themselves in a hostile environment—or simply the absence of any transcendent meaning. For Paul Smith allegory always exhibits a "nostalgia for a plenitude and security of reference, for 'truth' as a stay against the individual's alienation from himself and from the world."[16] Martel's insufficient, incomplete allegories reveal a similar nostalgia for that absent "plenitude and security," but they bear witness, also, to the impossibility of returning to such plenitude. In many ways *La niña santa* can be read as a film about a lost faith, an aspect of her own personal experience to which Martel often refers in public and that she herself suggests to be the impetus behind *La ciénaga*.[17] Her characters are tragically cut loose from anything that might lend transcendence to the petty selfishness of their existence. The alienation of her characters is traced with a particular anguish: here is no straightforwardly postmodern celebration of individual liberation at the collapse of traditional bastions of authority and morality.

This crisis of religion as a signifying structure that could lend a degree of protection against the banality and futility of individual lives reflects a more general collapse of distinctions in these films between the private and the public. Emphasis in both films is placed on lived, bodily experience: the touching of other bodies, sensations of heat and pain, the body's immersion in water (a repeated motif in both films), fever, infection, and parasites. Action in *La ciénaga* is largely reduced to the private household, to bedrooms and bathrooms, as the most intimate of spaces. Both films evoke the insularity, the inertia, the secret fears and pleasures of private life. These intimate cinematic worlds, like those of many of Martel's contemporaries, would appear to suggest a withdrawal from political signification, expressing cynicism in respect of art's capacity to interact with the political and testifying to the collapse of collective identities and utopian discourses. However, the anxiety evident in Martel's work in relation to the boundaries between the private and the public suggests a more nuanced reading. The conscious conflations noted above—between the private and the public, the literal and the symbolic, the material and the spiritual—indicate that Martel's intimate, private films do not simply perform a withdrawal from that which transcends the individual; they register a crisis in the very structures of signification that embed the individual and the private within the general and the public. They stage a collapse of distinctions between public and private spheres on which more conventional political filmmaking has been predicated.

This collapse has been explored in different ways by Hannah Arendt, Michel Foucault, and Giorgio Agamben, among others. A brief discussion here of their theoretical insights will lay the foundation for a more historicized reading of Martel's films. For Arendt the conflation of public and private realms is contemporaneous with the rise of the nation-state and the modern idea of society: "with the rise of society, that is, the rise of the 'household' (oikia) or of economic activities to the public realm, housekeeping and all matters pertaining formerly to the private sphere of the family have become a 'collective' concern." Classical politics, by contrast, had maintained sharp distinctions between biological life and political life. Politics in the classical world was a higher calling: Aristotle's "good life" referred to that which was not simply bound up with survival and "biological life" (the private realm of the household). It was these distinctions, the gap between political life and biological life, that allowed for the possibility of transcendence and protection against what Arendt calls "the futility of individual life." Indeed, Arendt notes a parallel between the opportunities offered for public life by early Greek and Roman forms of citizenship and those of the Catholic Church, which acted as a substitute after the fall of the Roman Empire: both granted a form of transcendence through the maintenance of sharp distinctions between private and public life and the insertion of individual life into a "higher" order of signification.[18]

Agamben, who reads Arendt in conjunction with Foucault's biopolitics, makes particular reference to Europe's experience of Nazi repression to demonstrate the extent to which "bare life" and political life have entered "a zone of irreducible indistinction":

> Every attempt to rethink the political space of the West must begin with the clear awareness that we no longer know anything of the classical distinction between zoç and bios, between private life and political existence, between man as a simple living being at home in the house and man's political existence in the city. . . .
>
> There is no return from the camps to classical politics. In the camps, city and house became indistinguishable, and the possibility of differentiating between our biological body and our political body—between what is incommunicable and mute and what is communicable and sayable— was taken from us forever.[19]

Given Argentina's own, even more recent, experience of the mass murder of civilians under dictatorship, it is unsurprising, perhaps, that Argentine cinema should testify to a similar collapse of distinctions. But in the more recent context of the Crisis, its retreat into private spheres acquires further possible meanings, many of which can be linked to the power of the state over biological life, but a power that is expressed to most devastating effect in weakness: the state's inability to uphold its part in the social contract. Fredric Jameson reminds us that it was the structural opposition between public and private spheres that made possible the existence of a specialized "political" literature about public life and that both of these categories have been "decisively modified, if not transformed beyond all recognition, by the enlargement of the social totality or operative context out into the uniquely distended proportions of the new world system of late capitalism."[20] The banking crisis of 2001 in Argentina demonstrated the extent to which what Arendt calls "housekeeping" has now become a global, not even a national, concern, dissolving even further the boundaries between private and public; it revealed the inability of the state to provide a space for public action that was not entirely taken up with the business of survival. It also demonstrated its failure to protect citizens against the very consequences of financial ruin to which it had exposed them through neoliberal policies. Cinema's retreat into the private sphere may in this respect be read as a critical intervention, signaling the failure of a bankrupt, dysfunctional state and emphasizing the primacy of biological life in times of severe economic crisis. This retreat implies a refusal of political significance that becomes, by virtue of its context only, a profoundly political gesture. Both reflexivity and minimalism in Martel's work can be read as aesthetic responses to the same phenomenon, a folding-in of structures of signification associated with the merging of public and private spheres and the erosion of a distinct space for meaningful political action.

As it charts the breakdown of the relationship between state and nation, Argentine cinema carves out a particular role for itself in mobilizing a national imaginary in the effective absence of the state. As Zygmunt Bauman writes, "The centuries-long romance of nation with state is drawing to an end; not so much a divorce as a 'living together' arrangement is replacing the consecrated marital togetherness grounded in unconditional loyalty."[21] In Argentina, even this more flexible arrangement has come under severe strain, given the state's amorous affair with foreign creditors and its shirking of responsibilities at home. Arendt notes the importance of art in transforming individual lives into politicized lives, lending them a more solid existence through being seen and heard: "Compared with the reality which comes from being seen and heard, even the greatest forces of intimate life—the passions of the heart, the thoughts of the mind, the delights of the senses—lead an uncertain, shadowy kind of existence unless and until they are transformed, deprivatized and deindividualized, as it were, into a shape to fit them for public appearance. The most current of such transformations occurs in storytelling and generally in artistic transposition of individual experiences."[22] If politics took on this role of lending transcendence to private lives in the classical world, cinema arguably performs at least some of these functions in our own, making individual lives visible by deprivatizing them, protecting in some measure against the futility of individual life. Cinema's partial supplanting of the role of the state becomes a distinctly ambivalent activity, however, particularly in relation to this emphasis on the private sphere. If, as Agamben argues, "bare life" becomes "both subject and object of the conflicts of the political order, the one place for both the organization of State power and emancipation from it,"[23] we can expect the space created by contemporary cinema to be shot through with contradictions: complicit with the rise of mass society, with its erosion of boundaries between private and political spheres, yet providing an important space for its critique.

CONCLUSION

Fredric Jameson's claim that "all third-world texts are necessarily . . . *national allegories*" has perhaps been unjustly discredited over the years for its generalizations about the "Third World," objections properly anticipated by Jameson himself.[1] No theory can take exhaustive account of difference. A more interesting challenge, and one directly relevant to the Argentine case, lies in Aijaz Ahmad's observation that Jameson's Third World appears to be suspended outside the First World system of capitalism.[2] This allows Jameson to contrast "the radical split between the private and the public"[3] that—according to him—characterizes capitalism, with the inseparability of these two spheres in the Third World text. There is much to suggest, however, that Argentina's experience of Third World status is articulated precisely in relation to the capitalist system. Indeed, it is surely the case that the experience of most Third World nations is very much defined by their position as dependent within a global system of capitalism and unequal trade. Furthermore, and curiously, Jameson's argument concerning the public and the private appears oddly unfitting in the context of Argentina's experience of neoliberalism since the 1990s, which has been most intent on *eroding* the boundaries between the private and the public by subsuming politics into economics.

This process is clearly delineated by Maristella Svampa, who traces the increasing loss of autonomy of politics with regard to economics in Menemist Argentina, as neoliberal reform was made to appear the only possible choice, arising from economic necessity rather than a political decision.[4] For

Hannah Arendt, as we saw in chapter 7, the conflation of the public and the private in the modern nation-state is linked to the primacy of economics (or biological life) within the political sphere. While Jameson's contrast between the public and the private is mapped onto a distinction between the social and the psychological, "Marx and Freud," rather than the political and the economic per se, it becomes clear that his model of the relationship between the public and private in the Third World is less adequate in this case than that which emerges through a reading of Arendt in the light of recent Argentine sociological thought (such as that of Svampa). The inseparability of the public and the private that Jameson nostalgically attributes to a kind of originary, precapitalist (or at least noncapitalist), Third World experience—the nostalgia is abundantly clear in his reflections on the "political intellectual" in Cuba, no longer a figure in First World culture[5]— becomes in Argentina a burden imposed by neoliberalism and not the glimpse of utopia Jameson is looking for.

In part due to the contradictions that arise from Argentina's position both within the First World and the Third (poverty levels would place it in the latter category, but urban development and industrialization in the former), and from the experience of global capitalism at the periphery, the relationship between individual experience and collective experience that emerges in contemporary Argentine cinema is far from the straightforwardly allegorical one Jameson depicts. The films studied in this book do not allow us to develop simple political readings in which the individual "stands for" the collective or the nation. However, by staging the disappearance of the political, and by commenting (explicitly or through formal means) on their own position as cultural texts and commodities within a global market, these films do present possibilities for political readings, but ones that would be more properly regarded as reflexive than allegorical.

The vision that emerges in fiction film is overwhelmingly negative with regard to the possibility of subverting market control or of reestablishing collective identity or collective action. This is all the more remarkable given that it has fallen to documentary film to account for emergence of new social movements in the wake of the Crisis: the *asambleas barriales*, the *piqueteros*, and the *fábricas tomadas* that have been well publicized as examples of grassroots organization and collectivization in post-Crisis Argentina. Instead, fiction film reflects what Svampa, following Robert Castel, terms the "inédito proceso de 'descolectivización' de vastos sectores sociales" (the unprecedented process of "decollectivization" of vast social sectors), referring to "la pérdida de los soportes colectivos que configuraban la identidad del sujeto (sobre todo referidos al mundo del trabajo y la política)" (the loss of the collective scaffolding that shaped the identity of the subject [particularly in relation to the world of work and politics]), which resulted from the dramatic social transformations of the 1990s.[6] If fiction film has focused to a much greater extent on the atomization of the social and the erosion of the public sphere, it is perhaps because of its insertion (in comparison to documentary video production) in a higher-cost, more competitive global market. It can also be argued that fiction film—again consonant with its longer "shelf life"—has focused on the much deeper social and economic problems that have characterized the 1990s and the early years of the twenty-first century, rather than the comparatively short-lived examples of collectivization that appeared in the aftermath of the Crisis; as Svampa notes, "cuatro años después de que la Argentina se transformara en un novedoso laboratorio de movimientos sociales, parece haber una escasa traducción político-institucional de esos procesos de autoorganización" (four years since Argentina was transformed into a laboratory for experimentation with social movements, there seem to have been few political repercussions of those processes of self-organization), with most becoming reembedded in private or institutional spheres of action.[7]

While attesting to the subsumption of both politics and culture into neoliberal economics, fiction film does succeed, marginally, in reestablishing a limited public sphere. It does so by staging in its very form the struggle between art and its market, thereby creating and fomenting public debate on the proper role of the state in relation to national culture and denaturalizing the discourse of globalization. It is here that the significant continuity between contemporary productions and the films of older directors Solanas and Subiela (contesting the subjection of independent art to "rational" market forces) becomes evident. Contemporary films rarely address the issue explicitly within their own discourse, in the manner of *La nube* or *No te mueras sin decirme adónde vas*, tending instead toward interventions of much greater reflexive subtlety, as exemplified in films by Lisandro Alonso or Martín Rejtman; they can also be seen to enter the public sphere decisively in a metadiscursive sense, and this will be the focus of my concluding remarks below.

The public debate over the question of a national film culture returns economic decisions over trade protection for the film industry to their properly political sphere and takes on—as might be expected—a strongly nationalist tone. Jorge Coscia, in his capacity as president of the Instituto Nacional de Cine y Artes Audiovisuales, makes the case for "la excepción

cultural"—the protection of the culture industry, and particularly the cinematic industry—claiming, "Lo que está en juego es mucho más que el éxito
o fracaso de una industria y sus empresas. Naciones enteras se juegan en
este debate su 'lugar en el mundo' o la definitiva exclusión" (What is at stake
is much more than the success or failure of an industry and its companies.
Whole nations are gambling their "place in the world"—or a definitive
exclusion from it—on this debate).[8] His rhetoric does not seem as excessive
if we observe that cinema was the only national industry that did not see a
reduction in activity during the aftermath of the Crisis in 2002.[9] The following extract from a speech by Néstor Kirchner (then president of Argentina)
reveals the extent to which cinema has become an important stage on which
Argentina's national identity, and its relationship with the capitalist First
World, is being played out, in a material, economic sense as well as in a
discursive or imaginary one:

> Es evidente hoy que las naciones grandes tienen un cine grande y tras-
> cendente. La historia demuestra también que la cinematografía muchas
> veces ha sido en el siglo XX y en este siglo XXI clave esencial de esa
> grandeza; mucha se expresa en el potencial del país que la impulsa y la
> genera, como Estados Unidos, Inglaterra o Francia, pero es imposible
> olvidar el papel que esas cinematografías han ocupado y ocupan en el
> afianzamiento de los proyectos de crecimiento e identidad de esos países.
> Es evidente entonces que las naciones también devienen grandes en la
> medida del cine que han hecho.

> [It is clear today that great nations have a great and transcendent cinema.
> History also shows that the cinematography of the twentieth and twenty-
> first centuries has often been a key to that greatness; much is expressed
> about the power of countries that drive and create such cinema, such as
> the United States, England, or France, but it is impossible to forget the
> role that those cinemas have played, and continue to play, in the financ-
> ing of those projects of national growth and identity. It is clear, therefore,
> that the greatness of nations is commensurate with the greatness of their
> cinema.][10]

Kirchner's rhetoric is telling. Contemporary Argentine cinema would find a
much closer affinity with the new cinemas of other developing nations, such
as Iran or Brazil: there are significant thematic and formal convergences to
be noted here in their preference for neorealist techniques, the rise of documentary filmmaking, and the use of documentary styles within fiction film,

and their adherence to nonindustrial modes of production. That the discourses surrounding cinema in contemporary Argentina persist in defining national film in relation to Hollywood or European styles and industries reveals the extent to which the success of national cinema is directly related to Argentina's First World aspirations. This is explicitly the case in Kirchner's comparisons above. If contemporary cinema has been intent on narrating the collapse of the nation-state, therefore, it is paradoxically also part of its reconstruction.

Such extratextual discourses obviously result in the overdetermination of the films they refer to: those partial, often unassuming, minimalist texts that shy away from the task of speaking for the nation. The task of criticism, as suggested in the introduction, becomes a difficult one of trying to negotiate between "intrinsic" and "extrinsic" meanings: between what the films seem to be "saying" (if anything) and the meanings they acquire as a result of their position within a global culture industry. However they may shrug off the burden of "representing the nation" within their diegesis, or through stylistic choices, these films become overdetermined by virtue of the inescapably public, and global, nature of cinema. The critic may well wish to point out the errors of constructing simplistic, nationalist discourses on the rather shaky ground provided by these films, in which such discourses are often undermined. However, it is also the case that the "meaning" of these films cannot be reconstructed in isolation from their position within the market and that the complexity of their interactions with their political and economic contexts comes to light through a kind of criticism that attempts to hold the "intrinsic" and "extrinsic" meanings of film in tension.

In presenting these arguments, I am not exclusively interested in analytical accuracy. In the context of contemporary, neoliberal Argentina, emphasizing the public significations of ostensibly private films responds to two imperatives. The first is the hermeneutical importance of reading these films within their context, in which the relationship between the public and the private is a beleaguered and contradictory one. The second imperative is the growing political urgency of insisting on the public (which still, in many cases, means the national) sphere in the context of the erosion of the state under globalization. Zygmunt Bauman, meditating on "the plight of critical theory in the society of individuals," concludes that "the table, so to speak, has been turned: the task of critical theory has been reversed. The task used to be the defence of private autonomy from the advancing troops of the 'public sphere,' smarting under the oppressive rule of the omnipotent impersonal state and its many bureaucratic tentacles or their smaller-scale replicas. The task is now to defend the vanishing public realm."[11] The aim of this study has been to uncover some of the many ways in which contemporary Argentine films, together with the cultural and political debates they have provoked, have often worked to denaturalize the discourses and practices of neoliberal capitalism and thereby to support the activity of a public sphere, encouraging critical reflection on the role of culture in a global age that remains marked by inequalities in transnational exchange.

NOTES

INTRODUCTION

1 Data compiled from www.cinenacional.com (accessed June 13, 2008).

2 Llach, "A Depression in Perspective," 40.

3 Klein, "Stumbling on the Verge of the Abyss," 5.

4 Batlle, "De la virtual extinción a la nueva ley," 19–20.

5 Quintín, "De una generación a otra," 114.

6 Xavier, "Allegories of Underdevelopment," 18 (quoted in Johnson, "Brazilian Cinema Novo," 103).

7 Law 24.377 for the "Fomento y Regulación de la Actividad Cinematográfica Nacional" provided for a significant increase in funding available for national films, achieved partly through a 10 percent tax on video rentals and sales and on other taxes relating to the broadcasting of films on television and cable channels. Like previous legislation, it also provided for a screening quota, under which exhibitors were obliged to screen one Argentine film for every six foreign films. As Diego Batlle notes, however, this stipulation was not always enforced. See Batlle, "De la virtual extinción a la nueva ley," 19.

8 Batlle, "De la virtual extinción a la nueva ley," 25.

9 Wolf, "Las estéticas del nuevo cine argentino," 29.

10 Aguilar, Otros mundos, 215–19.

11 See Moguillansky and Ré, "Nueva crítica, nuevo cine," for a detailed exploration of the symbiosis between filmmakers and critics in this period.

12 Jameson, Signatures of the Visible, 144.

13 Deleuze, Cinema 2, 75.

14 Grimson, "La experiencia argentina y sus fantasmas," 187–88; Svampa, El dilema argentino, 387.

15 See Svampa, *La sociedad excluyente*, 95–96.
16 Baud, foreword to Fiorucci and Klein, *The Argentine Crisis at the Turn of the Millennium*, xi.
17 Svampa, *La sociedad excluyente*, 296.
18 Statistics reveal the extent of the gap between the richest and poorest in Argentina: in 1974 the family income of the richest 10 percent in Gran Buenos Aires was 12.7 times that of the poorest 10 percent; by 2001 it was almost 52 times greater. In 1991, 16 percent of homes were below the poverty line; in 2002 this figure surpassed 54 percent. See Svampa, *La sociedad excluyente*, 294.
19 Massey, *Space, Place and Gender*, 154–55.
20 Jameson, *Signatures of the Visible*, 22.

1. NATION, STATE, AND FILMMAKING IN CONTEMPORARY ARGENTINA

1 Hart, *A Companion to Latin American Film*, 13–14.
2 King, "Cinema in Latin America," 304.
3 Hart, *A Companion to Latin American Film*, 13 (quoting Pérez Soler, "Pup Fiction," *Sight and Sound*, May 2001, 29).
4 Sarlo, *Escenas de la vida posmoderna*, 167.
5 Getino, *Cine y televisión en América Latina*, 72.
6 Coscia, "Cuota de pantalla, un paso esencial," 22.
7 Stock, "Migrancy and the Latin American Cinemascape," 19–20.
8 Newman, "National Cinema after Globalization," 244.
9 D'Lugo, "Authorship, Globalization, and the New Identity of Latin American Cinema," 103.
10 King, *Magical Reels*, 265.
11 Chanan, "Latin American Cinema in the 90s," n.p.
12 Data compiled from www.cinenacional.com (accessed June 13, 2008).
13 Batlle, "De la virtual extinción a la nueva ley," 17, 27.
14 Perelman and Seivach, *La industria cinematográfica en la Argentina*, 130.
15 Resolution 2016/2004 was prompted by the alarming figures for the first six months of 2004, in which North American films captured 90 percent of all ticket sales, compared to just 6.5 percent for local films. See Batlle, "El año del cine," *La Nación*, July 4, 2004, Espectáculos section, www.lanacion.com.ar (accessed June 13, 2008).
16 For an overview of the impact of new legislation and the role of the state in contemporary Brazilian cinema, see Moisés, "A New Policy for Brazilian Cinema"; and Diegues, "The Cinema That Brazil Deserves."
17 See Segre, "'La *desnacionalización* de la pantalla,'" 43. Stephen Hart, who believes that this law heralds "irreversible changes in the film industry in Latin America," does not mention more recent legislation, which suggests that these changes were not, in fact, irrevocable (Hart, *A Companion to Latin American Film*, 13).

18 See Vargas, "El cine mexicano postindustrial (1990–2002)"; and Estrada, "Cine de contrastes."

19 See Estrada, "Cine de contrastes," and "Más cines y menos espectadores."

20 Johnson, "In the Belly of the Ogre," 207.

21 This is the subject of Tamara L. Falicov's *The Cinematic Tango*, which provides a very useful survey of the impact of political events and state policy on film production from the 1930s to the present day. Also of value in this respect is Finkielman, *The Film Industry in Argentina*.

22 Burton-Carvajal, "South American Cinema," 198.

23 Stock, "Migrancy and the Latin American Cinemascape," 20–21.

24 Bourdieu, *Acts of Resistance*, 94–96, 102.

25 Massey, *For Space*, 82–83.

26 Harvey, *Spaces of Hope*, 13.

27 García Canclini, "Will There Be Latin American Cinema in the Year 2000?" 247.

28 Ibid., 251–52.

29 See García Canclini, *Culturas híbridas*, 347.

30 Stock, "Migrancy and the Latin American Cinemascape," 20, 24.

31 This argument is also advanced by King, who suggests that "awareness of the culturally specific is all important and an approach that considers the pressures on *national* cinemas in a changing international order would still seem to be the best way to keep the picture in focus" (*Magical Reels*, 255).

32 King, "Cinema in Latin America," 304.

33 Smith, *Amores perros*, 87.

34 Miyoshi, " 'Globalization,' Culture, and the University," 264.

35 Sarlo, "El relativismo absoluto, o cómo el mercado y la sociología reflexionan sobre estética," 31.

36 Macdonald, "Third Cinema and the Third World," 30–31.

37 Willemen, "The Third Cinema Question," 18.

38 From 1989 to 1994 an average of fourteen national films were released each year in Argentina, compared to twice that number in the previous six-year period, 1983–88 (figures compiled from data available at www.cinenacional.com [accessed June 13, 2008]).

39 King notes that the number of cinemas in Argentina fell by 50 percent between 1967 and 1985 (*Magical Reels*, 92).

40 Batlle, "De la virtual extinción a la nueva ley," 17.

41 Adorno and Horkheimer, *Dialectic of Enlightenment*, 137.

42 Solanas (quoted in Mahieu, "Fernando Solanas," 88–89).

43 Arlt, *Los siete locos*, 122.

44 Castagna, "Un grito en la oscuridad," 5.

45 This image is a play on *derretirse*, which means both "to melt" and "to be besotted."

46 See *El amante* 47 (January 1996): 47–50.

47 Cavallari, "El exilio sin fin," 266.

48 Montes-Bradley, "All We Need Is Love," 13–15.

49 Grant, "Giving Up Ghosts," 106, 109.

50 Sarlo, *Tiempo presente*, 118–19.

51 Quintín, "El carnaval de las almas," 3.

52 Ibid.

53 Quintín, "Subiela y nosotros," 7.

54 Diego Batlle, "Eliseo Subiela," *Clarín*, August 12, 1994, Espectáculos section, www.elarin.com.

55 Quintín, "De una generación a otra," 113.

2. NEW ARGENTINE CINEMA AND THE PRODUCTION OF SOCIAL KNOWLEDGE

1 Beceyro et al., "Estética del cine, nuevos realismos, representación," 2.

2 See, e.g., Lerer, "Pablo Trapero," 62–66.

3 Bernini, "Un proyecto inconcluso," 89.

4 See Kantaris, "Visiones de la violencia en el cine urbano latinoamericano," 42; and Jameson, *The Seeds of Time*, 8.

5 Bourdieu, *Acts of Resistance*, 82 (my emphasis).

6 Ibid., 83.

7 Wolf, "Aspectos del problema del tiempo en el cine argentino," 172–76.

8 Deleuze, *Cinema 1*, 210.

9 See Rodowick, *Gilles Deleuze's Time Machine*, 12, 15.

10 Deleuze, *Cinema 1*, 211.

11 Rodowick, *Gilles Deleuze's Time Machine*, 143.

12 Deleuze, *Cinema 2*, 2–3.

13 Rodowick, *Gilles Deleuze's Time Machine*, 17.

14 Deleuze, *Cinema 2*, 3.

15 Bazin, "De Sica," 204, 203.

16 Castells, *End of Millennium*, 364.

17 Svampa, *La sociedad excluyente*, 82.

18 Sarlo, *Tiempo presente*, 114; Castells, *End of Millennium*, 162.

19 Ray, *The Avant-Garde Finds Andy Hardy*, 30, 35. For Roland Barthes's notion of a third or "obtuse" meaning see Barthes, "The Third Meaning," where Barthes proposes that

> the filmic begins only where language and metalanguage end. Everything that can be *said* about *Ivan* or *Potemkin* can be said of a written text (entitled *Ivan the Terrible* or *Battleship Potemkin*) except this, the obtuse meaning; I can gloss everything in Euphrosyne, except the obtuse quality of her face. The filmic, then, lies precisely here, in that region where articulated language is no longer more than approximative and where another language begins (whose science, therefore, cannot be linguistics, soon discarded like a booster rocket). The third meaning—theoretically locatable but not describable—can now be seen as the *passage* from language to *signifiance* and the founding act of the filmic itself. (64–65)

20 A similar sequence, again of extremely long duration, is used to close *Extraño* (Santiago Loza, 2003), with the same effect of making us aware of how little we have come to know or understand the protagonist.

21 Rangil, *Otro punto de vista*, 69.

22 Barthes, "The Third Meaning," 61.

23 Lyotard, *Heidegger and "the jews,"* 47.

24 Restivo, *The Cinema of Economic Miracles*, 35.

25 Babino, "Pablo Trapero" (interview), 25.

26 Bazin, "De Sica," 204.

27 Castagna, "Mundo panza," 4. Strangely, Castagna claims that the film "no tiene planteos estéticos de importancia ni una cámara con la cual se perciba la presencia (y la autosuficiencia) de un director" (does not advance anything of importance in aesthetic terms and does not use the camera in a way that would reveal the presence [and the self-sufficiency] of a director).

28 Diego Lerer claims, for example, that "*Mundo grúa* no es una película habitada por gente, es gente que habita una película" (*Mundo grúa* is not a film inhabited by people, but people who inhabit a film) ("Como vos y yo," *Clarín*, June 17, 1999, Espectáculos section, www.clarin.com [accessed June 13, 2008]). Likewise, Paraná Sendrós praises its realism: "Esta película es, y aquí está su mérito, lo más parecido a la vida que podamos ver en la pantalla" (This film, and herein lies its merit, is the closest to life we will see on the screen) ("Sobresale un film nacional," *Ámbito Financiero*, June 17, 1999, Espectáculos section, 4).

29 Russell, *Experimental Ethnography*, 123.

30 Clifford, "On Ethnographic Allegory," 100.

31 Hopenhayn, *Ni apocalípticos ni integrados*, 23, 26.

32 Clifford, "On Ethnographic Allegory," 98.

33 Ibid., 99.

34 Ibid., 112.

35 Russell, *Experimental Ethnography*, 123.

36 Ibid., 278.

37 See Svampa, *La sociedad excluyente*, 120–24.

38 Pratt, "Arts of the Contact Zone," 64.

3. LABOR, BODIES, AND CIRCULATION

1 Svampa, *La sociedad excluyente*, 34–35.

2 Ibid., 42.

3 Bourdieu, *Acts of Resistance*, 82.

4 Grimson, "La experiencia argentina y sus fantasmas," 181, 189.

5 Gundermann, "The Stark Gaze of the New Argentine Cinema," 244.

6 Ibid., 241.

7 Sennett, *The Corrosion of Character*, 32–39.

8 Ibid., 43.

9   Noriega, "Freddy toma soda,"15.

10 Neruda, "Sobre una poesía sin pureza," n.p.

11 Deborah Young, review of *Fantasma*, *Variety*, June 5, 2006, www.variety.com (accessed June 13, 2008).

12 Gundermann, "*La libertad* entre los escombros de la globalización," n.p.

13 Aguilar, *Otros mundos*, 77–78.

14 Although *La libertad* was screened briefly in mainstream cinemas, neither *Los muertos* nor *Fantasma* were released commercially: they were shown exclusively in the Sala Lugones.

15 Borges, *Otras inquisiciones*, 55.

16 Aguilar, *Otros mundos*, 67.

17 Aguilar observes that "El efecto documental se ve disminuido ya que la cámara, a diferencia de los documentales etnográficos o de aquellos sobre la naturaleza, no avanza con el personaje sino que lo espera de frente" (the documentary effect is diminished as the camera, unlike in ethnographic or nature documentaries, does not advance with the character but moves ahead and waits for him) (*Otros mundos*, 81).

18 Ibid., 80–81.

19 Julián Gorodischer, "No me interesa lo pretencioso," *Página 12*, September 18, 2005, Espectáculos section, www.pagina12.com.ar (accessed June 13, 2008).

20 Oubiña, "Martín Rejtman," 5–6.

21 Gorodischer, "No me interesa lo pretencioso."

22 Suárez, "Martín Rejtman," 47.

23 Unsigned interview with Martín Rejtman, "La importancia de llamarse Silvia Prieto," *Página 12*, May 23, 1999, Radar section, www.pagina12.com.ar (accessed June 13, 2008).

24 See Marx, *Capital*, 247–57.

25 Ibid., 250–51.

26 Ibid., 713, 719.

27 Ibid., 717–18.

28 Harvey, *Spaces of Hope*, 102–3.

29 Oubiña, "Martín Rejtman," 9.

30 Ibid.

31 See Bauman, *Liquid Modernity*, 149.

32 Hopenhayn, "Nueva secularización, nueva subjetividad," 83–84.

33 Sarlo, "Plano, repetición," 128.

34 Ibid.

35 Bauman, *Liquid Modernity*, 149.

36 Ibid., 139.

37 Ibid., 163.

38 Hyde, *The Gift*, 4.

39 Ibid., 37.

40 Ibid., 5.

41 Mauss, *The Gift*, 67, 64.

42 Ibid., 1.

4. CRIME AND CAPITALISM IN GENRE CINEMA

1 Ludmer, *El cuerpo del delito*, 13–14.

2 Ibid., 229, 228.

3 Ibid., 232, 233.

4 Avelar, *The Untimely Present*, 93.

5 Jameson, *The Geopolitical Aesthetic*, 3.

6 Ibid., 26.

7 Copertari, "*Nine Queens*," 280.

8 Shaw, "Playing Hollywood at Its Own Game?" 69.

9 The reference is to teaching notes on *Nueve reinas* published online at www
.mml.cam.ac.uk/Spanish/SP12/cine/nuevereinas (accessed June 13, 2008).

10 Referring to the film's ending, Bielinsky comments: "Ese final para mí es forzar,
un minuto antes de que la película termine, el hecho cinematográfico básico: la
película, aunque no hubiera terminado así, también es una clase de estafa, de
ilusión. El cine como fenómeno de comunicación es ilusorio. En este caso en vez
de haber una ilusión, que es la película, hay una ilusión dentro de otra ilusión"
(That ending to me drives home, one minute before the close of the film, the
basic fact of cinema: the film, even if it had not ended like that, is also a kind of
fraud, an illusion. The idea of cinema as a mode of communication is an illusory
one. In this case, instead of there being just one illusion—the film—there is an
illusion within that illusion). Cynthia Sabat, "Ilusionista del millón" (interview
with Bielinsky), *Espacio Cine Independiente*, November 23, 2000, www.cineinde
pendiente.com.ar (accessed July 7, 2007).

11 Harvey, *The Condition of Postmodernity*, 297.

12 Marx, *Theories of Surplus-Value*, part 1, 375–76.

13 Piglia, *Crítica y ficción*, 27–28.

14 Harvey, *The Condition of Postmodernity*, 163.

15 Sabat, "Ilusionista del millón."

16 Wolf, Castagna, and Quintín, "Los inconvenientes del éxito," 34.

17 Piglia, *Crítica y ficción*, 228.

18 Wolf, Castagna, and Quintín, "Los inconvenientes del éxito," 34.

19 Arlt, *Los siete locos*, 10.

20 Close, *La imprenta enterrada*, 120.

21 Martín Pérez, "Hay que echar mano a la historia propia" (interview with Caetano), *Página 12*, October 1, 2002, Espectáculos section, www.pagina12.com.ar
(accessed June 13, 2008).

22 Jameson, *Signatures of the Visible*, 31–32.

23 See, e.g., Emilio Toibero, "Zumban las balas en la tarde última," *Enfocarte* 4, no.
23 (2004), www.enfocarte.com (accessed June 13, 2008); Moira Soto, "Una ap-

uesta ganada," *Página 12*, March 12, 2004, Las 12 section, www.pagina12.com.ar (accessed June 13, 2008).

24 Foster Hirsch, for example, argues that "the place of women, both at home and on the job, changed radically. It is, in fact, in the way that it reflects the new status of women in American society that *film noir* is most closely connected to its period" (Hirsch, *The Dark Side of the Screen*, 19). Janey Place discusses the two major female archetypes found in film noir, "the deadly seductress and the rejuvenating redeemer," and argues that the instability of the representation of women reflects a moral universe in which "values, like identities, are constantly shifting and must be redefined at every turn" (Place, "Women in *Film Noir*," 52, 41); Sylvia Harvey relates the visual "dissonances" of noir to the displacement of "the normal representation of women as the founders of families" (Harvey, "Woman's Place," 25).

25 Reid and Walker, "Strange Pursuit," 63.

26 Krutnik, *In a Lonely Street*, 90–91.

27 Munby, *Public Enemies, Public Heroes*, 215.

28 Krutnik, *In a Lonely Street*, 47.

29 Telotte, *Voices in the Dark*, 21–22.

30 Hirsch, *The Dark Side of the Screen*, 17.

31 See Krutnik, *In a Lonely Street*, 54. Krutnik goes on to suggest that this line of argument is too simplistic, as "the very escape from the realm of the social can be seen in itself to constitute an implicitly negative representation of the idea of social conformity. Contemporary American society becomes something to escape from rather than to 'find one's place' within—there is a strong sense in which it can be seen as failing in its obligations towards the individual" (55).

32 Munby, *Public Enemies, Public Heroes*, 214–15.

33 Hirsch, *The Dark Side of the Screen*, 67.

34 For further details on the film's use of the actual sites of repression used during the dictatorship see Mariano Blejman, "Playaterminal," *Página 12*, February 19, 2004, "No" section, www.pagina12.com.ar (accessed June 13, 2008).

35 Jameson, *Postmodernism, or, the Cultural Logic of Late Capitalism*, 20.

36 Reid and Walker, "Strange Pursuit," 65.

37 Jameson, *The Geopolitical Aesthetic*, 5.

38 Amado, "Cine argentino, cuando todo es margen," 88. The reference to "contrarian fables" alludes to the concept developed by Jacques Rancière in his *La fable cinématographique*.

5. NATION, MIGRATION, AND GLOBALIZATION

1 Grimson, "La experiencia argentina y sus fantasmas," 178.

2 Sarlo, "¿Hay un país llamado Argentina?" n.p.

3 Figures quoted by *Clarín* from INDEC, the Instituto Nacional de Estadística y Censos. Ismael Bermúdez, "En doce meses 2,6 millones de personas salieron de

la pobreza," *Clarín*, March 22, 2007, El país section,www.clarin.com (accessed June 13, 2008).

4 Gorelik, "*Mala época*," 33–34.

5 Ibid., 35.

6 Grimson, "La experiencia argentina y sus fantasmas," 179–81.

7 Anderson, *Imagined Communities*, 32.

8 Morley, "Bounded Realms," 157.

9 For an account of the construction of rural images in cinema of this period see Tranchini, "El cine argentino y la construcción de un imaginario criollista," 103–69.

10 Rapoport, *Tiempos de crisis, vientos de cambio*, 221.

11 Martínez Estrada, *Radiografía de la pampa*, 341.

12 Jameson, *Signatures of the Visible*, 34.

13 Harvey, *The Condition of Postmodernity*, 302.

14 Mora, "*Bombón*," n.p.

15 Spinazzola, *Cinema e pubblico*, 101–21.

16 Restivo, *The Cinema of Economic Miracles*, 23.

17 Ibid., 36.

18 Ibid., 35.

19 Veaute, "Sesgar el discurso civilizado," 109.

20 Tranchini, "El cine argentino y la construcción de un imaginario criollista," 137.

21 Augé, *Non-Places*, 118–19.

22 Apezteguia, "Bolivia," 22. Apezteguia was the film's director of photography.

23 Bhabha, *The Location of Culture*, 2.

24 Bauman, *Liquid Modernity*, 173.

25 Bhabha, *The Location of Culture*, 5.

26 Naficy, "Phobic Spaces and Liminal Panics," 131.

27 Naficy proposes a very broad definition of *transnationalism* in film, arguing that "in the age of internationalized capital . . . it is not necessary to leave home to enter the spaces of liminality and transnationality" and that, as a result, "not only filmmakers but people the world over are always already transnational" (Naficy, "Phobic Spaces and Liminal Panics," 124).

28 *Bolita* is a pejorative term for a Bolivian.

29 Sarmiento, *Facundo*, 65.

30 Naficy, *An Accented Cinema*, 5.

31 Ibid., 103.

32 Ibid., 25.

33 Dostoevsky, *Crime and Punishment*, 2.

34 Naficy, *An Accented Cinema*, 105.

35 Sarlo, *Tiempo presente*, 15.

36 Sarlo, "Ya nada será igual," 5.

37 Sarlo, *Tiempo presente*, 18.

38 See García Canclini, *Culturas híbridas*, 288–305.

39 D'Lugo, "Authorship, Globalization, and the New Identity of Latin American Cinema," 112–13, 119–20.

40 Agustín Mango and Naza Chong, "El hombre como especie cultural" (interview), *Espacio Cine Independiente*, April 3, 2004, www.cineindependiente.com.ar (accessed July 7, 2007).

41 Ibid.

42 Diego Lerer, "Los mapas del deseo," *Clarín*, January 15, 2004, Espectáculos section, www.clarin.com (accessed June 13, 2008).

43 Mango and Chong, "El hombre como especie cultural," n.p.

44 Lorena García, Martín Wain, and Carlos Jaramillo, "Secretos de puertas adentro," *La Nación*, January 9, 2004, Vía Libre section, www.lanacion.com.ar (accessed June 13, 2008).

45 Molinari, "Un film argentino usa la fotografía digital," n.p. Molinari was the director of photography for the New York sequence of the film.

46 Mango and Chong, "El hombre como especie cultural," n.p.

47 Acland, *Screen Traffic*, 39.

48 García Delgado, *Estado-nación y la crisis del modelo*, 13.

49 Many of the actions of the IMF actually exacerbated the Crisis. According to Mark Weisbrot and Luis Sandoval, "the IMF was opposed to most of the major economic policies that contributed to the country's rapid economic recovery" (Weisbrot and Sandoval, "Argentina's Economic Recovery," 16).

50 Mabel Thwaites Rey, " 'Si la sociedad no puede organizarse, gana el mercado' " (interview with Robert Boyer), *Clarín*, January 12, 2003, Opinión section, www .clarin.com (accessed June 13, 2008).

51 Rojas, *Historia de la crisis argentina*, 36–37.

52 *Bar El Chino* Web site, 2003, www.barelchinofilm.com.ar (accessed June 13, 2008).

53 Hall, "Cultural Identity and Cinematic Representation," 706.

54 Harvey, *The Condition of Postmodernity*, 295–96.

55 Ibid., 303.

56 Massey, *Space, Place and Gender*, 155.

57 Durham Peters, "Exile, Nomadism, and Diaspora," 33.

58 See Bourdieu, "The Forms of Capital," 252–55.

59 Julia Montesoro, "Pasado mañana llega 'Bar El Chino,' " *La Nación*, October 14, 2003, Espectáculos section, www.lanacion.com.ar (accessed June 13, 2008).

60 See *The Economist* Web site, www.economist.com / cities.

6. MEMORY AND SUBJECTIVITY

1 Avelar, *The Untimely Present*, 36.

2 Svampa, *La sociedad excluyente*, 23. In British English, these numbers would be rendered $13,000 million to $46,000 million.

3 Gramuglio, "Políticas del decir y formas de la ficción," 9.

4 Sturken, *Tangled Memories*, 20.

5 The much earlier date of the play complicates what I (and others) analyze more generally as a historical shift in debates over memory in Argentina. While there has been a tendency in recent artistic productions to move away from a strictly testimonial function, many earlier texts exhibited an experimentalism altogether absent in later ones, such as Adrián Caetano's *Crónica de una fuga (Buenos Aires 1977)* (2006). Such "anachronisms" reveal something of significance in relation to the operations of collective memory. As Nancy Wood observes, "If particular representations of the past have permeated the public domain, it is because they embody an intentionality—social, political, institutional and so on—that promotes or authorizes their entry" (*Vectors of Memory*, 2). The debates sparked off in 2001 and surrounding *Los rubios* since 2003 can be seen to have "authorized" new versions of the past, in the same way that future debates may "reveal" the contestatory role of texts lying unnoticed in the present.

6 D'Angiolillo's long and successful career in montage includes some of the most celebrated Argentine productions of the 1980s, such as *Camila* (María Luisa Bemberg, 1984), *Hombre mirando al sudeste* (Eliseo Subiela, 1986), and several films by Fernando Solanas.

7 Turim, *Flashbacks in Film*, 228–29.

8 Smith, *Engaging Characters*, 83.

9 Ibid., 84.

10 Freud, "Screen Memories," 320.

11 Néstor Tirri, "Pavlovsky, del teatro al cine," *La Nación*, January 18, 2002, Espectáculos section, 4, www.lanacion.com.ar.

12 Freud, "Remembering, Repeating and Working-Through," 150.

13 Vezzetti argues:

> Hay que recordar que el régimen, en verdad, fue cívico-militar, que incorporó extensamente cuadros políticos provenientes de los partidos principales y que no le faltaron amplios apoyos eclesiásticos, empresariales, periodísticos y sindicales. De modo que la representación, ampliamente instalada después del renacimiento democrático, de una sociedad víctima de un poder despótico es sólo una parte del cuadro y pierde de vista que la dictadura fue algo muy distinto de una ocupación extranjera, y que su programa brutal de intervención sobre el Estado y sobre amplios sectores sociales no era en absoluto ajeno a tradiciones, acciones y representaciones políticas que estaban presentes en la sociedad desde bastante antes.

> [It must be remembered that the regime, in truth, was a civilian-military regime that incorporated a number of politicians from major political parties and was not short of support from the Church, businesses, journalists, and trade unionists. Such that the depiction—fully established after the renaissance of democracy—of a society that was victim to a despotic power represents only part of the picture and loses sight of the fact that the dictatorship

was hardly a foreign occupation, and that its brutal program of intervention in the State and across broad social sectors was not at all alien to the kind of traditions, actions, and political representations that had been present in society long before] (Vezzetti, *Pasado y presente*, 39).

14 Pilar Calveiro, *Política y/o violencia*, 12.
15 Calveiro, *Poder y desaparición*, 165.
16 Vezzetti, *Pasado y presente*, 15.
17 Sarlo, *Tiempo presente*, 45–46.
18 Schmucler, "Las exigencias de la memoria," 9.
19 Vezzetti, "Lecciones de la memoria," 12–13.
20 Schmucler, "Las exigencias de la memoria," 8.
21 Terán, "Tiempos de memoria," 11.
22 Ibid., 12.
23 Bordwell, *Narration in the Fiction Film*, 31.
24 Ibid., 30.
25 Bordwell, "Contemporary Film Studies and the Vicissitudes of Grand Theory," 8.
26 Stam, *Film Theory*, 245.
27 Prince, "Psychoanalytic Film Theory and the Problem of the Missing Spectator," 73.
28 Diego Papic and Jorge Bernárdez, "Pequeñas anécdotas sobre las instituciones," 2003, www.cinenacional.com/notas/index.php?nota=427 (accessed June 13, 2008).
29 Lorena García, "Albertina Carri: 'La ausencia es un agujero negro,'" *La Nación*, April 23, 2003, Espectáculos section, www.lanacion.com.ar (accessed June 13, 2008).
30 Julián Gorodischer, quoted in María Moreno, "Esa rubia debilidad," *Página 12*, October 23, 2003, Radar section, www.pagina12web.com.ar (accessed June 13, 2008).
31 Bruzzi, *New Documentary*, 153–54.
32 Kohan, "La apariencia celebrada," 30.
33 Sarlo, *Tiempo pasado*, 153.
34 Macón, "*Los rubios* o del trauma como presencia," 47.
35 Both Kohan and Sarlo insist that Carri's vision is essentially different from that of other children of the disappeared, citing as counterexamples María Inés Roqué's film *Papa Iván* (2000), Juan Gelman and Mara La Madrid's compilation of testimonies in *Ni el flaco perdón de Dios* (1997), and the work of HIJOS. See Kohan, "Una crítica en general y una película en particular," 48; Sarlo, *Tiempo pasado*, 153–54.
36 Sarlo, *Tiempo pasado*, 146.
37 Halbwachs, *On Collective Memory*, 53.
38 The relevance of Hirsch's concept of postmemory seems to have been the happy discovery of a number of critics working independently on the film. See, for

example, my own earlier article on the film, "Memory and Mediation in *Los rubios*"; Nouzeilles, "Postmemory Cinema and the Future of the Past in Albertina Carri's *Los rubios*"; and Macón, "*Los rubios* o del trauma como presencia."

39 Hirsch, "Projected Memory," 8.

40 Sarlo, *Tiempo pasado*, 129–30.

41 LaCapra, *History and Memory after Auschwitz*, 21.

42 Vezzetti, *Pasado y presente*, 192.

43 María Moreno, "Esa rubia debilidad," *Página 12*, October 23, 2003, Radar section, www.pagina12web.com.ar (accessed June 13, 2008).

44 Ibid.

45 Nichols, *Representing Reality*, 31.

46 Aguilar, *Otros mundos: Un ensayo sobre el nuevo cine argentino*, 145. An "escrache" is the public exposure and denunciation of an individual connected with the repression of the dictatorship. It usually takes the form of a demonstration outside the individual's home.

47 Jelin, *Los trabajos de la memoria*, 61–62.

48 Amado, "Órdenes de la memoria y desórdenes de la ficción," 49.

49 Ibid., 50.

50 Sarlo, *Tiempo pasado*, 62.

51 Ibid.

52 García, "Albertina Carri," (see note 29 above).

53 See, e.g., Jelin, *Los trabajos de la memoria*, 72.

54 Sarlo, *Tiempo pasado*, 147.

55 Aguilar, *Otros mundos*, 145.

56 Ibid., 187.

57 Sarlo, *Tiempo pasado*, 90–91.

58 Ibid., 82.

7. THE POLITICS OF PRIVATE SPACE

1 See, for example, *Últimas imágenes del naufragio* (1989), in which Roberto finds inspiration for his novel when he meets Estela and her family, living in poverty and touched by psychosis and crime; or *El lado oscuro del corazón* (1992), in which Oliverio finds the object of his desire in a prostitute working in a Montevideo cabaret. In both *Hombre mirando al sudeste* (1986) and *No te mueras sin decirme adónde vas* (1995), the outsider who comes to teach the protagonists how to live is even further removed from their daily existence: a possible extraterrestrial in the former and a spirit waiting for reincarnation in the latter.

2 Sarlo, *Tiempo presente*, 59.

3 The film's other settings include birthday parties reuniting old high school friends and Mar del Plata, a popular middle-class holiday resort not far from the capital.

4 An exception would be Jorge Gaggero's *Cama adentro* (2004), which deals explicitly with the transformation of relationships between social classes in the wake of the Crisis of 2001.

5 Solanas's films present a series of parodic symbols and metaphors that operate within the traditions of satire and the grotesque rather than constructing a sustained allegory. Nevertheless, they draw on the well-established conventions of allegorical interpretation in order to suggest a frame of reference beyond the literal frame of representation.

6 Monteagudo, "Lucrecia Martel," 69.

7 See, e.g., García and Eduardo, "Desbordes del deseo" (interview with Martel), 13; Monteagudo, "*La ciénaga* por tele, al terminar el domingo," *Página 12*, August 4, 2002, Espectáculos section, www.pagina12.com.ar (accessed June 13, 2008); Babino, "Lucrecia Martel, directora de *La ciénaga*" (interview with Martel), 40; Peña, Félix-Didier, and Luka, "Lucrecia Martel" (interview), 123.

8 Monteagudo, "Lucrecia Martel," 76.

9 See Peña, Félix-Didier, and Luka, "Lucrecia Martel," 123–24.

10 Babino, "Lucrecia Martel, directora de *La ciénaga*," 40.

11 Ocampo, "La casa natal," 80.

12 Ocampo, "El pecado mortal," 440.

13 Mariana Enriquez, "Ese oscuro objeto del deseo" (interview with Martel), *Página 12*, May 2, 2004, Radar section, www.pagina12web.com.ar (accessed June 13, 2008).

14 Ocampo, "El pecado mortal," 437.

15 Babino, "Lucrecia Martel, directora de *La ciénaga*," 41.

16 Smith, "The Will to Allegory in Postmodernism," 108.

17 Rangil, *Otro punto de vista*, 99.

18 Arendt, *The Human Condition*, 33, 34, 36–37, 56.

19 Agamben, *Homo Sacer*, 9, 187–88.

20 Jameson, *The Geopolitical Aesthetic*, 48–49.

21 Bauman, *Liquid Modernity*, 185.

22 Arendt, *The Human Condition*, 50.

23 Agamben, *Homo Sacer*, 9.

CONCLUSION

1 Jameson, "Third-World Literature in the Era of Multinational Capitalism," 69.

2 Ahmad, "Jameson's Rhetoric of Otherness and the 'National Allegory,'" 13.

3 Jameson, "Third-World Literature in the Era of Multinational Capitalism," 69.

4 Svampa, *La sociedad excluyente*, 54.

5 Jameson, "Third-World Literature in the Era of Multinational Capitalism," 74–75.

6 Svampa, *La sociedad excluyente*, 47.

7 Ibid., 296.

8 Coscia, "Cuota de pantalla, un paso esencial," 20. Coscia makes reference here to *Un lugar en el mundo* (1991), a successful film by Adolfo Aristarain that takes as its theme the importance of finding a place in the world where one feels a sense of belonging and is able to play a part. Aristarain's career spans the late 1970s until the present day; as a director he is as prominent a figure within Argentine cinema as Eliseo Subiela or Fernando Solanas, although his productions are significantly more conventional in narrative and stylistic terms.

9 Perelman and Seivach, *La industria cinematográfica en la Argentina*, 132.

10 Kirchner, "El estado y el cine argentino," 10–11.

11 Bauman, *Liquid Modernity*, 38–39.

BIBLIOGRAPHY

Acland, Charles R. *Screen Traffic: Movies, Multiplexes, and Global Culture*. Durham, N.C.: Duke University Press, 2003.

Adorno, Theodor W., and Max Horkheimer. *Dialectic of Enlightenment*. London: Verso, 1997.

Agamben, Giorgio. *Homo Sacer: Sovereign Power and Bare Life*. Translated by Daniel Heller-Roazen. Stanford, Calif.: Stanford University Press, 1998.

Aguilar, Gonzalo. *Otros mundos: Un ensayo sobre el nuevo cine argentino*. Buenos Aires: Santiago Arcos, 2006.

Ahmad, Aijaz. "Jameson's Rhetoric of Otherness and the 'National Allegory.'" *Social Text* 17 (autumn 1987): 3–25.

Amado, Ana. "Cine argentino, cuando todo es margen." *Pensamiento de los confines* 11 (September 2002): 87–94.

——. "Órdenes de la memoria y desórdenes de la ficción." In *Lazos de familia: Herencias, cuerpos, ficciones*, compiled by Ana Amado and Nora Domínguez, 43–82. Buenos Aires: Paidós, 2004.

Anderson, Benedict. *Imagined Communities: Reflections on the Origin and Spread of Nationalism*. London: Verso, 1983.

Apezteguia, Julián. "Bolivia." *Revista ADF* 5, no. 11 (2002): 22–23.

Arendt, Hannah. *The Human Condition*. Chicago: University of Chicago Press, 1998.

Arlt, Roberto. *Los siete locos*. Buenos Aires: Losada, 1958.

Augé, Marc. *Non-Places: Introduction to an Anthropology of Supermodernity*. London: Verso, 1995.

Avelar, Idelber. *The Untimely Present: Postdictatorial Latin American Fiction and the Task of Mourning*. Durham, N.C.: Duke University Press, 1999.

Babino, Ernesto. "Lucrecia Martel, directora de *La ciénaga*." Interview. *Sin cortes* 22, no. 130 (May 2001): 40–42.

———. "Pablo Trapero." Interview. *Sin cortes* 21, no. 119 (July 1999): 24–26.

Barthes, Roland. "The Third Meaning: Research Notes on Some Eisenstein Stills." In *Image, Music, Text*, translated by Stephen Heath, 52–68. London: Fontana, 1977.

Batlle, Diego. "De la virtual extinción a la nueva ley: El resurgimiento." In Bernades, Lerer, and Wolf, *El nuevo cine argentino*, 17–28.

Baud, Michiel. Foreword to Fiorucci and Klein, *The Argentine Crisis at the Turn of the Millennium*, xi–xii.

Bauman, Zygmunt. *Liquid Modernity*. Cambridge: Polity Press, 2000.

Bazin, André. "De Sica: Metteur-en-scène." In *Film Theory and Criticism: Introductory Readings*, edited by Leo Braudy and Marshall Cohen, 203–11. 5th ed. Oxford: Oxford University Press, 1999.

Beceyro, Raúl, Rafael Filippelli, David Oubiña, and Alan Pauls. "Estética del cine, nuevos realismos, representación." *Punto de vista* 23, no. 67 (August 2000): 1–9.

Bernades, Horacio, Diego Lerer, and Sergio Wolf, eds. *El nuevo cine argentino: Temas, autores y estilos de una renovación*. Buenos Aires: FIPRESCI, 2002.

Bernini, Emilio. "Un proyecto inconcluso: Aspectos del cine contemporáneo argentino." *Kilómetro* 111, no. 4 (October 2003): 87–106.

Bhabha, Homi K. *The Location of Culture*. London: Routledge, 1994.

Birgin, Alejandra, and Javier Trímboli, comps. *Imágenes de los noventa*. Buenos Aires: Libros del Zorzal, 2003.

Bordwell, David. "Contemporary Film Studies and the Vicissitudes of Grand Theory." In Bordwell and Carroll, *Post-Theory*, 3–36.

———. *Narration in the Fiction Film*. London: Methuen, 1985.

Bordwell, David, and Noël Carroll, eds. *Post-Theory: Reconstructing Film Studies*. Madison: University of Wisconsin Press, 1996.

Borges, Jorge Luis. *Otras inquisiciones*. Buenos Aires: Alianza, 1976.

Bourdieu, Pierre. *Acts of Resistance: Against the New Myths of Our Time*. Translated by Richard Nice. Cambridge: Polity Press, 1998.

———. "The Forms of Capital." Translated by Richard Nice. In *Handbook of Theory and Research for the Sociology of Education*, edited by John G. Richardson, 241–58. New York: Greenwood, 1986.

Bruzzi, Stella. *New Documentary: A Critical Introduction*. London: Routledge, 2000.

Burton-Carvajal, Julianne. "South American Cinema." In *World Cinema: Critical Approaches*, edited by John Hill and Pamela Church Gibson, 194–210. Oxford: Oxford University Press, 2000.

Calveiro, Pilar. *Poder y desaparición: Los campos de concentración en Argentina*. Buenos Aires: Colihue, 2004.

———. *Política y/o violencia: Una aproximación a la guerrilla de los años '70*. Buenos Aires: Norma, 2005.

Castagna, Gustavo J. "Un grito en la oscuridad." *El amante* 7, no. 78 (September 1998): 4–5.

——. "Mundo panza," *El amante* 8, no. 88 (July 1999): 4–6.

Castells, Manuel. *End of Millennium*. Oxford: Blackwell, 1998.

Cavallari, Hector Mario. "El exilio sin fin: De Subiela a Bioy Casares." *Alba de América: Revista literaria* 15, nos. 28–29 (July 1997): 262–71.

Chanan, Michael. "Latin American Cinema in the 90s: Representational Space in Recent Latin American Cinema." *Estudios interdisciplinarios de América Latina y el Caribe* 9, no. 1 (January–June 1998): www.tau.ac.il/eial/IX_1/chanan.html (accessed June 13, 2008).

Clifford, James. "On Ethnographic Allegory." In *Writing Culture: The Poetics and Politics of Ethnography*, edited by James Clifford and George E. Marcus, 98–121. Berkeley: University of California Press, 1986.

Close, Glen S. *La imprenta enterrada: Baroja, Arlt y el imaginario anarquista*. Rosario: Beatriz Viterbo, 2000.

Copertari, Gabriela. "*Nine Queens*: A Dark Day of Simulation and Justice." *Journal of Latin American Cultural Studies* 14, no. 3 (December 2005): 279–93.

Coscia, Jorge. "Cuota de pantalla, un paso esencial." In *El estado y el cine argentino*, 19–23. Santa Fe: Instituto Superior de Cine y Artes Audiovisuales de Santa Fe, 2005.

Deleuze, Gilles. *Cinema 1: The Movement-Image*. Translated by Hugh Tomlinson and Barbara Habberjam. London: Continuum, 2005.

——. *Cinema 2: The Time-Image*. Translated by Hugh Tomlinson and Robert Galeta. London: Continuum, 2005.

De Toro, Alfonso. "La postcolonialidad en Latinoamérica en la era de la globalización: Cambio de paradigma en el pensamiento teórico-cultural latinoamericano?" In *El debate de la postcolonialidad en Latinoamérica: Una postmodernidad periférica o cambio de paradigma en el pensamiento latinoamericano*, edited by Alfonso de Toro and Fernando de Toro, 31–77. Madrid: Iberoamericana and Frankfurt: Vervuert Verlag, 1999.

Diegues, Carlos. "The Cinema That Brazil Deserves." In *The New Brazilian Cinema*, edited by Lúcia Nagib, 23–35. London: I.B. Tauris, 2003.

D'Lugo, Marvin. "Authorship, Globalization, and the New Identity of Latin American Cinema: From the Mexican 'Ranchera' to Argentinian 'Exile.'" In *Rethinking Third Cinema*, edited by Anthony Guneratne and Wimal Dissanayake, 103–25. London: Routledge, 2003.

Dostoevsky, Fyodor. *Crime and Punishment*. Translated by Constance Garnett. London: Folio Society, 1957.

Durham Peters, John. "Exile, Nomadism, and Diaspora: The Stakes of Mobility in the Western Canon." In Naficy, *Home, Exile, Homeland*, 17–41.

El estado y el cine argentino. Santa Fe: Instituto Superior de Cine y Artes Audiovisuales de Santa Fe, 2005.

Estrada, Marién. "Cine de contrastes." *Revista mexicana de comunicación* 80 (March-April 2003): www.mexicanadecomunicacion.com.mx. (accessed June 13, 2008).

——. "Más cines y menos espectadores." *Revista mexicana de comunicación* 85 (February-March 2004): www.mexicanadecomunicacion.com.mx (accessed June 13, 2008).

Falicov, Tamara L. *The Cinematic Tango: Contemporary Argentine Film*. London: Wallflower Press, 2007.

Finkielman, Jorge. *The Film Industry in Argentina: An Illustrated Cultural History*. Jefferson, N.C.: McFarland, 2004.

Fiorucci, Flavia, and Marcus Klein, eds. *The Argentine Crisis at the Turn of the Millennium*. Amsterdam: Aksant, 2004.

Freud, Sigmund. "Remembering, Repeating and Working-Through." In *The Standard Edition of the Complete Psychological Works of Sigmund Freud*. Translated by J. Strachey. Vol. 12, 147–56. London: Hogarth Press, 1958.

——. "Screen Memories." In *The Standard Edition of the Complete Psychological Works of Sigmund Freud*. Translated by J. Strachey. Vol. 3, 303–22. London: Hogarth Press, 1958.

García, Jorge, and Eduardo Rojas. "Desbordes del deseo." Interview with Lucrecia Martel. *El amante* 13, no. 145 (May 2004): 12–14.

García Canclini, Néstor. *Culturas híbridas: Estrategias para entrar y salir de la modernidad*. Mexico: Grijalbo, 1989.

——. "Will There Be Latin American Cinema in the Year 2000? Visual Culture in a Postnational Era." In *Framing Latin American Cinema: Contemporary Critical Approaches*, edited by Ann Marie Stock, 246–58. Minneapolis: University of Minnesota Press, 1997. Originally published as "¿Habrá cine latinoamericano en el año 2000?" *Jornada Semanal* 193 (February 17, 1993): 27–33.

García Delgado, Daniel. *Estado-nación y la crisis del modelo*. Buenos Aires: Norma, 2003.

Getino, Octavio. *Cine y televisión en América Latina*. Buenos Aires: Ciccus, 1998.

Gorelik, Adrián. "*Mala época*: Los imaginarios de la descomposición social y urbana en Buenos Aires." In *Imágenes de los noventa*, compiled by Alejandra Birgin and Javier Trímboli, 19–46. Buenos Aires: Libros del Zorzal, 2003.

Gramuglio, María Teresa. "Políticas del decir y formas de la ficción: Novelas de la dictadura militar." *Punto de vista* 25, no. 74 (December 2002): 9–14.

Grant, Catherine. "Giving Up Ghosts: Eliseo Subiela's *Hombre mirando al sudeste* and *No te mueras sin decirme adónde vas*." In Rix and Rodríguez-Saona, *Changing Reels*, 89–120.

Grimson, Alejandro. "La experiencia argentina y sus fantasmas." In *La cultura en las crisis latinoamericanas*, compiled by Alejandro Grimson, 177–93. Buenos Aires: CLACSO, 2004.

Gundermann, Christian. "*La libertad* entre los escombros de la globalización." *Ciberletras: Revista de crítica literaria y de cultura*, 13 (July 2005): www.lehman.cuny.edu/ciberletras/v13/gunderman.htm (accessed June 13, 2008).

——. "The Stark Gaze of the New Argentine Cinema: Restoring Strangeness to the Object in the Perverse Age of Commodity Fetishism." *Journal of Latin American Cultural Studies* 14, no. 3 (December 2005): 241–61.

Halbwachs, Maurice. *On Collective Memory*. Edited, translated, and introduced by Lewis A. Coser. Chicago: University of Chicago Press, 1992.

Hall, Stuart. "Cultural Identity and Cinematic Representation." In *Film and Theory: An Anthology*, edited by Robert Stam and Toby Miller, 704–14. Oxford: Blackwell, 2000.

Hart, Stephen. *A Companion to Latin American Film*. Woodbridge, U.K.: Tamesis, 2004.

Harvey, David. *The Condition of Postmodernity: An Enquiry into the Origins of Cultural Exchange*. Oxford: Blackwell, 1989.

——. *Spaces of Hope*. Edinburgh: Edinburgh University Press, 2000.

Harvey, Sylvia. "Woman's Place: The Absent Family of *Film Noir*." In Kaplan, *Women in Film Noir*, 22–34.

Hirsch, Foster. *The Dark Side of the Screen: Film Noir*. San Diego: A.S. Barnes; London: Tantivy, 1981.

Hirsch, Marianne. "Projected Memory: Holocaust Photographs in Personal and Public Fantasy." In *Acts of Memory: Cultural Recall in the Present*, edited by Mieke Bal, Jonathan Crewe, and Leo Spitzer, 3–23. Hanover, N.H.: University Press of New England, 1999.

Hopenhayn, Martín. *Ni apocalípticos ni integrados: Aventuras de la modernidad en América Latina*. Santiago: Fondo de Cultura Económica, 1994.

——. "Nueva secularización, nueva subjetividad: El descentramiento del trabajo y de la política." *Revista de estudios sociales* 5 (January 2000): 81–88.

Hyde, Lewis. *The Gift: Imagination and the Erotic Life of Property*. New York: Random House, 1979.

Jameson, Fredric. *The Geopolitical Aesthetic: Cinema and Space in the World System*. Bloomington: Indiana University Press, 1995.

——. *Postmodernism, or, The Cultural Logic of Late Capitalism*. London: Verso, 1991.

——. *The Seeds of Time*. New York: Columbia University Press, 1994.

——. *Signatures of the Visible*. London: Routledge, 1990.

——. "Third-World Literature in the Era of Multinational Capitalism." *Social Text* 15 (autumn 1986): 65–88.

Jelin, Elizabeth. *Los trabajos de la memoria*. Buenos Aires: Siglo XXI, 2002.

Johnson, Randal. "Brazilian Cinema Novo." *Bulletin of Latin American Research* 3, no. 2 (1984): 95–106.

——. "In the Belly of the Ogre: Cinema and the State in Latin America." In King, López, and Alvarado, *Mediating Two Worlds*, 204–13.

Kaplan, E. Ann, ed. *Women in Film Noir*. London: BFI, 1978.

Kantaris, Geoffrey. "Visiones de la violencia en el cine urbano latinoamericano." *Cuadernos del Centro de Estudios en Diseño y Comunicación* (Universidad de Palermo, Buenos Aires) 18 (May 2005): 39–46.

King, John. "Cinema in Latin America." In *The Cambridge Companion to Modern Latin American Culture*, edited by John King, 282–313. Cambridge: Cambridge University Press, 2004.

——. *Magical Reels: A History of Cinema in Latin America*. 2nd ed. London: Verso, 2000.

King, John, Ana M. López, and Manuel Alvarado, eds. *Mediating Two Worlds: Cinematic Encounters in the Americas*. London: BFI, 1993.

Kirchner, Néstor. "El estado y el cine argentino" (speech given by the president during the 19th Festival Internacional de Cine, Mar del Plata, March 13, 2004). In *El estado y el cine argentino*, 10–15. Santa Fe: Instituto Superior de Cine y Artes Audiovisuales de Santa Fe, 2005.

Klein, Marcus. "Stumbling on the Verge of the Abyss (Without Falling into It): Argentina and Its Crisis of the Millennium." In Fiorucci and Klein, *The Argentine Crisis at the Turn of the Millennium*, 1–14.

Kohan, Martín. "La apariencia celebrada." *Punto de vista* 27, no. 78 (April 2004): 24–30.

——. "Una crítica en general y una película en particular." *Punto de vista* 28, no. 80 (December 2004): 47–48.

Krutnik, Frank. *In a Lonely Street: Film Noir, Genre, Masculinity*. London: Routledge, 1991.

LaCapra, Dominick. *History and Memory after Auschwitz*. Ithaca, N.Y.: Cornell University Press, 1998.

Lerer, Diego. "Pablo Trapero: El hombre suburbano." In Bernades, Lerer, and Wolf, *El nuevo cine argentino*, 61–68.

Llach, Lucas. "A Depression in Perspective: The Economics and the Political Economy of Argentina's Crisis of the Millennium." In Fiorucci and Klein, *The Argentine Crisis at the Turn of the Millennium*, 40–63.

Ludmer, Josefina. *El cuerpo del delito: Un manual*. Buenos Aires: Perfil, 1999.

Lyotard, Jean-François. *Heidegger and "the jews."* Translated by Andreas Michel and Mark S. Roberts. Minneapolis: University of Minnesota Press, 1990.

Macdonald, Gerald M. "Third Cinema and the Third World." In *Place, Power, Situation, and Spectacle: A Geography of Film*, edited by Stuart C. Aitken and Leo E. Zonn, 27–45. Lanham, Md.: Rowman and Littlefield, 1994.

Macón, Cecilia. "*Los rubios* o del trauma como presencia." *Punto de vista* 28, no. 80 (December 2004): 44–47.

Mahieu, José Agustín. "Fernando Solanas: Del cine político a las metáforas del país." *Cuadernos hispanoamericanos* 592 (October 1999): 83–89.

Mango, Agustín, and Naza Chong, "El hombre como especie cultural" (interview). *Espacio Cine Independiente*, April 3, 2004, www.cineindependiente.com.ar (accessed July 7, 2007).

Martínez Estrada, Ezequiel. *Radiografía de la pampa*. Buenos Aires: Losada, 2001.

Marx, Karl. *Capital*. Vol. 1. Translated by Ben Fowkes. London: Penguin, 1990.

——. *Theories of Surplus-Value*. Edited by S. Ryanzanskaya. Translated by Emile Burns. Moscow: Foreign Languages Publishing House, 1964.

Massey, Doreen. *For Space*. London: Sage, 2005.

——. *Space, Place and Gender*. Cambridge: Polity Press, 1994.

Mauss, Marcel. *The Gift: Forms and Functions of Exchange in Archaic Societies*. Translated by Ian Cunnison. London: Cohen and West, 1954.

Miyoshi, Masao. "'Globalization,' Culture, and the University." In *The Cultures of Globalization*, edited by Fredric Jameson and Masao Miyoshi, 247–70. Durham, N.C.: Duke University Press, 1998.

Moguillansky, Marina, and Valeria Ré. "Nuevo crítica, nuevo cine." www.iigg.fsoc .uba.ar/Jovenes_investigadores/3JornadasJovenes/Templates/Eje%20represen taciones/Moguillansky%20Re%20Discursos.pdf (accessed June 13, 2008).

Moisés, José Álvaro. "A New Policy for Brazilian Cinema." In *The New Brazilian Cinema*, edited by Lúcia Nagib, 3–21. London: I.B. Tauris, 2003.

Molinari, Mariano. "Un film argentino usa la fotografía digital" (n.d.). www.foto mundo.com and www.molinaripixel.com.ar/notas/film_arg.htm (accessed June 13, 2008).

Monteagudo, Luciano. "Lucrecia Martel: Susurros a la hora de la siesta." In Bernades, Lerer, and Wolf, *El nuevo cine argentino*, 69–78.

Montes-Bradley, Eduardo. "All We Need Is Love." *El amante* 10, no. 113 (August 2001): 13–15.

Mora, Orlando. "*Bombón*: El regreso de un director." *El ojo que piensa* 7 (March 2005): www.elojoquepiensa.com.

Morley, David. "Bounded Realms: Household, Family, Community, and Nation." In Naficy, *Home, Exile, Homeland*, 151–68.

Munby, Jonathan. *Public Enemies, Public Heroes: Screening the Gangster from Little Caesar to Touch of Evil*. Chicago: University of Chicago Press, 1999.

Naficy, Hamid. *An Accented Cinema: Exilic and Diasporic Filmmaking*. Princeton, N.J.: Princeton University Press, 2001.

——, ed. *Home, Exile, Homeland: Film, Media, and the Politics of Place*. London: Routledge, 1999.

——. "Phobic Spaces and Liminal Panics: Independent Transnational Film Genre." In *Global/Local: Cultural Production and the Transnational Imaginary*, edited by Rob Wilson and Wimal Dissanayake, 119–44. Durham, N.C.: Duke University Press, 1996.

Nagib, Lúcia, ed. *The New Brazilian Cinema*. London: I. B. Tauris, 2003.

Neruda, Pablo. "Sobre una poesía sin pureza." *Caballo verde para la poesía* 1 (October 1935): n.p.

Newman, Kathleen. "National Cinema after Globalization: Fernando Solanas's *Sur* and the Exiled Nation." In King, López, and Alvarado, *Mediating Two Worlds*, 242–57.

Nichols, Bill. *Representing Reality: Issues and Concepts in Documentary*. Bloomington: Indiana University Press, 1991.

Noriega, Gustavo. "Freddy toma soda." *El amante* 11, no. 120 (April 2002): 14–15.

Nouzeilles, Gabriela. "Postmemory Cinema and the Future of the Past in Albertina Carri's *Los rubios*." *Journal of Latin American Cultural Studies* 14, no. 3 (December 2005): 263–78.

Ocampo, Silvina. "La casa natal." In *Poesía completa*. Vol. 2, 79–80. Buenos Aires: Emecé, 2003.

——. "El pecado mortal." In *Cuentos completos*. Vol. 1, 437–41. Buenos Aires: Emecé, 1999.

Oubiña, David. "Martín Rejtman: El cine menguante." In *Martín Rejtman*, edited by David Oubiña, 5–23. Buenos Aires: Fundación Eduardo F. Costantini, 2005. Published in conjunction with the release of the Colección Malba Cine's edition on DVD of Rejtman's films.

Page, Joanna. "Memory and Mediation in *Los rubios*: A Contemporary Perspective on the Argentine Dictatorship." *New Cinemas* 3, no. 1 (2005): 29–40.

Peña, Fernando Martín, Paula Félix-Didier, and Ezequiel Luka. "Lucrecia Martel" (interview). In *Generaciones 60/90: Cine argentino independiente*, edited by Fernando Martín Peña, 117–24. Buenos Aires: Fundación Eduardo F. Costantini, 2003.

Perelman, Pablo, and Paulina Seivach. *La industria cinematográfica en la Argentina: Entre los límites del mercado y el fomento estatal*. 2nd ed. Buenos Aires: Centro de Estudios para el Desarrollo Económico Metropolitano, 2004; www.cedem.gov.ar/areas/des_economico/cedem/pdf/estudios_especiales/ind_cine_arg2.pdf (accessed June 13, 2008).

Pérez Soler, Bernardo. "Pup Fiction." *Sight and Sound*, May 2001, www.bfi.org.uk/sightandsound/feature/78 (accessed June 13, 2008).

Piglia, Ricardo. *Crítica y ficción*. Buenos Aires: Seix Barral, 2000.

Place, Janey. "Women in *Film Noir*." In Kaplan, *Women in* Film Noir, 35–67.

Pratt, Mary Louise. "Arts of the Contact Zone." In *Mass Culture and Everyday Life*, edited by Peter Gibian, 61–72. New York: Routledge, 1997.

Prince, Stephen. "Psychoanalytic Film Theory and the Problem of the Missing Spectator." In Bordwell and Carroll, *Post-Theory*, 71–86.

Quintín. "El carnaval de las almas." *El amante* 4, no. 40 (June 1995): 2–3.

——. "De una generación a otra: ¿Hay una línea divisoria?" In Bernades, Lerer, and Wolf, *El nuevo cine argentino*, 111–17.

——. "Subiela y nosotros: Un diario." *El amante* 1, no. 5 (May 1992): 7–8.

Rangil, Viviana. *Otro punto de vista: Mujer y cine en Argentina*. Rosario: Beatriz Viterbo, 2005.

Rapoport, Mario. *Tiempos de crisis, vientos de cambio*. Buenos Aires: Norma, 2002.

Ray, Robert B. *The Avant-Garde Finds Andy Hardy*. Cambridge, Mass.: Harvard University Press, 1995.

Reid, David, and Jayne L. Walker. "Strange Pursuit: Cornell Woolrich and the Abandoned City of the Forties." In *Shades of Noir: A Reader*, edited by Joan Copjec, 57–96. London: Verso, 1993.

Restivo, Angelo. *The Cinema of Economic Miracles: Visuality and Modernization in the Italian Art Film*. Durham, N.C.: Duke University Press, 2002.

Rix, Rob, and Roberto Rodríguez-Saona, eds. *Changing Reels: Latin American Cinema against the Odds*. Leeds: Trinity and All Saints University College, 1997.

Rodowick, D. N. *Gilles Deleuze's Time Machine*. Durham, N.C.: Duke University Press, 1997.

Rojas, Mauricio. *Historia de la crisis argentina*. Buenos Aires: Distal, 2003.

Russell, Catherine. *Experimental Ethnography: The Work of Film in the Age of Video*. Durham, N.C.: Duke University Press, 1999.

Sarlo, Beatriz. *Escenas de la vida posmoderna: Intelectuales, arte y videocultura en la Argentina*. Buenos Aires: Ariel, 1994.

———. "¿Hay un país llamado Argentina?" *Revista criterio* 76, no. 2280 (March 2003): www.revistacriterio.com.ar (accessed June 13, 2008).

———. "Plano, repetición: Sobreviviendo en la ciudad nueva." In *Imágenes de los noventa*, compiled by Alejandra Birgin and Javier Trímboli, 125–49. Buenos Aires: Libros del Zorzal, 2003.

———. "El relativismo absoluto, o cómo el mercado y la sociología reflexionan sobre estética." *Punto de vista* 27, no. 48 (April 1994): 27–31.

———. *Tiempo pasado: Cultura de la memoria y giro subjetivo; Una discusión*. Buenos Aires: Siglo XXI, 2005.

———. *Tiempo presente: Notas sobre el cambio de una cultura*. Buenos Aires: Siglo XXI, 2001.

———. "Ya nada será igual." *Punto de vista* 24, no. 70 (August 2001): 2–11.

Sarmiento, Domingo Faustino. *Facundo: Civilización y barbarie*. Madrid: Alianza, 1988.

Schmucler, Héctor. "Las exigencias de la memoria." *Punto de vista* 23, no. 68 (December 2000): 5–9.

Segre, Erica. " 'La *desnacionalización* de la pantalla': Mexican Cinema in the 1990s." In Rix and Rodríguez-Saona, *Changing Reels*, 33–57.

Sennett, Richard. *The Corrosion of Character: The Personal Consequences of Work in the New Capitalism*. London: Norton, 1998.

Shaw, Deborah. "Playing Hollywood at Its Own Game? Bielinski's [sic] *Nueve reinas*." In *Contemporary Latin American Cinema: Breaking into the Global Market*, edited by Deborah Shaw, 67–85. Lanham, Md.: Rowman and Littlefield, 2007.

Smith, Murray. *Engaging Characters: Fiction, Emotion, and the Cinema*. Oxford: Clarendon Press, 1995.

Smith, Paul. "The Will to Allegory in Postmodernism." *Dalhousie Review* 62, no. 1 (spring 1982): 105–22.

Smith, Paul Julian. *Amores perros*. London: BFI, 2003.

Spinazzola, Vittorio. *Cinema e pubblico: Lo spettacolo filmico in Italia, 1945–1965*. Milan: Bompiani, 1974.

Stam, Robert. *Film Theory: An Introduction*. Oxford: Blackwell, 2000.

Stock, Ann Marie. "Migrancy and the Latin American Cinemascape: Towards a Post-National Critical Praxis." *Revista Canadiense de estudios hispánicos* 20, no. 1 (autumn 1995): 19–27.

Sturken, Marita. *Tangled Memories: The Vietnam War, the AIDS Epidemic, and the Politics of Remembering*. Berkeley: University of California Press, 1997.

Suárez, Pablo. "Martín Rejtman: La superficie de las cosas." In Bernades, Lerer, and Wolf, *El nuevo cine argentino*, 43–48.

Svampa, Maristella. *El dilema argentino: Civilización o barbarie*. 2nd ed. Buenos Aires: Taurus, 2006.

———. *La sociedad excluyente: La Argentina bajo el signo del neoliberalismo*. Buenos Aires: Taurus, 2005.

Telotte, J. P. *Voices in the Dark: The Narrative Patterns of Film Noir*. Urbana: University of Illinois Press, 1989.

Terán, Oscar. "Tiempos de memoria." *Punto de vista* 23, no. 68 (December 2000): 10–12.

Tranchini, Elina Mercedes. "El cine argentino y la construcción de un imaginario criollista." In *Concurso Anual de Ensayos 1998 Legislador José Hernández: El cine argentino y su aporte a la identidad nacional*, compiled by the Honorable Senado de la Nación: Comisión de Cultura, 103–69. Buenos Aires: FAIGA, 1999.

Turim, Maureen. *Flashbacks in Film: Memory and History*. New York: Routledge, 1989.

Vargas, Juan Carlos. "El cine mexicano postindustrial (1990–2002)." *El ojo que piensa* 2 (August 2003): www.elojoquepiensa.udg.mx/espanol (accessed June 13, 2008).

Veaute, Adrián. "Sesgar el discurso civilizado: Una aproximación a la idea de barbarie en el cine argentino." In *Civilización y barbarie en el cine argentino y latinoamericano*, edited by Ana Laura Lusnich, 99–110. Buenos Aires: Biblos, 2005.

Vezzetti, Hugo. "Lecciones de la memoria: A los 25 años de la implantación del terrorismo de estado." *Punto de vista* 24, no. 70 (August 2001): 12–18.

———. *Pasado y presente: Guerra, dictadura y sociedad en la Argentina*. Buenos Aires: Siglo XXI, 2002.

Weisbrot, Mark, and Luis Sandoval. "Argentina's Economic Recovery: Policy Choices and Implications." Washington: Center for Economic and Policy Research, 2007; www.cepr.net/index.php/publications/reports/argentina-s-economic-recovery-policy-choices-and-implications (accessed June 13, 2008).

Willemen, Paul. "The Third Cinema Question: Notes and Reflections." In *Questions of Third Cinema*, edited by Jim Pines and Paul Willemen, 1–29. London: BFI, 1989.

Wolf, Sergio. "Aspectos del problema del tiempo en el cine argentino." In *Pensar el cine 2: Cuerpo(s), temporalidad y nuevas tecnologías*, compiled by Gerardo Yoel, 171–85. Buenos Aires: Manantial, 2004.

———. "Las estéticas del nuevo cine argentino: El mapa es el territorio." In Bernades, Lerer, and Wolf, *El nuevo cine argentino*, 29–39.

Wolf, Sergio, Gustavo J. Castagna, and Quintín. "Los inconvenientes del éxito." Interview with Fabián Bielinsky. *El amante* 9, no. 103 (August 2000): 34–37.

Wood, Nancy. *Vectors of Memory: Legacies of Trauma in Postwar Europe*. New York: Berg, 1999.

Xavier, Ismail. "Allegories of Underdevelopment: From the 'Aesthetics of Hunger' to the 'Aesthetics of Garbage.'" Ph.D. diss., New York University, 1982.

96; *Nueve reinas*, 5, 12, 84, 86–96, 100, 207n10

Birri, Fernando, 35

Body Heat, 107

Bolivia, 36, 52, 55, 58–63, 112, 125–29, 134, 181

Bombón, el perro, 112, 120–25

bonaerense, El, 85

Bordwell, David, 166–67

Borges, Jorge Luis, 66, 86; "El evangelio según Marcos," 118

Bourdieu, Pierre, 14, 38, 58, 146, 151

Boyer, Robert, 145

Bruzzi, Stella, 168

Buena Vida Delivery, 58, 77, 113

Buenos Aires Festival de Cine Independiente (BAFICI), 3

Burak, Daniel, *Bar El Chino*, 115, 136, 143–51

Burman, Daniel, *El abrazo partido*, 113

Burton-Carvajal, Julianne, 14–15

Caballos salvajes, 83–85, 100, 109

Cabinet of Dr. Caligari, The, 161–62

Caetano, Adrián Israel: *Bolivia*, 36, 52, 55, 58–63, 112, 125–29, 134, 181; *Crónica de una fuga*, 211n5; *Un oso rojo*, 5, 84, 96–100, 109; *Pizza, birra, faso*, 34, 36–42, 55, 57, 61

Calveiro, Pilar, 162–63

Camila, 135, 182, 211n6

capitalism, 10–11, 20–22, 37–38, 44, 59–61, 70–74, 77–80, 82–84, 86–96, 99, 116–17, 119–21, 193, 195–96, 198, 200. *See also* neoliberalism

Carri, Albertina: *Géminis*, 181; *Los rubios*, 153, 167–79

casa del ángel, La, 124

Castagna, Gustavo J., 25–26, 205n27

Castells, Manuel, 44

Cavallari, Hector Mario, 28

Chanan, Michael, 12

cielito, El, 112, 117–19

ciénaga, La, 181–93

Cien años de perdón, 84

City of God, 10, 56

civilization and barbarism, 97, 99, 112, 115–17, 118–19, 124

class, 48, 55–58, 69, 71–73, 126, 180–84, 214n4

Cleopatra, 112, 116–17, 119

Clifford, James, 52–53

Close, Glen S., 95

Copertari, Gabriela, 86

Coppola, Francis Ford, *The Godfather*, 97, 99

coproduction, 2, 9–10, 12–15, 134–36

Coscia, Jorge, 12, 197–98

country, 111–12, 114–24

crime, crimes: as analytical tool, 81–82; "just," 82–85; representation of, in films, 38–42, 57, 82–108, 128–29, 132–33, 162; rise in, in Argentina, 3, 181; of the state, 21, 82–85, 89, 100. *See also* dictatorship of 1976–83, film representations of

Crime and Punishment, 132–33

Criminal, 90

Crisis of 2001–2, 1–3, 6, 78, 90–91, 110–11, 114–16, 143–44, 153, 193, 197–98, 202n18; impact of, on film production, 2, 13, 33–34

Cronenberg, David, *Videodrome*, 85

Crónica de una fuga, 211n5

cruz del sur, La, 85, 100–107, 109

cumple, El, 181

D'Angiolillo, Luis César, *Potestad*, 153–67

De la Rúa, Fernando, 114

Deleuze, Gilles, 5; movement-image and, 40; time-image and, 37, 40–42

dependencias, Las, 186

Derrida, Jacques, 132

De Sica, Vittorio, 49; *The Bicycle Thieves*, 50, 75

36, 55–56, 90, 111–51; role of cinema in imaginary of the, 7–8, 114–15, 193–94, 197–200. *See also* film criticism

neoliberalism, 4, 6–7, 10, 14–15, 17, 21, 44, 56, 83–84, 116, 124, 152, 193, 195–97, 199–200

neorealism, 25, 33–38, 40–43, 48–50, 68–69, 75, 101–2, 106, 122–24

Neruda, Pablo, 62–63

New Argentine Cinema: general characteristics of, 4, 26–27, 32–33, 68; relationship of, with neorealism, 34–43, 123–24; rise of, 3, 18–19; treatment of social knowledge by, 36–43, 49–56, 69

Newman, Kathleen, 12

Nichols, Bill, 173

niña santa, La, 181–93

1960s cinema in Latin America, 2, 33, 35, 124, 182–83

Nobleza gaucha, 124

noir, 86, 100–109, 208n24

No quiero volver a casa, 5

Noriega, Gustavo, 61

No te mueras sin decirme adónde vas, 19, 27–33, 197, 213n1

nube, La, 19–27, 32, 64, 197

Nueve reinas, 5, 12, 84, 86–96, 100, 207n10

Ocampo, Silvina, 186, 190

oso rojo, Un, 5, 84, 96–100, 109

Ossessione, 101

Oubiña, David, 35, 69, 73–74

Papá Iván, 176, 212n35

Paparella, Aldo, *Hoteles*, 115, 136–43, 149, 151

Parapalos, 54

Pavlovsky, Eduardo, 20, 22, 25, 154

película del rey, La, 120

Perrone, Raúl, *Tarde de verano*, 48–49

Piglia, Ricardo, 89–91

Piñeyro, Marcelo, *Caballos salvajes*, 83–85, 100, 109

Pizza, birra, faso, 34, 36–42, 55, 57, 61

Polan, Dana, 104–6

Poliak, Ana: *La fe del volcán*, 43–48, 53–54; *Parapalos*, 54

postcolonialism, 17, 56, 86, 142

Postiglione, Gustavo, *El cumple*, 181

postmemory, 168–70, 212–13n38

postmodernism, 7, 24, 35, 55, 90, 107–8, 191

Potestad, 153–67

Pratt, Mary Louise, 56

Preminger, Otto, *Laura*, 103

prima Angélica, La, 156

Prince, Stephen, 167

psychoanalysis: in noir film, 104–6; in *Potestad*, 154–67; psychoanalytical models of spectatorship and, 154–67

public sphere: private sphere vs., 168–69, 175–76, 181–82, 184, 191–96; role of culture in, 5–7, 14–16, 19, 27, 164, 197–200

Puenzo, Luis, *La historia oficial*, 135, 153, 160

Quintín, 2, 31–32

Quiroga, Horacio, "Las medias de los flamencos," 98

Rapado, 68–69, 73, 75

Rapoport, Mario, 116

Ray, Robert B., 45

reflexivity, 5, 7, 24–25, 35–36, 48–49, 54–55, 63–68, 108–9, 114–15, 124, 143, 149–50, 168–69, 182–93, 196–97

Reid, David, 103, 107

Rejtman, Martín, 58, 197: *Los guantes mágicos*, 5, 69, 71, 73–78, 80; *Rapado*, 68–69, 73, 75; *Silvia Prieto*, 58, 69, 71–74, 76–79

Restivo, Angelo, 48, 123–24

Joanna Page is a lecturer in Latin American
cultural studies, University of Cambridge.

Library of Congress Cataloging-in-Publication Data
Page, Joanna
Crisis and capitalism in contemporary
Argentine cinema / Joanna Page.
p. cm.
Includes bibliographical references and index.
ISBN 978-0-8223-4457-5 (cloth : alk. paper)
ISBN 978-0-8223-4472-8 (pbk. : alk. paper)
1. Motion picture industry—Argentina.
2. Motion pictures—Argentina.   3. Argentina—
Economic conditions—1983–   I. Title.
PN1993.5.A7P344 2009
791.43′635882065—dc22   2008048038